Face to Face

Richard Cork

Face to Face
Interviews with Artists

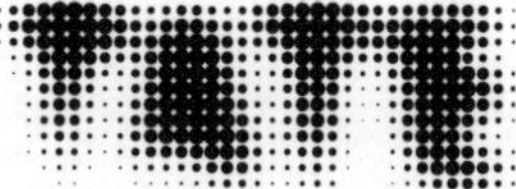

First published 2015 by order
of the Tate Trustees
by Tate Publishing, a division
of Tate Enterprises Ltd,
Millbank, London SW1P 4RG
www.tate.org.uk/publishing
Paperback edition first published 2022

A catalogue record for this book is
available from the British Library
ISBN 978 1 84976 808 5

Distributed in the United States
and Canada by ABRAMS, New York

Library of Congress Control Number
applied for

Designed by Esterson Associates
Printed and bound in the United
Kingdom by TJ Books Ltd

Photo credits
Photograph © Julia Auerbach 66
Michael Craig-Martin, April 2012.
    Photo Chloe Barter. Courtesy
    Gagosian Gallery 100
Rachel Whiteread from the series
    First Women by Anita Corbin,
    March 2011 226
Photograph by Polly Cork jacket
Photograph by John Deakin 30
rita donagh 40
Photography by Terrence Donovan 78
Portrait of Langlands & Bell by
    Lucinda Douglas-Menzies 160
Photograph Charles Duprat 124
© Jillian Edelstein 152
Photo credit: Peter Gidal 1996 142
Photo credit: John Fitzherbert 90
Photograph by Jeff McMillan 172
© Nick Morrish, British Airways 206
Lorcan O'Neill 114
Photography © Philippa Perry 190
Photograph by Jim Rakete 240
Sir Anthony Caro, London, 1992.
    Photograph by Nicholas Sinclair 48

Acknowledgements

My thanks must go to all the artists who took part in these interviews. I am delighted that they responded so well to my questions when we sat down to talk. But I also want to pay tribute to three distinguished radio producers who played such a crucial role in recording and editing many of the interviews: Judith Bumpus, Leonie Cohn and John Goudie were all a great pleasure to work with.

Several of these interviews were staged as live events: Tony Caro, Tracey Emin and Cornelia Parker at the Courtauld Institute of Art, Richard Hamilton at the Royal Academy, Michael Craig-Martin at Tate Modern, Tacita Dean at the Goethe-Institut London, Langlands & Bell at the Architectural Association, and Grayson Perry at the Cheltenham Festival. Thanks are due to everyone at these institutions who looked after us before, during and after our sessions.

Four of the interviews – Francis Bacon, Anish Kapoor, Richard Long and Thérèse Oulton – were broadcast on BBC radio. I appreciate the BBC's willingness to let me publish them. I am especially grateful to all the artists and their estates for allowing the interviews to be gathered together in these pages.

Finally, I would like to pay tribute to Alice Dill, and later Norah Perkins, my admirable agents at Curtis Brown, and to my excellent publishers at Tate for making this project such a positive experience. Roger Thorp, Publishing Director at Tate Publishing when the book was first published, made his enthusiasm for this book clear to me from the outset, and his encouragement was fortified at every stage by my invaluable Project Editor Nicola Bion. Colin Grant was equally estimable, and I am fortunate to have received their professional support.

I have also benefited immeasurably from the love of my wife Vena and my children Adam, Polly, Katy and Joe.

This book is dedicated
to my darling grandson,
James, with all my love

Contents

Introduction

Some critics shy away from interviewing artists, preferring instead to write solely about their own reactions to the work. But ever since the summer of 1965, when at the age of eighteen I chanced on Picasso, talked to him and drew his portrait in Cannes, I have always welcomed opportunities to talk to the artists I respect. Meeting Picasso taught me that even the greatest of them are not automatically remote figures, engaged in superhuman tasks and impatient with the whole notion of answering questions. They are, above all, intensely human. And often very frank about their own supposed failings. However much they might seem to contest my previous understanding of their work, I invariably end up feeling that my mind has been enlarged by our conversations – often in very surprising ways. Whether the artist is an inveterate loner like the uncompromising rural wanderer Richard Long, or a painter as wedded to his urban studio as Frank Auerbach, I emerge from my encounters realising that one quality unites all these disparate individuals: a fundamental, fiercely held belief that art itself is indispensable.

Talking to artists is like embarking on voyages of discovery. Inevitably, I arrive at their house or the recording studio with preconceptions based on my response to their work. But from the moment we start conversing, those earlier ideas are challenged in fascinating ways. The artists turn out to be subtly or even dramatically different from the image already in my mind. Even if they look familiar from photographs or TV programmes, their personalities and views on both art and life never wholly conform to my expectations. Take Francis Bacon, whose violent and obsessive emphasis on isolated figures had led me to feel very wary about entering his Kensington mews for the first time. I was only twenty-four, and imagined that Bacon would be neurotic, withdrawn, suspicious or even explosive. But to my astonishment, he proved from the outset both warm and communicative – probably the most companionable artist I have ever encountered.

The last time we met, in 1991, I visited Bacon to record an interview for the BBC's *Kaleidoscope* programme on Radio 4. Convivial as ever, he made me and the programme's young producer John Goudie feel very welcome. John remembers that, before we began the interview, Bacon talked eloquently and enthusiastically about his recent trip to Paris, where he had marvelled at an 'absolutely superb' exhibition of Seurat's paintings and drawings. Even so, Bacon had not lost his ability to be dismissive of other artists. Seeing a new Gilbert & George book on his table, I asked him if he admired their work. 'Admire?' he said indignantly. 'No, I think they're terrible, but for some ridiculous reason a friend imagined that I like them, and gave me this awful book as a present!'

Eventually, both John and I thought it was time to start recording the interview. 'Are you ready now, Francis?' I enquired. 'Ready for what?' he replied. 'Well,' I said, trying to hide my puzzlement, 'your radio interview, of course.' There was a dramatic pause, and then Bacon erupted. 'Radio interview?' he echoed in an astonished voice, as if we had never discussed it with him at all. I quietly reminded Bacon that he had already promised John Goudie and the BBC to do this recording. Another pause. 'Well, yes I did,' he admitted quietly, before adding in a loud and impatient voice: 'But what's the point?' Fearing that he had decided against the idea, I argued that 'a lot of listeners will be fascinated to hear you talk about your work'. Bacon considered this for a while, and then – to our intense relief – said with great reluctance: 'Oh, all right, then.'

Once we started the interview, he rewarded us with a whole range of pithy, memorable remarks. Early on, Bacon said: 'Ideally one would just like to pick up a lump of paint and throw it at the canvas.' But at another point, he declared: 'I'd like a very, very ordered chaos.' Later, he insisted: 'I can't draw.' And then he remarked: 'There's a natural feeling that, after all, the human race is not going on with homosexuality. Because, in a sense, it's a dead end.' When I asked him if the urge to paint was just as strong at this stage of his life, he replied without hesitation: 'Yes, stronger. The nearer to death I am, the stronger it gets.' Why? 'I've no idea, but I just feel more inventive, in a way.' Then he went further, declaring: 'I certainly hope I'll go on till I drop dead.' And when I asked him if he feared the prospect of death, Bacon replied: 'Fear? I've got nothing to fear about it, because as I believe in absolutely nothing, I know I just won't exist.' Those defiant words came back to haunt me when, only months later, I heard that Bacon had died of a heart attack in Madrid at the age of eighty-two.

In some respects, Richard Hamilton could not have been more different from Bacon. Visiting Hamilton at home, I discovered an artist very much at ease in the quiet Oxfordshire farmhouse where he lived for many years with his wife and fellow-artist Rita Donagh. His capacious rural studio contrasted absolutely with the urban confinement of Bacon's window-less studio in a narrow Kensington mews. And Bacon was entirely self-taught, whereas Hamilton received his early training at the Royal Academy Schools. But the last time I talked to him, early in 2010, Hamilton revealed just how bizarre his experience there had been. He cherished vivid memories of this traumatic, little-known period in his life, which ended in an explosive rumpus.

Even after the Second World War, the RA Schools were full of reactionaries, apoplectic about the sheer ghastliness of modernism, as Hamilton told me:

> *Alfred Munnings had become the President, and he used to appear after riding in Rotten Row. Dressed in a rakish hat and boots, with a riding crop in his hand, he would shout: 'Are you one of those bastards who talk about Picasso?' Munnings was frightening, and my teacher Thomas Monnington also got angry when he looked at my Cézanne-influenced life drawings. He said: 'Augustus John could knock spots off Cézanne!' I roared with laughter – it was hysterically funny. But Monnington was not amused. Some of my work was a bit cubist, and he got red in the face and exploded: 'They're not even good, honest Frenchmen – they're fucking dagoes!' By that time I wasn't a kid, and this was all a bit silly. Sir Walter Russell was still kind to me, but he called me in and said: 'The President has been told that you are not profiting from your studentship. Therefore it is terminated.' I was expelled!*

Hamilton, twenty-four by now, 'was dragged screaming into the bloody army for a year and half's service with the Royal Engineers'. But his negative experiences at the Royal Academy did him no harm in the long run. They may even have sharpened his rebellious urges. He ensured that his final solo show in London, at the Serpentine Gallery, focused on works alive with images of protest. They ranged from his celebrated picture of the handcuffed art dealer Robert Fraser and Mick Jagger, arrested by the police for suspected drug offences, to the tragic shooting of a student by National Guardsmen at Kent State University, Ohio. 'It's a demonstration of the stupidity of mankind,' Hamilton told me, and I can still hear in his voice the passion that impelled him to produce this powerful, elegiac work.

When I interviewed him at the Royal Academy in 1991, Hamilton's intense involvement with Marcel Duchamp came to dominate much of our discussion. I had been fascinated by their relationship ever since visiting, at the age of nineteen, the landmark Duchamp exhibition that Hamilton curated with admirable, pioneering flair at the Tate Gallery. The year was 1966, and nobody in Europe had ever seen a retrospective survey of Duchamp's work before. It was a complete revelation to me, overturning all my own teenage ideas about what modern art could be. So in our 1991 interview I questioned Hamilton closely about his fruitful relationship with the French iconoclast, and Hamilton summed up Duchamp's heretical achievements by pithily declaring that 'he invented fire'.

But Hamilton also revealed how tough it had been for him to become such a radical artist in the Britain of the 1950s, when there was still widespread opposition to the whole notion of avant-garde experiment. 'I felt completely out on a limb,' he said, recalling: 'I thought that I was being tremendously adventurous and alone, going out into the sea with absolutely nothing in front of me.' This sense of openness led him to anticipate pop art with his 1956 collage *Just what is it that makes today's homes so different, so appealing?* Yet Hamilton told me: 'I didn't show it in a gallery context until 1964, at the Hanover Gallery. I tried for eight years to persuade dealers around London to give me an opportunity to show.'

After artists become successful, the viewing public tends to imagine that they have always felt secure and confident about their careers. Even a sculptor as internationally fêted as Anthony Caro, however, started out saddled with an astonishing lack of knowledge. When I asked him, during our interview at the Courtauld Institute of Art in 1992, whether he was interested as a young man in the modernist tradition, he replied: 'I didn't know anything about it.' Caro then told me that his 'great-uncle was a painter, and he stood up on a chair in the Picasso show at the V&A and said: "It's all rot!" His paintings weren't very good. I did go to that Picasso show, but it was far too out for me. It took a long time for me to get to modern art.'

That is why Caro was so lucky to become Henry Moore's studio assistant for a couple of years. 'I was learning, and he was a kind of parent to me, sculpture-wise, which was wonderful,' Caro recalled. He described his time with Moore as 'an enormous eye-opening experience', although the young Caro also enjoyed making fun of Moore's obsession with the shells, pebbles and stones he would pick up on a walk through the countryside. Caro and his mischievous fellow-assistants secretly put small stones on the path where Moore walked, 'and he'd pick them up and he'd say: "Look what I've found!"' Even so, Moore made Caro realise how important it was, in his own sculpture of the 1950s, to make work 'to do with feeling and getting to know the body. And all that is very important in my later work.' Even if he made his reputation in the 1960s by moving dramatically away from Moore's influence, Caro still believed that 'this thing about the body' is 'very much what sculpture's about, because sculpture, however far it goes towards the visual, is still very physical'.

Ultimately, Caro's contact in the early 1960s with two American artists proved more decisive than his earlier experience with Moore. Talking to Kenneth Noland made Caro determined to make 'very big things in my one-car garage studio. And I couldn't see them! I just had to make what I wanted, and during those first three years, from '60 to '63, I did actually make one or maybe two which I put outside. And when I put them outside, I started to make balanced judgements.' Then in 1963, after taking up a teaching job at Bennington College, Vermont, he went to see David Smith at a little pub called The Rainbow. 'He was a very big man, and he was gnawing a chicken-bone,' Caro recalled, describing how 'he wore these big welding boots, and I just felt so shrunk by the time I got to him, because he seemed to be this giant saying: "I smell the blood of an Englishman!"' Caro remembers that 'there was a more competitive thing with him than with Henry [Moore]', but in the end Smith 'was all right'.

Even in 1992, after Caro had revolutionised British sculpture with audacious works like *Early One Morning*, he was self-critical enough to think: 'I never really could get colour right. I never was that interested, and I'm not still.' But the abstraction he explored in these seminal pieces was exhilarating, and he felt that 'it really cut through all the stuff that was irrelevant. That's not purity – people say it was purity. It was a cutting-through situation, you know, and getting right down to what I felt.' Caro realised that he would encounter a great deal of opposition, and he told me that most people still did not 'feel very comfortable with abstract sculpture. And steel sculpture, I don't think people like it very much. I don't think I'm being too paranoid. But I don't really give a damn.'

This exuberant spirit of defiance can be felt in the work he produced during the 1960s. He and his closest allies at St Martin's School of Art in London, where Caro taught, 'were regarded as very mad, and as a hostile, difficult bunch of people'. Yet he learned to withstand his opponents, even when they behaved brutally towards his work. 'I did once have a sculpture which somebody bought and welded into their gate,' he declared. 'I heard about it, and I wasn't very pleased. I couldn't do anything about it – it wasn't worth making a fuss. Then suddenly, it came up at Sotheby's with an extra bit of gate on it!'

Caro would never allow himself to become too downhearted about such an act of vandalism. He was too energetic and powered by plentiful ideas about future work. Refusing to sit still as an artist, he became fascinated for a while by the possibilities of working with architects.

I worked with Gehry and we talked about the idea that an architect could work like a sculptor. Architects could pick units and put them and attach them like

<blockquote>a sculptor does, instead of making drawings – or as well as making drawings. And we did it together a bit, and when I made something that people could get into, I said: 'It's not really architecture … It's not a sculpture, it's a sculpitecture.'</blockquote>

Caro showed no sign of slowing up. His appetite for renewal was still formidable, and he concluded our interview in 1992 by declaring: 'I'm interested really in pushing the possibilities of sculpture in every direction that comes along. Because I think sculpture has been a very constricted art – it got very bad, and it's suddenly being taken seriously again. So we've got to try and give it a chance by going every way you can.'

In a far smaller Camden Town studio, only a few streets away from Caro's immense cluster of buildings and team of assistants, Frank Auerbach pursues his lonely goal as a painter with a similar amount of zeal. For several decades he has stayed very close to this particular area of North London, and when I interviewed him in 1983 he immediately made clear that 'knowing something well' served for him as 'a corrective factor'. Speaking with an impassioned conviction, Auerbach argued: 'I think people do start painting because of a sort of anxiety about time. One knows that the experience is going to go, one knows the people are going to disappear, so one tries to pin them down.'

After being sent over as a child from his native Germany to escape the Nazis in 1939, Auerbach never saw the rest of his family again. This devastating tragedy informs his art, but he has never sought comfort from predictability in his work. On the contrary, he told me: 'If I paint somebody, what happens is that I paint them once and I do my damnedest to discover something that I hadn't known before, and that stands up as a coherent whole.' Auerbach is convinced that, 'unless one has an absolutely set method, which to me would be boring, the possibilities are infinite'. He thinks of all his work 'as drawing – whether with charcoal or paint. It's a question of trying to throw a lasso to capture the organic fact in a way that doesn't throttle the life out of it.' And he is not afraid of pushing himself to the outermost limits, in the belief that 'people, when brought to a desperate situation, behave in a certain way. And that is what real style is. It's how one behaves in a crisis.'

Auerbach's commitment to scraping off paint and starting again has become legendary. When he was young, 'I felt I would really be throwing the whole painting away if I scraped it all off, so I would always leave some of it on and scrape some of it off, so that the paintings were thicker then, were an accretion – not only over weeks and months but sometimes over years of paint.' As time went on, though, his attitude changed dramatically. 'I have become aware that I can finally only work one way, which is to try to do the whole thing at one go. Many times I have scraped it off, and what you may be seeing is a single layer over a scraped-down canvas, which yet is the result of a long period of working.'

Striving to sum up the essence of his aims as an artist, Auerbach told me that painting 'is distilled experience. And because the thing has been inhabited and worked through and understood, one makes the marks to conjure up the sense of something haptic – which actually is, for me, the magic of all painting. From Cimabue and Giotto right through to Matisse.' Although his work is informed by an immense and discerning awareness of the European tradition, Auerbach insists that, 'like every emigrant, I feel passionately English'. He hardly travels at all,

<blockquote>and because of the emigrant's anxiety, I actually hate to leave the place that I am at. What you'd call my repetition of subjects may have to do with it. I hate leaving my studio, I hate leaving the district, I hate leaving London.</blockquote>

> *I don't think I've spent four weeks abroad since I was seven, because
> I hate travelling so much.*

Unlike many artists, who loathed their teachers and are never willing
to acknowledge a debt to their student years, Auerbach readily describes the
stimulus he received from David Bomberg's evening classes at the Borough
Polytechnic. He first went there in January 1947, at the age of sixteen, and
studied under Bomberg 'for longer than anybody else'. When interviewing
Auerbach, I was immersed in researching and writing my book on Bomberg,
so his remarks about the Borough Polytechnic classes proved revelatory to
me. After asking Auerbach to define the value of Bomberg's teaching, I found
his reply inspirational:

> *He was enormously courageous and enormously serious in a way that very
> few painters are. He had no gift at all for prevarication or for fitting in. He had
> a deep instinct as to how a painting should go. The link is tenuous, but his art
> teaching was not like verbal teaching, there was an element in it of something
> like teaching ballet: certain things are transmitted that don't have to be fully
> articulated, and there was a line stretching back from Bomberg to Sickert
> to Degas to Ingres to David, which had a deeper understanding of how
> drawings are made.*

One particular aspect of Bomberg's approach must have stimulated
Auerbach's subsequent work. 'He would suggest a total destruction of what
the students were doing, and they would destroy it and go on. Probably at some
point of destruction, at some point where they were not in the least aware of
having done a picture, he might stop suddenly and say: "There is some quality
in this form."' Auerbach described it as 'a hint of something very grand and noble
and profound in painting', and his own breakthrough as an artist must have
benefited from Bomberg's advice. On Auerbach's first day at the Royal College
of Art, he felt offended, 'went home and in anger repainted my picture. It was,
in fact, the picture that is now called *Earl's Court Building Site*.' And when he
had finished it, 'I recognised that somehow I had cut through my habits. I had
made some shapes that seemed to conjure up a coherent, plastic fact, and I felt
I had done my own painting. I didn't know whether I would ever be able to do
it again, but I knew what it felt like.' And it encouraged him to become 'as
courageous as I could possibly be, not caring what the things looked like, driving
myself to every possible extreme'.

In order to visit Howard Hodgkin's studio, you have to leave Camden
Town and make your way to Bloomsbury. The last time I went there, the
schizophrenic London weather turned ferocious as I rang Hodgkin's antique
doorbell near the British Museum. Sunshine gave way to an epic rainstorm,
and water was streaming off me by the time the door opened. But Andy Barker,
his amiable studio assistant, quickly provided shelter. And as he led me through
to meet the artist, all thoughts of the downpour disappeared from my mind.
Crossing an iron bridge between the Georgian house and the mighty Victorian
studio beyond, I was delighted to find a colossal palm tree and a flourishing
cluster of loquats – big-leaved oriental plants that bear sweet, reddish and
irresistibly edible fruit. The sun unexpectedly returned when we entered
the studio, flooding the lofty glass roof above us with luminosity. In Victorian
times this remarkable building was a dairy, and horses with milk-carts would
enter and move around on a turntable. Far larger than most artists' studios,
its space and light must be a perpetual source of inspiration to Hodgkin.

I have long regarded him as one of our most impressive painters,
but in our 1984 interview he recalled that, at the outset of his career, 'the kind
of painting I was doing at the time was hardly taken seriously by anybody but
myself, and I felt that I was being slightly "tolerated" by my abstract-painting

friends'. They regarded him as far too 'idiosyncratic'. When the influential critic Lawrence Alloway agreed to view his work, the verdict was dismissive: 'You are too slow. I think you might one day perhaps find something to paint that would interest other people, but I probably won't be around to see it.' The words were, as Hodgkin wrily remembered, 'hardly encouraging. But they did make me feel, in an old-fashioned, boarding-school way, "try harder"'.

He certainly succeeded in his wish, and Hodgkin proved himself alive to the finest radical painting of the period. Yet he was acutely conscious of the past as well as the present. When I asked him about this in our interview, he told me: 'I cannot understand how any painter or sculptor now could work without being aware of art history, because an awareness of art history is part of being alive now.' Hodgkin feels free to roam around the rich legacy that we have all been given from the past, and he described this ability as 'one of the amazing things about living now and working as a painter, which wouldn't have existed fifty years ago'. Far from feeling oppressed by the burden of vying with the achievements of past masters, Hodgkin feels liberated by their legacy. 'Because when I am painting, I would like to feel that I can do anything I like within the context of the situation I am in – so that anything can be used, anything is useful as a means of expression.'

As a result, Hodgkin thrives on a sense of freedom as his imagination feeds off unpredictability. At one point in the interview, I told him: 'I have a feeling that you may often be very surprised by the end result.' Hodgkin said: 'You are quite right.' And he explained:

> *To me, a picture is really finished when, in theory at least, it's as far away from me as it would be from anyone else. So that the emotion – which is often extremely intense, the subject of the picture, the situation – becomes so completely turned into an object, a thing, in other words a painting, that I look at it as a painting that is being transformed.*

Although the works often originate in private, very intense moments that Hodgkin has experienced in his own life, he made clear to me that 'the actual subject matter of my pictures is not something I want to share with anybody'.

Hodgkin said he felt 'very touched' by my suggestion that 'ultimately you want to celebrate things, to affirm something which you value, something which you cherish'. When I asked him why celebration was so important, his reply was as impassioned as Auerbach's:

> *I don't care about mortality in the slightest, but I certainly want to beat time. I certainly want to defy time. And in the first writing I ever did, which was about classical art when I was thirteen or fourteen, I remember saying that these pictures should be like 'war memorials'. Why I said 'war memorials' I don't know, but the point being that really they should be like memorials, that's what paintings were.*

I wondered if he felt pained by the transitory nature of the experiences he valued. But Hodgkin's response was admirably defiant: 'No, because they have been regained, they can be regained. I've put them into pictures.'

David Hockney, whom I interviewed in 1984, began his precocious career by revelling in stylistic diversity. Looking back on his swift emergence in the early 1960s, he wrily recalled showing

> *some pictures at the Young Contemporaries and I deliberately gave a name to each style and claimed I was being versatile. But looking back, I don't think they were very different styles, and I suspect now there is less than I think. There are more connections between one and another than I thought. But I liked the idea of being able to use any style you wanted.*

He certainly did, and yet Hockney soon decided to shy away from abstraction. 'So did Picasso. He too never really painted abstract pictures, ever.' While retaining the freedom to dart from one idiom to another, Hockney concluded that 'everything I do begins with something real. To me, abstraction is too internal, in the end. I see its achievement, of course. It's marvellous, but I think in a sense it will settle down till it's kind of a branch of painting, like landscape painting.'

But by the time he had completed one of his most widely hailed figurative paintings, the portrait of Ossie Clark and Celia Birtwell with their cat Percy, Hockney underwent a crisis. After working for a long while on a large double portrait of George Lawson and Wayne Sleep, he decided to destroy it. 'I finally gave it up because I thought I was doing something that has gone really wrong,' he told me. 'The way of looking is wrong, and I completely abandoned it, went off to live in Paris and spent a year or two just drawing. I hardly did any painting. I thought: "I'll draw, I'll learn to draw better."' When I asked Hockney what had afflicted him in his attitude to painting, his reply was fascinating. 'In the end, what I didn't realise at the time – I realise it much clearer now – was frankly I began to paint pictures in a way we never see, we do not see that way.' Hockney underwent a related crisis with the photographs he began taking, in prodigious quantities, during the same difficult period. Although he regarded his photographs with great seriousness, Hockney 'thought about them and then I would go off it and think: "This is crazy, these photographs. They are not very real, either." That was always my problem, and it took quite a few years for me to figure out what was wrong.'

The first review I ever wrote of Hockney's work was for a Cambridge student newspaper in 1968, when his prodigious new Californian swimming-pool paintings were exhibited at Kasmin gallery in London. I felt convinced that a photographic way of seeing must have influenced the show's masterpiece, *A Bigger Splash*, and Hockney agreed with me in our 1984 interview. 'I think *A Bigger Splash* is the only one where it's frozen, in the sense of the splash you never see. You never see the splash stopped. And that was done because I was amused by the photograph of the splash and I thought: "Well, it would be nice to paint it slowly."' Hockney's later experiments with polaroid photographs yielded some memorable results, and I was intrigued to hear him relate this experiment back to Picasso. After admitting that Picasso always thought photographs 'were dead, they weren't lively enough', Hockney remembered a 'curator of the Beaubourg' telling him that 'the only time Picasso ever picked up a camera, he just pointed it everywhere taking pictures, saying: "This is the only thing to do with it."' Such an approach made absolute sense to Hockney, who maintained:

> *In the end, of course, that's what I had done. And when you do that, it's amazing: you get these perceptions of space you've never quite seen in photographs. Things happen. You don't worry whether somebody has four or five legs, it doesn't seem to affect how you see. And you are aware that time has just done it. I mean, it delighted me.*

Just before we taped this 1984 interview, Hockney had been enjoying himself working on stage designs for 'a French triple-bill' at the Metropolitan Opera in New York. Once again, he responded to the fact that 'it makes you look at things in a different way'. Hockney loves music, 'and trying to think of visual equivalents for it I found quite exciting. Suddenly, you don't think naturalistically at all – you then think in another way.' He responded with special warmth to Ravel's music for Colette's 'little story that kindness is our only hope in the end, that destruction is self-destructive. I agree with it, I think it is true.' Hockney's voice became very urgent at this stage in our interview, emphasising: 'I shy away from violence, am not attracted to it in any way. Yet I know that people like it, people are attracted to it, there is beauty there. But I cannot grasp it.'

Michael Craig-Martin is in many respects very different from Hockney, but both men have benefited from living in places far removed from the ones where they grew up. In Craig-Martin's case, he was educated in the US and then, at the age of twenty-five, he surprised himself by moving to Britain. Offered a teaching job, he ended up settling in London. But he still felt, when I interviewed him at Tate Modern in 2006, that he has

> *a funny position in Britain, because in a way I've become an insider on everything in the English art world, and at the same time I feel a sense of distance. But that sense of distance is also very useful when you're trying to gain a sense of a place, and a sense of what's going on. You always have a bit of space between you and it, which is quite useful and which other people may not have.*

Although Craig-Martin made his most radical early work in London, he had an extraordinarily open mind towards art even when he was a student at Yale. For his graduation, he decided to travel over to a remote area of Ireland – 'a very bleak place, but strangely beautiful' – and make a film. Craig-Martin told me that he 'already had an interest in things that were not hierarchical and not dramatic', but he was also honest enough to admit that

> *when I got there to film, I realised that I had no idea what I was doing. I didn't have a plan, I had nothing. I just had the camera, and I'd never used the camera before I got it to do the film. And I can remember that one of the first things that really struck me was – I went to shoot my first shot, and suddenly I thought: 'How long is a shot? How long do you hold the button?' I had no idea, and I'm in a field all by myself wondering how long.*

The year was 1963, and the completed film turned out to be a remarkably bold, eloquent achievement. This willingness to explore unknown territory benefited Craig-Martin enormously in his subsequent London-based work. He became preoccupied with a fundamental question: 'What is the use of art? What is it for? I was very conscious of the fact that, in a lot of art that used real objects, the one thing the artist got rid of was usage. In Duchamp's urinal, you're not supposed to have a pee in the urinal.' As a result, Craig-Martin successfully evaded categorisation, and he was stimulated by the emergence in London of a new generation of young artists 'who thought about the world completely differently, and I remember quite clearly in the early 1970s that there were artists of the older generation who were really in a panic about themselves and their own practice'. There was indeed an enormous amount of hostility directed at these young heretics, as I can testify from my own embattled experience as the Art Critic of the *Evening Standard*. Craig-Martin rightly pointed out that 'it's summed up in the idea that "painting is dead", but actually there were many other aspects to it, because there was also an aspect of sculpture being dead, too. So there was art that changed the whole idea of what art might be.'

Craig-Martin arrived at the ultimate heresy in 1974, when his solo show at the large and luminous Rowan Gallery in London turned out to be empty – apart from one wall where a glass of water was resting on an equally simple glass shelf. He called this work *An Oak Tree* and accompanied it with a pamphlet containing an auto-interview full of subversive statements like: 'What I've done is change a glass of water into a full-grown oak tree without altering the accidents of the glass of water.' Looking back on that extraordinary work during our interview in 2006, Craig-Martin explained how he arrived at *An Oak Tree*:

> *I felt that I was trying to find something that interested people a lot at the time,*

which was about the nature of art itself. The question about what is art and what isn't art, how do you define it, how do you recognise it when you see it? And I had the idea – because I'd also by that point been attacked a lot in the press – of trying to make a work that was invulnerable.

He realised that

the only way to do it was to make it entirely on the basis of claim. So that's really the genesis of the Oak Tree.

Since then Craig-Martin has continued to thrive on an essentially questioning approach to art. He made wall drawings, but 'what intrigued me about the wall drawings was that I thought of them as sculptures'. He became an immensely influential teacher at Goldsmith's, where in the late 1980s Craig-Martin helped Damien Hirst and his fellow-students to create 'a context for each other that enabled them to be artists, and to grow in the way that they did. I felt that that's what I had come from.' Then, in the early 1990s, Craig-Martin made a work at the British School in Rome, where 'I painted all the walls in the gallery. I'd never done that before. I added images, but essentially I painted the walls. And it was just a revelation to me – a complete revelation.' From that point on, he has 'never done a single installation that was not site-specific, or that did not use colour'.

In a different way, Richard Long discovered a new terrain for art when he left the confines of the artist's studio and moved out into the natural world. He defined this singular vision at a very early stage in his career, too. Long was only twenty-two when, in the summer of 1967, he took a train from Waterloo and found an empty field outside London. Walking repeatedly up and down a straight line, he flattened the grass and created *A Line Made by Walking*. The boldness and simplicity of Long's work announced a new determination to open up adventurous possibilities for working in a landscape. But he thrives on exhibiting in a gallery context as well as making art outdoors. When I interviewed him in 1988 he made it clear that 'I enjoy both ways of working, and for me it is necessary to use both possibilities. I think if I only worked outdoors it could perhaps be seen as romantic escapism.'

Even so, the act of making marks in the countryside, or placing stones in primal configurations, remains fundamental to Long's pioneering practice as an artist. And he pointed out to me:

People can go to the places of my walks. Also, it is not true to think that my landscape sculptures are never seen. They are sometimes seen by local people in the country, occasionally as I make them, or discovered by chance by people who might not recognise them as art but who would nevertheless see them. I am sort of interested in all the different contexts that work can be put into the world and then also received back by different people in different circumstances.

I once wandered out into an epic landscape in search of the stones that Long had left there. Finding them, and seeing how well they related to the dramatic countryside around, made me appreciate even more his ability to gain inspiration from isolated encounters with natural settings. He told me in our interview:

I am happy to make it in solitude. I think part of the energy in my work is that I have the opportunity to make art in amazing, beautiful landscapes which are very strong and powerful. Somehow part of the power and the energy comes from being alone in that place. The simplicity and feeling of being alone is actually part of the work.

Not that Long wants to spend his whole life wandering on his own. Rather than roaming ceaselessly and without a goal, he likes 'to go to places for a certain reason, following a certain idea, and to do a piece of work which lasts for a certain amount of time. Then when I have finished that work I always like to come home. So it is a necessary part of my life to be quiet at home in Bristol.'

This is the city where Long was born. And here, in a house not far from Clifton Gorge where he has often collected the mud for making freely splashed wall-works, Long is able to rest and regain his appetite for the ambitious walks ahead of him. I could never walk out on my own in places as deserted as the Sahara, so I asked Long if he ever felt lonely. 'Oh no', he replied. 'It never occurs to me to feel lonely. I just think I am very lucky to have these pockets of freedom and silence, escaping from the normal chaos of everyday life in the art world. It is like another dimension I can have in my life.' Walking many hours a day, he explained, has a 'rhythmic relaxation' that 'puts me into a state of mind which frees the imagination'. He is fascinated by 'homing in on the universal similarities between things, but also on the great differences between places, because each place on the earth is absolutely unique, and no stone is like another'.

Long is the very opposite of a hesitant artist who finds difficulty deciding when to stop walking and make a work. 'When I come to an incredible place I don't have to make that decision,' he told me. 'I have an instantaneous feeling that this is the place and here are the stones and I just get on with it.' Since lines and circles have always been the basis of his work, I asked him if they gave him freedom. 'A circle is such an open system,' he replied, before declaring that 'it can be a vehicle for perhaps any idea under the sun. It is a freedom, as you say.' Above all, though, he made clear that 'the long walking, the physical toil, the sweating and the getting tired' did not 'come from a kind of angst or discontent. A sculpture in a landscape, when it really happens well in a good way, is like a celebration of the place and my feelings of me being there and having the right idea at the right time and everything coming together.' He hoped that his work 'does tie up in some ways with the Green philosophy, "small is beautiful", and of seeing the world as one place, and using its raw materials with respect. I like to see art as being a return to the senses.'

Tony Cragg also discovered his *métier* by going outdoors and finding raw material there, but the work he made was at the opposite extreme to Long. Walking along the River Rhine, he discovered an array of discarded plastic fragments. They provided him with the material for a major 1978 sculpture called *New Stones – Newton's Tones*. Laid out on the floor, hundreds of unwanted bits and pieces – including a spoon, a cigarette lighter, a spade and much else besides – were given a life of their own. Its overall vitality is still astonishing, and in our 1992 interview I asked Cragg if he remembered the very first time he came upon plastic detritus. 'I do, yes,' he replied. 'The first time I used the material was in 1970, when I was a student in the first year at Wimbledon and made some work on a beach. I didn't know how to use it, but I really started looking at the things on the beach, swept up from the waves, and there was a lot of plastic in that.'

When Cragg began working with plastic all the time, in the late 1970s and 1980s, he wallowed in its astonishing potential. 'I knew, in the instant I had it in my hand, that it was leading somewhere, because it just tingled – the whole thing! The colour excited me, and when I really started to look at the forms, they excited me.' By the time he made the immense wall-work *Britain Seen from the North*, Cragg had become a major British sculptor, and I was one of the judges who recognised his early achievement by awarding him the Turner Prize in 1988. When we did this interview four years later, he had moved on as an artist to other materials. But Cragg still felt passionately about plastic and insisted that 'to classify it as rubbish is a great disservice to our own culture, in a sense. I actually do like it: I am very, very interested in it. That's not an irony – I do find it very beautiful, I really do.'

When I asked Cragg if the isolated figure who looks slightly askance

in *Britain Seen from the North* was a self-portrait, he said without any
ambiguity: 'Yes, it is.' And he agreed with me that it was reflective of his
detachment from the UK, as someone who had left his native country and
settled in Wuppertal with his German wife. He enjoyed working there, but
at the same time confessed that 'sometimes I would really love to be back
in England, and regret that I don't spend more time here'. Cragg still regarded
himself as 'a British sculptor', and he emphasised that 'making sculpture is
an eminently useless thing. You can't do anything with it, it doesn't belong to
a functional kind of world. It's a tool for thinking about things, or maybe seeing
things differently for analysing and making up a new proposition, different
from the way sculpture has been made in the past. It's changing radically.'

It certainly is, and Cragg surprised me when he admitted: 'I am just
aghast at the amount of work which is left to do'. But he agreed with my
suggestion that a fundamental sense of wonder underlay everything he made.
'Yes,' he said, before explaining that

> *most human beings have the idea of being very big for our egos, because we see
> and touch and appreciate everything through our own senses and appetites.
> But at the same time we are also aware of what a tiny little meaningless speck
> of organic stuff we are in all this mass, in the sea of time. So one is being
> constantly torn between the picture of oneself as something very, very
> important, and infinitesimally unimportant. It is something that terrifies,
> and it is just wonder.*

Some artists are unwilling to open up their feelings during an
interview, but towards the end of our session Cragg became very frank and
talked about humanity's alarming predicament:

> *We are just drifting away, as if we were a separate entity to nature – which
> we are not, of course. And I think we have become very, very lonely. When
> it gets to the point where we have killed off all the other animals on this planet,
> we are just looking into the firmament thinking: 'Is there an ET to come down
> and be nice to me?' [Laughs.] So making sculpture must be a comfort.*

Most of these interviews occurred well away from the artists'
workplaces. But talking to Richard Deacon in his South London studio,
where he was busy preparing for a solo exhibition, I found myself confronted
by a large, looming sculpture in laminated wood. Deacon had made spectacular
use of the glue squeezed out of its sides, and in the other works-in-progress he
was equally prepared to expose how they had been put together. Our interview,
recorded two years after he won the 1987 Turner Prize, began by discussing his
schooldays in Plymouth, where the teenage Deacon had even worked for a time
in its art centre. This holiday job was stimulating, he recalled,

> *because the difference between hanging art on the wall and looking at it in
> galleries is a major one. I have a memory of handling a Jackson Pollock, which
> is very different from seeing the same painting purely as a spectator. Since I was
> already interested in making things anyway, to handle art as physical objects
> seemed to be a good thing to do.*

All the same, the young Deacon proved far more reluctant to commit
himself to creating art.

> *I felt very awkward about the business of declaring 'I'm an artist.' That seemed
> to imply that what you made was 'art', and I really wasn't sure that was what
> I did – in the sense that things that I deeply love and move me very much belong
> to that category, and therefore to think of myself as the producer in that
> category just felt uncomfortable.*

Why, I wondered, did it take him so long to decide to become a sculptor?

> *Because it seemed to be making claims for what I did that I didn't know, at that
> age, I could really support.*

In view of Deacon's later development, I was very intrigued by the fact that at art school he was fascinated by the idea of the body in action, especially on the dance floor. When I asked him if he liked to dance himself, Deacon replied with a smile: 'Yes, I enjoy dancing very much. I always have done.' Looking at the big, finished sculpture in his studio, I told him that although it looked quite abstract, it also seemed to bear on my knowledge of my own body. So I wondered if Deacon liked the idea of something that had its own formal existence apart from him, and yet drew him in to relate to things that are very intimate. 'Yes, if I can do that,' he said. 'I mean, if a physical object can transcend the boundary of subjectivity, then that seems to be what making art is about. In a nutshell, I think that my experience of looking at art is of physical substance trangressing subjective boundaries.' He emphasised that 'those subjective/objective dialogues do seem to me a fundamental part of what I think of as important in looking at art, or in looking at dance. But it does rely on finding something in the way I feel about my body, and the way I use my body, that is hard to describe.'

Compared with the new work that I scrutinised in his studio, Deacon's early sculpture was much more open and sometimes almost skeletal. He agreed that it had been 'extremely, intentionally light. But I think the concern seems to flow all the way through, in particular this almost double concern with the body on the one hand and, on the other, materials that you use when you're very aware of the machine age, the industrial age, the world that we live in.' I told Deacon that, when I looked at his sculpture, I usually found that it suggested a whole variety of possible meanings: one of the excitements of his work was its ability to spawn interpretations. In the end, though, Deacon affirmed that

> *clarity seems to me a crucial issue, so that when you look at something it seems to be distinct rather than a blur. The kinds of ambiguities that you mention are part of the way in which one handles one's perceptions. You bracket them according to different things. I don't actually think that there is an unlimited set of things that one can think of in relationship to any work.*

However much artists may want to control the meaning of their work, viewers often come up with very surprising interpretations. When Thérèse Oulton suddenly became a prominent young British painter, with the arrival of her 1984 exhibition *Fools' Gold*, some reviewers hailed her as an artist who had revived the Romantic landscape tradition. But when I interviewed Oulton in 1990, she said that 'it was somewhat of a shock that my work was so easily appropriated into the English or Northern Romantic sublime'. Oulton made it clear: 'I certainly am critical of Romanticism. The title of my 1984 show, *Fools' Gold*, was supposed to give a clue into how to read the paintings. It was meant to set the pictures in a critical relationship to that tradition.'

Later in the 1980s, she trained an equally critical eye on the Baroque tradition.

> *In Rubens the juxtaposition of the flesh next to hard metal … makes one very uneasy, or makes a very powerful tension or anxiety. And I thought that oil painting could still conjure up those kind of sensibilities, but not necessarily attached to that same kind of subject matter, which tended to be – particularly in Rubens – violence and sensuality as an unsolvable contradiction. It might still be possible to take on those issues, but not directly illustrative of those subjects, which are not very acceptable to me as a modern painter.*

Oulton was born in Shropshire, and during our interview she referred to a recent walk in the Lakes: 'I was deeply affected by them, so I can't deny it. But it influences me as a person, not as a painter.' Even so, when I asked Oulton to tell me more about her response to the Lakes, she replied:

> *If there is any connection with the paintings, it's in the kind of closeness to
> the elements. And I have never been to such a watery place. The only sounds
> were of water, from bricks to waterfalls, and the constant rain. There was
> one walk which actually was above cloud levels: it was raining beneath me,
> and the peaks were jutting out above the clouds into a clear sky, which was
> quite startling. So I think a landscape which stressed a watery element would
> be somehow quite close to my sensibilities, and in fact a lot of the paintings
> have referred to the effect of something liquid destroying form.*

Later in our interview, though, Oulton emphasised that, 'in the actual
substance' of her paint, 'I imbue it with as much light as I can, and that's the
true subject matter of my paintings. I take oil paint and make it as transparent
as possible, so that it can absorb, refract, sparkle, split up light, be elusive so
that the light flickers across the surface.' I asked her if this fascination with light
was a substitute for the Catholic certainties that had buttressed her childhood.
'Yes, that's probably very true,' she said. 'That's my inheritance, those are the
materials with which I have to work as a person. And if conflicts and
contradictions come out in those terms, it's probably because of a strict Catholic
upbringing.' So did she see herself now, I wondered, as a kind of heretical
figure? She replied:

> *Well, heresy is a most fascinating kind of strategy, which can be useful
> for an artist in a context where meaning is so over-laden, so over-burdened,
> that it appears as if there were no room to move. In order to strategise out
> of that situation, I have been interested in the parallels to Christianity,
> expressed in all kinds of heresies. They were a strategy for survival.*

But Oulton remained firmly opposed to the idea that her paintings
were, in the end, to do with her own state of mind. 'I am wary of that notion,'
she said. 'I have got a feeling that it's another of those fictions that you put
your heart and soul into your work, and they can be somehow extricated from
it again.' She was 'critical of a notion that says art is self-expression', and near
the end of our interview Oulton returned to the world as a whole by declaring:
'If there was a landscape painting tradition still possible, it would have to
acknowledge the death of this planet, or the death of nature as we've conceived
to fit it in our art and music.'

When I interviewed Anish Kapoor in 1990, he likewise emphasised
his distance from the idea of art as self-expression. 'I am against the cult of
personality,' he said. 'It seems that many of our twentieth-century art heroes
cultivated huge cults of personality. We've also come through a time in the
1980s when self-expression was the big thing.' Although Kapoor was talking
to me in Venice, where at the age of only thirty-six he represented Britain
at the Biennale, he had no time for the notion of the artist exploiting his own
ego. 'I have a great love for art of the earlier times. Medieval and earlier, I should
say, Eastern and Western. And in it there is very little artist.' With immense
conviction in his voice, Kapoor insisted: 'It seems to me that is the condition
worth aspiring to: a lot is said, a lot is touched. Great feelings are conveyed,
but with very little artist. I think that's a good way of going about it.'

This belief, which runs counter to so much of today's ego-obsessed
art, reflects Kapoor's long-term preoccupation with presence and absence.
In the main room of his highly impressive show at the British Pavilion in
Venice, I encountered twenty boulder-like lumps of red sandstone. But they
all turned out to be pierced by small circular apertures. So although these
dark, rough-hewn blocks seemed at first very different from Kapoor's earlier
pigmented work, their inner hollowness was crucial and he called the work
Void Field. It linked up with his previous decision to use pigment, which, he
told me, 'has a kind of material presence, and yet it's made of nothing'. Kapoor

explained that 'this kind of dichotomy ... is a central part of my whole being'.

That is why Kapoor decided, early in his prodigious career, to place almost all his work under the generic title *1000 Names*. It implied that each piece was a fragmentary contribution to his search for a larger whole, and Kapoor told me that 'with pigment powder being there and not there, this issue has been a part of what I do since I can remember making art, which is about what is present and what is not present'. Obsessed by the tension between material and immaterial, he regarded his pigment pieces as 'partial revelations of a bigger whole. I think, on a metaphoric level, this is a notion about passage. It's a language which I'm trying to form.'

For many years Kapoor was stimulated by the duality of the material he used. 'Powder pigment by its very nature is laid out,' he explained, before quickly adding:

> *One of the things I like about it, too, is that it seems to do the very opposite, that there is a way of laying out pigment which seems to remove the hand from the making of the object. It gives an impeccably pristine, clear surface, and this has always been important. So on the one hand, a very tactile, physical kind of contact. And then, on the other hand, a distance. A distance that seems to say: 'This is fragile, keep away, don't touch.'*

His 'discovery' of pigment was a revelation, and it occurred when Kapoor returned to his native India in 1979 after studying at art colleges in London. 'I'd spent five years or so in Britain by then, as a student, and felt alien from my culture,' he recalled. 'I didn't quite understand whether I was British or Indian, or what that amounted to. I do think I suffered quite a serious identity crisis, going back to India.' Even so, he subsequently returned to London 'feeling clearer about the kind of person I am'.

Kapoor's involvement with intense colour shows a strong kinship with painting, and he told me: 'I'm a sculptor who's a painter, really. It seems to me that painting deals with this space, with an illusory space of the mind, and that sculpture deals with the world – it's here, it's present.' Obsessed by 'the here, the present, implying some kind of illusory not-here', Kapoor declared in our 1990 interview:

> *I must be dealing with something there. I see making art not just as a process in which one deposits in the world more or less interesting objects. I do see it as an internal journey, which carries me where it carries me, and in a sense it's only of any use to me if, through it, I can act out my own internal drama. In the conjunction of my works at Venice there's a play between mass, as in* Void Field, *this mass of stones, and then their emptiness.*

Ben Langlands and Nikki Bell have embarked on another kind of journey, and their collaboration began soon after they met as art students in 1978. From the outset it disregarded the boundaries normally separating sculpture, painting, architecture and furniture. So they were out on their own, not least in their unusual decision to work together as partners, and I asked if they agreed with me that their art operated at a tangent to the rest of the art world. Langlands replied:

> *It's not a deliberate policy, although we do feel that at times, yes. Really we just follow our own interests and the things that excite us – and the things that we love. That's what has led us along this path. We haven't consciously sought to separate the course we're following from other art, or anything like that. But you're right.*

For the first work they made together as students, Langlands and Bell built two kitchens, side by side. 'As an installation, if you like,' recalled Bell. 'Originally, I was going to build the old half of it and Ben was going to build the new kitchen. But as it happened, we ended up collaborating and making both kitchens together.' What were these rooms like? Bell recalled that visitors who entered the old kitchen moved through a space 'full of rusty objects' along with 'the smell of old fat, rotten floorboards and an old window that you looked through – and there was a brand new kitchen. It was a mirror image of the old, and everything was brand new and sparkling and shiny. But you couldn't actually enter this space at all.' According to Langlands, he and Bell 'didn't actually know each other that well' before they made these rooms. 'We were just talking about making work – we were both fascinated by abandoned buildings and that kind of thing, just because it was interesting to explore them and to go through piles of rubbish, really.'

In this sense, they shared the appetite for scavenging detritus that fed the work of other young British artists like Tony Cragg. But Langlands and Bell were fascinated above all by 'architecture as a whole, we're interested in buildings because they're the biggest "found objects" you find in a city. We're surrounded by architecture, and we're both from London and grew up with buildings around us, so it became our subject quite naturally.' My interview with Langlands and Bell was staged in front of an audience at London's Architectural Association in 2001, and I asked them about their subversive piece inspired by the extraordinary prison that formerly occupied the site of Tate Britain at Millbank. Bell pointed out that this nineteenth-century penitentiary building was 'shaped like a giant flower with amazing radiant petals, where people were segregated according to whether you were a debtor or a female or a male. It was all categorised and very rational. We were struck immediately by just the shape of the plan. It seemed so beautiful, and yet it was a prison.'

But a wealth of meanings can be discovered in this work. As Langlands went on to explain, 'the irony is that both buildings – the art gallery and the prison – they had quite a lot of links'. When the Millbank penitentiary was designed, its creators decided 'in a very specific way that prisons should be about observation, surveillance. And, of course, galleries were also predicated upon observation. So both buildings were in many ways about looking, containing and observing.' Langlands also wrily emphasised that 'Millbank was the main prison in London for transporting people to penal colonies, for periods of enforced labour. And, of course, the Tate fortune was built up with a lot of plantation labour.'

Both he and Bell are committed to asking how buildings 'connect to other things. And in a way, part of our strategy is to isolate them and look at things with quite a strong stare.' Later in the interview, Langlands declared that 'there are no rules – art can be what you want it to be'. They were particularly excited by the idea of a far more active collaboration between architects and artists. 'They can be the same people,' Langlands said, referring back to the stimulating precedent of constructivism. And Bell felt convinced that 'architects are becoming less wary of artists, which I think is a good thing. Because up until about ten years ago, there was a real suspicion: people looked down on artists, they didn't want to include them, they were tokens to be added.' Whereas now, she argued, 'people are thinking that artists do have something to contribute, and can combine with engineers and developers and the whole process that you go about together. I think it's opening up, I do feel that.'

Architecture also played a crucial part in Cornelia Parker's installation at the 1997 Turner Prize exhibition. She suspended, in an arresting vertical downpour, the scorched fragments of a Texas Baptist church struck by lightning. And the theme of catastrophic destruction runs through much of her other work as well, most dramatically in *Cold Dark Matter: An Exploded View*, where Parker blew up a shed whose shattered contents were then

suspended in a light-filled space and cast powerful shadows on the surrounding
walls. So I asked Parker where this sense of apocalypse came from. 'As a child,
I was a loner, fearful, shy and introverted,' she recalled, before admitting: 'My
outlook on life has always been a bit doom-laden. I've been fighting these dark
thoughts, which have been with me since I was a child, but I'm making sense
of them through the work, trying to overcome it and project my optimistic side.'

I first felt impressed by Parker in 1990, when her *Thirty Pieces
of Silver* was suspended from the ceiling at the British Art Show. She had
arranged for them to be flattened by a steamroller, and told me how all the
hapless silverware pieces 'were trashed, basically, and then resurrected again.
I suspended them to hover just above the ground, to replace the volume they
once had. The steamroller was only ten tons, and I really wanted them to be
flatter. But it was still pretty brutal.' The work's meaning became even more
disturbing when Parker described how she had obtained some of the gleaming
goblets, teapots and other vessels. 'I remember a lot of friends giving me their
wedding presents', she said. Why were they willing to do that? 'Well, I'm not
sure, perhaps they were unwanted presents,' replied Parker, adding: 'Obviously
they got some perverse pleasure out of seeing their things smashed.'

When I asked her if she wanted people to recognise the biblical
reference in the title *Thirty Pieces of Silver*, Parker said: 'Yes, definitely, it was
a found title. I was brought up as a Catholic, now lapsed, but it was very much
part of my childhood.' She went on to reveal: 'I've just been in Jerusalem, and
the last couple of days I spent visiting the Garden of Gethsemane, which is
where Judas betrayed Christ for thirty pieces of silver. So I've finally returned
to the scene of the crime, literally.' Parker emphasised: 'I like to be out and
about, doing stuff on the hoof. I'm not at all interested in spending years
in the studio perfecting a technique. I want to try lots of different things.
And the idea of using natural disasters, as well as disasters I have orchestrated
myself, seems quite compelling to me.' Hence her decision to make a work from
the remnants of the Texan church struck by lightning. 'I talked to the minister
at the church and I said: "What about this fire being an act of God?" And he
replied: "Oh, I think God wanted me to have a better church!"'

The minister allowed her to take away some of the charred remains,
and the British army proved equally helpful when Parker blew up a garden
shed for *Cold Dark Matter: An Exploded View*. Visiting the Army School
of Ammunition in Banbury, she talked to a 'very gung-ho' major, who was
'an Arnie Schwarzenegger type', and then to Major Hewitt. He turned out
to be 'much more sensitive, and really got into the idea. So on a later trip
we took the shed and all the contents out to the ammunition grounds, where
they blow things up. We modelled the Semtex, plastic explosives which hung
inside the shed, and then I got to press the button.' When I told Parker how
impressive *Cold Dark Matter* was in the dialogue it created between solid
fragments and the extraordinary shadows they cast on the walls all round,
she explained: 'I like the fact that the viewer is standing in between the shadow
and the shed …You're caught in between, and then you become part of the
piece.' She also remembered that,

> *when the shadows proved to be so dramatic, that was a wonderful bonus.
> It appeared as if the fragments had reanimated themselves, like the shed was
> unexploding and reconstituting itself. That's the way things can often work
> out. I quite like working under pressure, building things in an exhibition
> space to a deadline. You haven't too much time to waste prevaricating about
> how things should look. You just do it swiftly, intuitively and instinctively.
> And I think that's when my best work comes out – when I'm under pressure.*

My interview with Grayson Perry occurred in front of an immense audience at the 2009 Cheltenham Festival. His outrageous transvestite outfit was greeted with loud gasps of astonishment and widespread applause when we walked onto the stage. So I began by asking him about his attire and how it was made.

> *I have grades of ponciness, really. When I work with students – this has been designed by a student at St Martin's, this romper suit with the teddy-bear-shaped breasts – I ask them to make the outfits where I need to take a deep breath before I leave the house. So I put this on today, because it's Frieze Week in London and as a transvestite I love it, because I can just dress up all the time.*

As someone who is usually bored by thinking about what to wear, I asked Perry if it was tremendously hard work having to devise all his outfits. 'It's my passion, though,' he explained. 'I'm driven lustfully – literally – to think about it. In the middle of the night I wake up, tossing and turning over what I'm going to wear the next day. It's so exciting! Of course, I have fantasies of being humiliated in my outfit, but they never really happen.'

Growing up in a rural part of Essex, Perry spent a lot of time on his own and, stimulated by 'a very strong fantasy life', became aware at an early age of what he described as 'S&M twinklings'. He told me that 'all my fantasy stories used to involve getting tied up and stuff – I would have been about six or seven. And then I tried on a dress at about twelve, thirteen.' Far from being aware of transvestite culture, he was 'completely unconscious' and 'lived in my bedroom, with my teddy bear Alan Measles. He was the king of my universe, and I played with model aeroplanes and Lego. And I built him fantasies and I just played out an imaginary world, which was very strong.' Perry's present-day work as an artist has clearly benefited from the intensity of these early years. He recalls that 'it wasn't until I bought from an Oxfam shop a bridesmaid's dress, and I tried it on when I was on one of my transvestite weekends, that it gave me new access to why I was a transvestite and these feelings of vulnerability and embarrassment. And I thought: "Ooh, that's interesting!" I didn't really look back from there.'

Although Perry said 'I've had enormous fun from being a tranny', he also had to battle with considerable anxieties during his years as an art student. Just before our interview in Cheltenham began, I was introduced to an old friend of Perry's and asked her what he had been like at Portsmouth college. To my astonishment, she replied: 'Oh, well, he hardly said a word … he would just grunt occasionally.' So I asked Perry about this silent phase in his life, and he admitted: 'I was probably a bit shy and unconfident, and I had what is very common with people from my background, which is Imposter Syndrome.' After I invited him to elaborate, he explained: 'It's often working-class people, when they're climbing the ladder and going out into the cultural world, you feel an imposter. You constantly think that someone's going to tap you on the shoulder and say: "Sorry, lad, you don't belong here."'

Perry encountered more hostility when he began experimenting with pottery. But he persisted, even though he had emerged from art college 'not being able to tell the difference between earthenware and stoneware'. Determined to be seen as an artist rather than 'a craftsperson', Perry knew that he did have 'the right sensibility, which was a certain sort of mischievous experimentation and willingness to be surprised and delighted'. He soon realised that a purely 'visual language' would not be enough to 'communicate the kind of ideas that I was interested in. So often I resort to language – a lot of my pieces have words on them. Because I was kind of stuck to get the complex social ideas onto the pot with just images – I find it really tricky sometimes.' Towards the end of the interview, I told Perry that some of his work had a very savage view of the modern world. So I asked him if he was really pessimistic.

'I definitely am,' he replied. 'Because I just feel, especially with global warming and everything, I just see it all and I think: "Oh god, we're not going to do anything about it, because we're so lazy and we're so addicted." I'm not very hopeful about it.'

Tracey Emin is likewise fascinated by words, and very willing to talk openly about her own troubled existence. She has placed it at the centre of her outspoken work, and showed no hesitation in discussing the relationship between art and life when I interviewed her in front of an audience filled with art historians at the Courtauld Institute. Although popularly known as one of the most notorious members of the Young British Artists (YBA) generation, Emin began our conversation by recalling her fifteen-year-old discovery, in a Margate bookshop, of Egon Schiele's work. She then told me: 'Edvard Munch is my favourite painter of all time.' And far from attending Goldsmith's College, like so many of her YBA friends, Emin studied painting at the Royal College of Art. Even though she was 'terribly unhappy' there, Emin said: 'I learned about the kind of artist I didn't want to be. I did not want to have the debutante's day out! There were so many people there who just went to art school like it was a finishing school, and I knew I really didn't want to do that.'

Instead, very surprisingly, she then took a Birkbeck Philosophy course. 'That was one of the best things I ever did,' Emin recalled, agreeing with me when I said that 'words are incredibly important to you'. She not only uses them in her work: 'I must write – on average, with letters I write to friends and different things – between 8 and 10,000 words a week.' But by the time she teamed up with Sarah Lucas in 1993, Emin had undergone a great deal of unhappiness. 'I actually hadn't made any work for about two years, and I'd been pregnant and had an abortion. And after I had an abortion, I decided that I couldn't make any art. I definitely couldn't paint.' But then she visited Sarah Lucas's solo show called *Penis Nailed to a Board*, and 'we just hit it off so well'. Walking down Brick Lane together, at a time when it was still quite shabby, 'we both said, at exactly the same time: "Let's have a shop."' So they leased The Shop for six months, and created objects for sale like a Rothko Comfort Blanket and an ashtray where people could stub out their cigarettes in Damien Hirst's face. Emin remembers that 'we had a really wild time!'

Soon after The Shop came to an end, Jay Jopling gave Emin her first solo show at White Cube. She called it *My Major Retrospective*, 'because I thought it was going to be my one and only show, so I'd get it all off my chest now, you know, definitely!' But looking back on it in our interview, Emin described this show as 'ground-breaking'. By focusing on her own life, with real objects and true stories, she opposed the prevailing 'glossiness' in art,

> *this veneer of making everything look all right, kind of stiff upper lip and everything being cool, you know. And I'm just not a cool person: never have been, never will be. And I was making a work of art about not being cool, about being on the outside of society looking in, but using myself as a vessel to talk about it.*

As the interview proceeded, Emin became increasingly frank about herself. After insisting that 'my loyalty to friends is amazing', she admitted: 'I'm really, really terrible at relationships – really awful. So I don't have one any more now I'm an adult. I'm useless at it, terrible. So I actually have in my life destroyed a lot of the love that's been around me, intentionally, because I couldn't have it close to me.' Emin was powered by a fundamental sense of anger. 'I was angry about being fucked up, I was angry about being psychologically unhinged, I was angry about being a mess. And when I make mistakes, I still get angry with myself now.' But she was able, as an artist,

to channel all this fury into her work. She had became aware of the importance
of 'being a woman as well and actually taking hold of all the subjects that
were taboo and you're not supposed to talk about. I really did grab hold
of them by the balls, and I just threw them back in the face of what hurt
me. I turned it around.'

In one of Emin's early video pieces her mother says: 'You would have
gone to the dogs if you hadn't gone to art school.' So I asked Emin if her mum
was right. 'Yeah, absolutely, 100 per cent!' Emin replied.

> *My mum actually thinks I'd be dead if I hadn't gone to art school. Which I think
> is true. Art saved me. Hence* I Need Art like I Need God. *Every time I try to run
> away from art, art has chased after me like some wanton lover: 'Don't leave
> me, don't leave me!' Art is always there to pick me up. Art is my best friend,
> art is my salvation.*

Memories of childhood are profoundly important for Rachel
Whiteread, too. But the sculpture inspired by them is very far removed from
the gritty autobiographical impact of Emin's work. Cast in 1990 from the
interior space of a London living room, *Ghost* convinced me immediately of
Whiteread's stature as a young artist. And her monumental *House*, tragically
demolished by a philistine local council soon after she won the 1993 Turner
Prize, was an outright masterpiece of modern British sculpture. Five years
earlier she had made *Closet* by taking an ordinary wardrobe, emptying the
inside, filling it with plaster and then jettisoning the wardrobe's outer shell.
It was, for her, 'absolutely a turning point, yes'. Whiteread told me, in our 1997
interview, that she 'was trying to illustrate a childhood experience of sitting
inside a wardrobe, of hiding inside wardrobes and finding these little dark
spaces to just go and dream in'.

Even so, she agreed with my suggestion that *Closet* was funereal as
well as idyllic. 'I think it's very sort of intentionally claustrophobic,' Whiteread
said, before recalling how difficult it was to make *Ghost* by casting 'every inch
of' a London living room by hand. At one point I was in there and had to cast
the door. I said to the people next door – I used to borrow their electricity –
and in the morning I said to them: 'If you don't see me by six o'clock, can you
come and find me because I am casting the door and I may not be able to get
out!' It was quite strange. I felt like a kind of wicked nun who had done
something terrible, and I was going to be bricked into my cell.'

When Whiteread made *Ghost*, she felt that it was to do with
'embalming lives, embalming the air, mummifying the space inside the room'.
Her father had died when she was young, but 'I didn't want to see him dead,
because I didn't want to live with that memory. I wanted to live with the
memory of him alive.' The elegiac quality of her work is bound up with the urge
to memorialise, and it is significant that she worked as a teenager in Highgate
Cemetery. She recalled:

> *The old part of the cemetery was derelict, and I helped to restore it – to enable
> people to walk round and look at it. It's incredibly peaceful. I love cemeteries.
> I love walking around cemeteries. I find them very calming, poetic places.
> I think they are so beautiful, and they are also incredibly sad. It's almost like
> walking into a cathedral when walking into a cemetery: you have this sense
> of awe, this sense of spirituality.*

Soon after she made *Ghost*, Whiteread thought about 'mummifying
a whole house. But it was a sort of dream at the back of my mind, really, and
then James Lingwood from Artangel asked me – maybe a couple of years later
– if I was interested in doing a project with them, and I said: "Well, I have got
this idea."' Eventually the right house came up, which Whiteread knew very
well, 'because I cycled past this road every day on my way to the studio, and

it was kind of perfect'. Why, I asked her, was there only one house left in this East End street? 'Because there was a very stubborn and extraordinary man called Mr Gale,' she replied. 'He refused to leave until he was really housed in another proper house, rather than pushed into some dreadful tower block. So he stayed and fought tooth and nail, and was rehoused in a house. When he and his son left, we moved in.' The work involved in creating an inside-out concrete house, after taking the original house down brick by brick, was formidable and gruelling. 'There were many stages when I thought I was mad,' Whiteread confessed. 'I felt very alien in the middle of it, and was going up on scaffolding with my head in bandages on the verge of a nervous breakdown. But I continued. No, it was an incredibly complicated thing to make – emotionally, physically, and all of those things. But I am very pleased that I did it, and very proud.'

Tacita Dean is another artist unafraid of executing intensely challenging projects. Working mainly in film during the 1990s, she often took on the role of a detective who follows trails of clues and amasses evidence. But the story always remains elusive, and the resultant absurdity is filled with a sense of wild yet poignant delight. When I interviewed her at the Goethe-Institut in 2002, Dean had just made an intense and powerful radio work for the BBC called *Berlin Project*. She called it 'the most personal piece I have ever made, the most autobiographical', and the main character is a family friend called 'Boots'. Dean told me:

> *His father was a silent movie actor called Jack Trevor in Berlin, just in the 1920s and '30s. Then, with the rise of National Socialism, he got enmeshed and stayed in Berlin. We don't really know the true story, but he ended up broadcasting for the Nazis in some manner or other. English-language propaganda broadcasts. He was eventually arrested, tried for treason, and spent four years in Pentonville Prison in Britain.*

By the time Dean finished recording all the diverse passages for *Berlin Project*, it had turned into a typically complex, fascinating and multi-layered work. Many kinds of unexpected elements came into play, including a paradoxical use of silence. 'My name means "silence", so that was another element,' said Dean, explaining:

> *I'm very interested in silence and what's perceived as silence, and the gaps between moments. It starts in my studio – I had a studio in the forest in Berlin, and literally there was this silence before a storm. I sensed the storm was coming, so I put on a recorder and then this wind comes, and that's a true piece of sound.*

While she was working on it, Dean 'wanted, radio-wise, to play with limits'. She emphasised:

> *I've always been interested in those bits of waste sound, as it were. Like for example where you hear people coughing at four o'clock in the morning in a courtyard, and at the beginning of the S-Bahn there's someone blowing their nose. There is that kind of wind in all sorts of places. I don't know if everyone noticed the fart in the ladies' loo, and then the hoover?*

Dean's subversive sense of humour has always been very strong. And she is so committed to daring experimentation that, while working on *Berlin Project*,

> *my unconscious was extremely busy. My conscious didn't know what was going on, because I was getting all these things that, at a certain point, suddenly made perfect sense. But it took me right up to the point of the editing, with boxes of sound, before I really understood what was going on. And I made a kind of map in the end, drawing it all to try and connect it, to try and understand what the hell I was going to do. It was quite a terrifying project in that sense, because*

I felt totally stuck. Also, I didn't really want to make it pedantically narrative. I wanted to make it elusive.

She has pursued that goal throughout her work – most frustratingly in an earlier sound piece that charts her doomed car journey through a remote area of Utah, with a patient driver called Greg, searching for Robert Smithson's iconic *Spiral Jetty* in the Great Salt Lake. 'We did follow these fax instructions that I'd rung up and got from Utah Arts Council,' said Dean, recalling that 'it was an incredibly difficult journey: further and further into this absolute waste-land, and then at the end we didn't find it'. But this failure only confirmed her obsession with projects in elemental surroundings that end up in disaster.

She has worked a great deal on Donald Crowhurst, the lone yachtsman who vanished during a 1969 race to sail around the world.

What attracted me first about him was that he faked his logbooks, and so it was the whole element of fact and fiction. But then what became more important was the fact that he got totally lost, and time-lost as well. He suffered from what was called 'time madness', and so I was very interested in and attracted to being able to get completely lost in a fairly contemporary age, although it was a pre-satellite age – losing all sense of time and space, really.

Fascinated in particular by the trimaran that Crowhurst had used for his ill-fated voyage, Dean tracked it down by travelling to Cayman Brac in the Caribbean. 'But the most amazing thing about going to Cayman Brac was that it also led me to Bubble House, which was the other place of neglect on this island.' Built by a man who ended up convicted of fraud for embezzling money, Bubble House was completely deserted. Dean realised that 'on this extremely tax-haven, pampered island, Bubble House and the trimaran were the only two pieces of neglect. It was extraordinary. Both had paid dearly for their fraud, and both had the same quality: out-of-timeness.' But in the end everything depended on how she transformed such subjects into her haunting artworks, so I asked Dean in my final question about the crucial role of editing. Her reply was succinct and revealing: 'The editing process is incredibly important, because you know I never pre-imagine things. It's the editing where everything happens.'

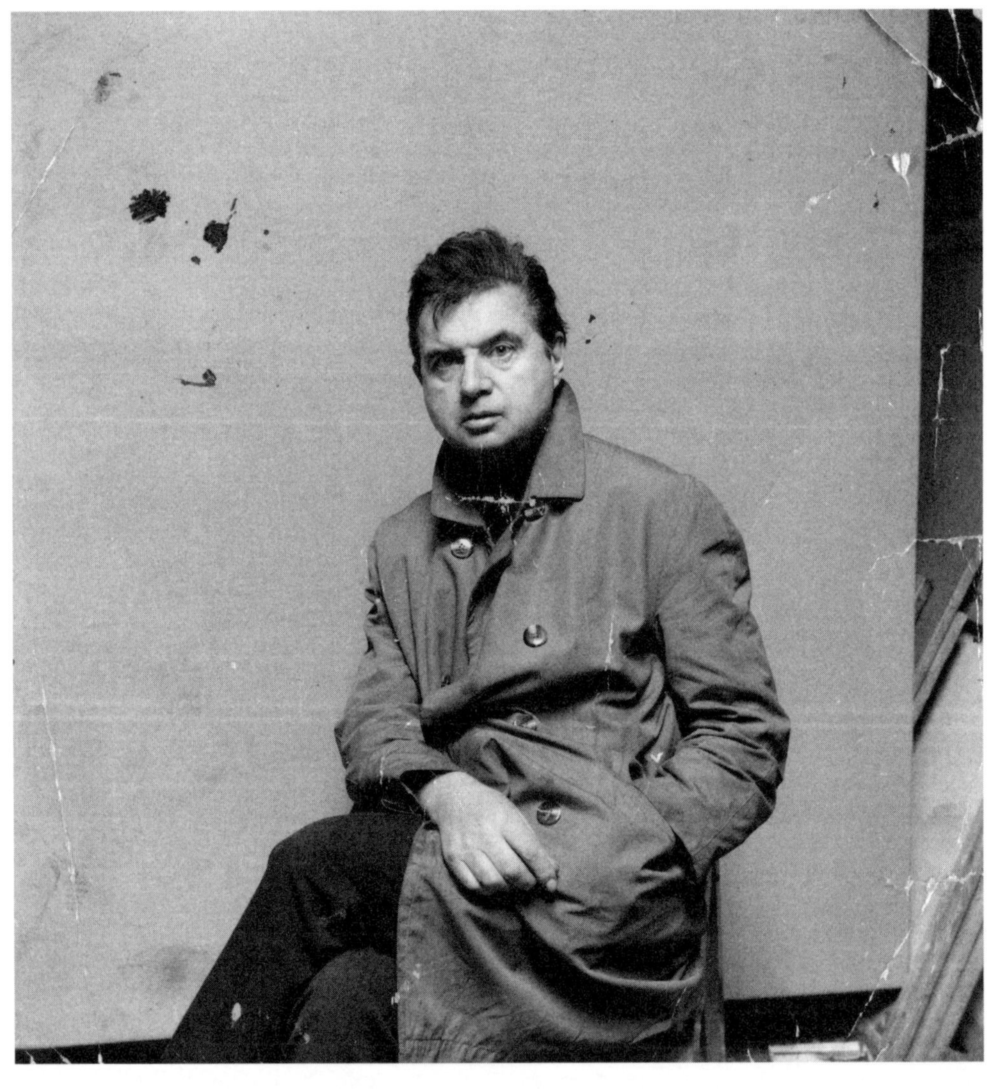

Francis Bacon

'If you really love life, things excite you, you're walking with the shadow of its opposite. You're walking with the shadow of death all the time. And the more you love life, the more conscious you are, perhaps, of death'

*Even though you have exhibited widely for well over forty years and your
paintings are instantly recognisable in reproduction, they continue to provoke
a sense of disquiet. Almost everybody in your relentless world is enclosed
by a claustrophobic structure from which there seems to be no escape. The
surroundings your people endure may not be as overtly prison-like as the cages
hemming in the baboon and chimpanzee, who in two of your 1950s paintings
roar with helpless rage at the confinement they suffer, but there's still something
very lacerating about the rooms inhabited by your human figures.*

*In your early paintings the interiors are murky, illuminated
only by a blurred face or a pale body passing indistinctly through curtains.
On the whole, though, you don't specify the cause of the disquiet which your
work creates with such macabre conviction. Shuttered like bedrooms where the
inmates are too distressed to expose themselves to the light beyond, these spaces
are permeated with unseen menace. In one tripartite work, which resembles
three stills from a strip of film, the grinning face on the left is transformed
into a yelling grotesque and then disintegrates completely, as if incapable
of withstanding his hellish environment any longer. Even the pope, who should
be better able than most to defend himself against the terrors of the void, suffers
an onslaught. Shorn of all the spiritual sustenance and power his position
should provide, he clings to his throne and screams like a condemned murderer
shuddering from lethal voltage in the electric chair.*

*Sometimes, your paintings do appear to break out of these unnerving
regions and enter more spacious locations, supposedly in the open air. But
they turn out to be just as disconcerting as the oppressive rooms. Your work
is utterly uncompromising. No one who sees it can remain indifferent to your
preoccupation with the violence of human existence, and you've often been
censured. But when the Tate honoured you with a second retrospective
exhibition in 1985, its director Alan Bowness described you as 'surely the
greatest living painter'. How do you react to such an accolade?*

I don't think that in one's lifetime anyone can come round to saying somebody
is great, because only time will sort things out. And you certainly can't talk
about yourself as being great. I try and work as closely to my instinct as I can.
Whether it's any good or not, only time will tell. When I started to try and paint,
I always thought I'd have to do some other work. I never expected to sell
anything at all. I've had all sorts of jobs, and I've been helped by different
people. I've painted because it excited me to try. I wanted to do something
that would excite me in painting. One hardly ever arrives at that, but that's
what I really wanted to do.

Do you think that the British understand your work?

Well, is there such a thing as understanding painting? I mean, when I look
at some of the late, great Rembrandt self-portraits, I can't say I 'understand'
them. I admire them and think they're among the most marvellous paintings
that have ever been done. But what they really do is unlock all sorts of valves
of sensation into other areas. So that the paint has such enormous implications:
the way it was put down, how it was put down.

*All the same, having encountered a considerable amount of hostility from the
British during your painting life, do you think that they are finally coming
round to your way of seeing?*

You see, I think that painting is such a limited instrument. Very, very few people
have really visual contact. Recently, the reason that people became so interested
in painting is because they've seen these enormous prices. But they don't mean
anything. There are so few people that have a feeling for painting, because

painting has not really been a British art. It's not been an art of England.
If you go to Spain, the people, having had this amazing succession of
remarkable paintings, are much more aware of painting and what it can do.

*There is a difference, and it's to do with the fact that we are essentially a literary
culture. You feel this all the time in Britain: it never really seems to change that much.*
No, I agree with you. But I don't believe that people understand a whole lot
of Shakespeare even now.

*It's very interesting that you should talk about a writer like that, because your
attitude is quite complex. In one way you're a very anti-literary artist, but in
another sense literature means a great deal to you, doesn't it?*
Certainly. Especially poetry means an enormous amount to me, and in my time
I always think that it's an astonishing thing to see a man like W.B. Yeats, how
he made himself into a very great poet. He started with great gifts. In the last
few years of his life, after a wonderful prophetic poem like 'The Second
Coming', he made himself into one of the greatest poets of the century.

*Could you say that you've been directly inspired by Yeats's poems, and in
particular the 'rough beast' of 'The Second Coming'?*
No, I couldn't. But I couldn't say I've been directly inspired by the poems of
anybody. Their astonishing quality is in itself: I don't know whether it's a help,
but it makes you conscious of the possibilities of things.

But you have painted one triptych which is pinned down, by its title, to T.S.Eliot.
It wasn't pinned down by me. It was pinned down by the Marlborough Gallery.

Oh really?
Yes, I certainly never called it that. They asked me how did this triptych come
about, and I said I'd been reading *The Waste Land* recently. But I never called
it that at all.

So are you unhappy about the fact that it has Eliot in the title?
Yes, I certainly am – much as I like Eliot and admire Eliot.

*On the other hand, some of your paintings' titles are attached to the Greek
Tragedies, aren't they? Do you object to that as well?*
I do really, because I don't think names … you see, I've only been able to read
The Oresteia in translation, unfortunately. But it's something that has meant
an enormous amount to me.

How do you think that it fed your imagination? Why were you so stimulated by it?
How does one know about anything? I mean, you can see an advertisement
or something lying in the street, anything can stimulate and excite you about
wanting to do something. It doesn't have to be a great or remarkable thing.
It can be just anything, lying on the floor. You see, when I start painting, I have
an idea of what I'd like to do, but generally the accidents in the paint suggest
the possibilities of developing the image in a way which seems to be very much
better than anything I had thought of.

And are you often surprised by what an accident can do to a painting?
Anything that helps me at all I'm surprised at. But of course, I know that in
my case, the things that are a bit better have come about really by accidental
movements of the brush.

You like starting very early in the morning, don't you?
> Well, that's just a habit. Some people like the afternoons, the evenings
> or the nights. I prefer the early morning.

But I do find it interesting, because you get up around six o'clock, don't you?
> Yes.

And you start fairly swiftly?
> Yes, I have a cup of tea, or something like that, and I start.

I also know that you don't, as a general rule, like the whole idea of painting
from the life, do you? You like to operate at a remove from that.
> I do, yes, myself. Certainly I do.

There have been certain occasions when you've painted portraits directly
from people, but on the whole you like to work from photographic sources.
> Well, I like people that I know well, and I know them visually well, when
> it comes down to portraits. But, you know, really I've done very few portraits.

Of the portraits that you have done, would you actually say to somebody:
'I'd quite like to have some photographs of you' or 'I'd quite like to take some
photographs of you', and use those?
> I do very often have photographs of people.

And how do you go about using them? Would you pin them up in the studio?
> No. Well, they're just like a reference. Ideally one would just like to pick up a
> lump of paint and throw it at the canvas, and there was the marvellous likeness
> – the whole thing was there.

It doesn't quite work like that, does it?
> Unfortunately not, no.

And also, you're not that kind of artist, are you? Because on the one hand
you like the idea of impulse and accident, but on the other hand you're
a very immaculate painter, strangely enough.
> Well, I'd like a very, very ordered chaos.

I've always been very intrigued by the fact that you don't seem to make
any drawings before you start. Some of your triptychs are very complicated,
but you don't feel the need to plot them before you begin the act of painting.
> I love many other people's drawings, but Picasso's drawings and his paintings
> are totally different things. The drawing is very often a wonderful thing in itself,
> but it's a totally different thing when it's translated into paint.

And yet, strangely enough, your paintings are in some senses quite
linear, aren't they?
> I think they are, yes.

So isn't it odd that you don't draw?
> I think it's because I can't draw [laughter].

I find that quite hard to believe, looking at your paintings.
> No, well, I don't think I can draw. I mean, if you asked me to draw something,
> I don't think I would be able to. And very often people have said: 'Well, he can't

draw, so there it is … that's why they're such awful paintings.' I can show you
a photograph of the new triptych. I can only show you one panel of it, because
I've redone the two other panels. Photographs don't give you much idea, but …

*We're looking at a painting where a large part of the surface is very plain,
almost austere. It's a kind of beige colour, around the lower half of the
composition. And then in the upper half, there's a strange pair of legs
that should lead up to the rest of the body, but instead there's a head …*
I've put a photograph.

So is that actually a photograph?
It is … Well, it's a painted photograph.

And it's a photograph of yourself?
Taken many years ago.

The young Francis Bacon …
Well, it's a younger one [laughter].

And he seems to be balancing, in a strange way, on top of these naked legs?
Yes, you see, that's the reason you can't talk about it.

The legs themselves are not as convulsive as they have been in your work.
Well, I never think of my work as a convulsive thing.

*But I have noticed, about your more recent work, that it is calmer, perhaps
more ordered than it once was.*
But then, you see, I like very ordered work.

*Yes, you went to see the great Seurat show in Paris recently. And he interests
you, doesn't he?*
Well, of course. I think they're absolutely superb. He died so young that
one doesn't know what he would have done, but it's absolutely astonishing
what he did. I think the sketches are the most beautiful things.

*But with someone like Seurat, where order is supreme, don't you ever feel,
being the artist you are, that there's something missing? After all, people
would never feel disturbed when they look at the great Seurat painting,*
Une Baignade, Asnières, *whereas your work is disturbing, in some cases
profoundly so. And it deals with an experience of extreme violence which
plays no part in Seurat's art.*
Yes, but I was born in 1909, and I lived through the First World War. And then
with all the things that have happened between the First World War, the Russian
Revolution and the Second World War, one has lived through a time of chaos,
in a sense. And I think that does affect one's way of feeling about things.

I'm sure you're right. Do you have any particular memories of the First World War?
I was only five, and I was in Ireland, but I remember my father telling us the war
had started. Then we came to London, because he was working in the War Office
or something of that kind. We lived near Kensington Gardens, and I remember
they used to spray the grass with phosphorescence. They imagined that the
Zeppelins would see it during their raids and think that it was the lights of
London, so the bombs would be dropped on Hyde Park or Kensington Gardens
or something – which was a mad idea.

I can't imagine that it worked, can you?
> I don't suppose it did at all. But then I don't think air warfare in 1914 was
> as efficient as it became in 1940. And at that age, of course, I wasn't as aware
> as I became during the last war. I was an asthmatic, and because of that
> I was turned down and put into a thing called the Rescue Service, in Chelsea.
> One did see then the war's effect on people, in an appalling state very often
> after bombardments.

You actually had to help pull people out of blitzed buildings?
> Yes, exactly.

But you've never tried to paint that kind of experience in a direct way, have you?
> Well, just look at … how bad it is.

Thinking about your 1944 triptych, which was such a landmark in your career,
I suppose that one of the things informing it must have been the experience of war
– the idea of these three strangely deformed figures at the base of a Crucifixion.
> No, I'd intended to do the Crucifixion, but I think that those figures really came
> out of Picasso's paintings – the beautiful images that he made on the beaches.
> I think it came out of his influence on me, of those things. But they were more
> to do with his love of the beauty of the imagery, and may have been with the
> rounded beauty of the girl he picked up.

Those Picasso images are very erotic, aren't they?
> They're very erotic and …

… distorted.
> Yes.

Would you say that some of your work has an erotic impulse?
> I don't know, really.

When I look at certain of your images, but by no means all of them,
I do get the feeling that the erotic element in them is very strong.
> It would be, but there are different eroticisms. As I'm homosexual, the eroticism
> is of a different type.

Yes, absolutely. But there are very often quite specific references to figures
embracing and beds. The act of making love is very often in your work, isn't it?
> Yes, it is, yes.

I always think that was actually a very brave thing for you to do. Because
when you started work as an artist, the climate in this country was very
much against the whole idea of homosexuality even being mentioned,
let alone put into images.
> But then it still is. And it probably always will be. There's a natural feeling
> that, after all, the human race is not going on with homosexuality. Because,
> in a sense, it's a dead end.

One at least of the recurring images of figures who seem to be making
love, struggling, embracing or whatever they're doing derives in fact
from a photograph by Muybridge of wrestlers.
> It does. I'd seen some Muybridge photographs and then somebody who used
> to be a friend of mine, called Dennis Wirth-Miller, discovered that you could

see the whole of Muybridge in the Victoria and Albert [Museum]. The thing
about it is, he wanted to make a record of human movement. I've always been
fascinated by the human body, and therefore this was a dictionary of it. Coming
back to the wrestlers, you've only got to go a point further and you could say that
the love act is a form of wrestling. So with wrestlers, it's fairly simple to turn
it into an erotic image. What the wrestlers themselves felt, one has no idea.

Mind you, in other paintings you have been stimulated by highly emotive
works of art. I'm thinking in particular of the Eisenstein still from his film
Battleship Potemkin.
> If I'd seen things like that when I was young, I would have tried to make films
> rather than been a painter, perhaps, because the possibilities in film are so
> enormous. But of course, the problems of money mean that the people who
> finance film think that they know what the public wants, whereas I think the
> public want something far, far more complicated than the people who put up
> the money for it do.

What was it about the Eisenstein image that really interested you? We're talking
about the face of a nurse with a pince-nez hanging down from her nose. There's
blood on her face, and she's screaming.
> She's screaming. And Eisenstein had such remarkable visual sense that, when
> you see the pram hurtling down those steps, it was just an extraordinary image.
> One of the greatest images that has been made.

What was it about the scream in the nurse's face that interested you? Because
the scream was – for a long time anyway, not so much now – very important
to you in your work.
> Well, you see, I never succeeded in doing what I wanted with the scream.
> I always thought that I could make the scream as beautiful as some of
> those late Monet landscapes. That's what I would have liked to have done.
> I thought, with the lips and the tongue and the teeth, one could have done
> that. But I didn't succeed in doing it.

And above all, your attempts to succeed with the scream centred on the Velázquez
portrait of Pope Innocent X, didn't they?
> Yes. They are things that I really hate now. And I wish … well, I suppose
> one criticises many things, but I just think it was only a form of sensationalism,
> and it never really worked.

That's a very harsh thing to say about your own work, isn't it?
> Well, I mean, if you can't be harsh about your own work, what else can you
> be harsh about?

Do you think that you are your own severest critic?
> I wouldn't say 'severest', because my work is really not liked at all,
> generally speaking.

Would you say that?
> I think so.

Well, how would you account for the fact that it now sells for several million
pounds per picture?
> Firstly, there are practically no good painters around. I'm not suggesting
> that I'm a good painter, but there are painters of really no quality at all

around. And the other thing is that I don't know how the market
is manipulated by the dealers.

*But this interests me very much, when you say that your work is not liked
at all. I mean, what do you base that statement on? From things that people
have said, or written?*
Sometimes people do come up and say that they like it. This is very nice, and
one's always very pleased if anybody does like the things. But I'm not a painter
who's liked in the way that, for instance, a painter like Hockney is loved.

*Yes, you're almost the antithesis of Hockney, aren't you, because Hockney is
an artist who – and he would be the first to confess it – cannot actually deal
with the darker side of life in his work.*
But then, am I dealing with the darker side of life? I'm only dealing with what
life is itself.

But you can't deal with the Hockney side of life, can you?
Well, I don't really want to. I mean, what is the Hockney side of life?

*I suppose we could sum it up by saying that it was to do with the idea
of celebration, a feeling of well-being.*
I would like to celebrate things, and I always think I do. But then there comes
into it the neurosis of my century. And of the time during which I've lived, and
grown up and exist in.

You can't ignore that, can you, in your work? I mean, it would be dishonest of you.
I don't want to ignore it, you see, because I think it's part of the very texture
of our existence.

But you're not at all downcast by it, are you?
No, I'm not. I have a very optimistic nature, but I'm optimistic about nothing,
because I don't believe in anything. I've nothing to be optimistic about, but
I am naturally optimistic. That just is a quirk of nature.

*Well, maybe the whole idea of having nothing to believe in is, for you, a curious
kind of emancipation, is it? A sort of release?*
But I never have believed in anything. You see, as children we were brought
up as Protestants in Ireland and taken to church every day. It took me, it's true,
until about the age of seventeen, when I suddenly realised that the whole thing
was just an absolute farce, and that one just had one's moments of life and that
was it. Yet I do remember when I did also come immediately to the knowledge
that life has no meaning except what certain people have done, through their
inventions or their images or other amazing things. But life in itself has no
other meaning than that.

Is this what drives you – that ambition to make something out of nothing?
I only know that when I started to paint, I tried. But you see, I didn't start till
very late. I was nearly thirty when painting really began to excite me. I think
it began after I had seen exhibitions of Picasso when I'd been in Paris. Although
a lot of the work of that period I don't happen to like at all, it was the excitement
of his work that started me wanting to try and paint myself.

And the urge to paint is clearly just as strong now in your life?
Yes, stronger. The nearer to death I am, the stronger it gets.

You think it's even stronger now?

Yes, I do.

Really? Why do you think that?

I've no idea, but I just feel more inventive, in a way.

That's one of the marvellous things about painting, isn't it? It's something that you can actually go on doing until you drop.

I certainly hope I'll go on till I drop dead. That's what I would like it to be.

Do you fear the prospect of death at all?

Fear … I've got nothing to fear about it, because as I believe in absolutely nothing, I know I just won't exist. Of course, it'll be horrible knowing that you're leaving everything – everything that has meant things to you.

It seems to me, looking at your work, that you've always been unusually aware of death. And it's almost as if you're a man who enjoys life so much, and relishes it so much, that somehow mortality offends you in some way. You don't like the idea of it all ending, do you?

No, of course I don't like the idea of it ending. But then, after all, if you really love life, things excite you, you're walking with the shadow of its opposite. You're walking with the shadow of death all the time. And the more you love life, the more conscious you are, perhaps, of death.

And shadows recur in your paintings, don't they?

They do. I don't think there's a great many shadows, though.

But when they appear, do you think that they are in a way to do with intimations of mortality?

No, I don't. I think they're entirely to do with the layout of the painting.

I knew you'd say that [laughter]. The curious thing is, I don't feel that I'm talking to an eighty-year-old at all.

But I'm very old [laughter]. I'm an eighty-year-old – you're talking to somebody over eighty!

I know. You're old on paper, but to meet you and talk to you, it's quite uncanny.

Yes, but then I mean obviously one's body decays and everything, but as long as the brain doesn't decay, there's no reason that one should bother too much about age.

Francis Bacon died in 1992, the year after this interview was recorded.

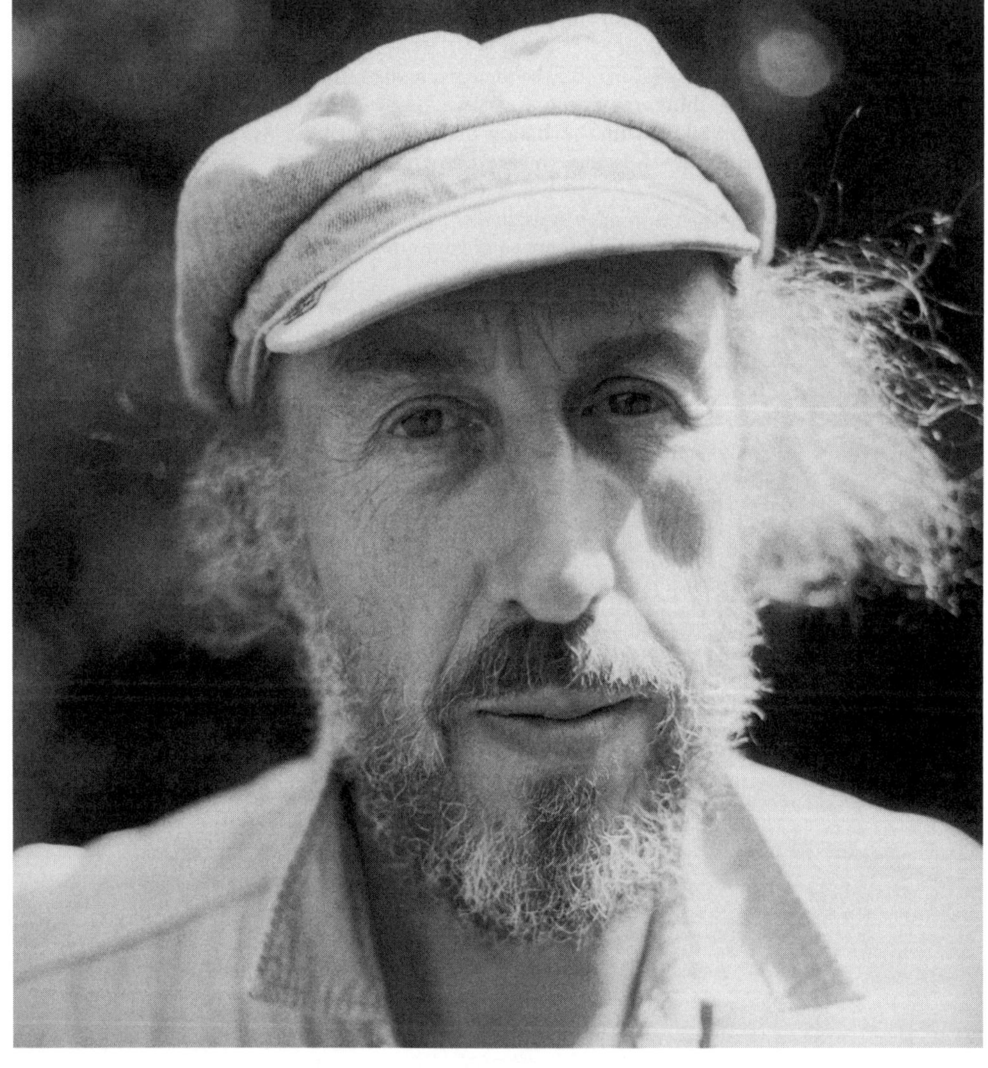

Richard Hamilton

'I felt completely out on
a limb: I thought that
I was being tremendously
adventurous and alone,
going out into the sea
with absolutely nothing
in front of me.'

*You always seem to welcome the scepticism that your work initially arouses.
It was, after all, one of the risks you had to take when helping to organise the
epoch-making London exhibition called* This Is Tomorrow *at the Whitechapel
Art Gallery back in 1956. Your section of the show, with its deliberate celebration
of images culled from advertising, comic books and film publicity, outraged
English opinion at the time. The critics viewed them as the subversive gestures
of someone who was planning to pollute fine art with the worst products of
American subculture. But what you were actually attempting, with a flair
that can only be called prophetic, was to extend the range of modern art by
unearthing the raw material for a new kind of picture-making: one that would
embrace the ephemeral kitsch bombarding the sensibilities of the city-dweller,
and acknowledge its powerful hold over contemporary civilisation. Your
temerity was justified, and the collage you made for the exhibition's poster,*
Just what is it that makes today's homes so different, so appealing?, *now looks
like a clarion call for the army of pop artists who would take the 1960s by storm.*

 *I want to start by asking you whether you had any inkling of what was
going on in US art during the 1950s – in terms of opening up the possibilities
summarised in your collage by Mr Universe, who clasps a shamelessly phallic
lollipop with the word 'Tootsie POP' splashed across its wrapping-paper?*

 No, not a clue. We were completely isolated here from the work going on in
New York, other than abstract expressionism or, I suppose in the mid-1950s,
hard-edged abstraction. You were either a hard-edged abstractionist or you
were a dribbler, and that was about it. Those were the options.

So where did you see yourself situated with regard to that kind of challenge?

 I didn't see myself situated at all. I felt completely out on a limb: I thought that
I was being tremendously adventurous and alone, going out into the sea with
absolutely nothing in front of me. There was a lot in the past, of course, and
the basis for my thinking I suppose was that I had done two exhibitions that
in some ways started off the idea that artists could make didactic shows about
things that interested them. In 1951 I had an exhibition called *Growth and
Form*, which was about the natural world, then in 1953 I had another
exhibition, *Man, Machine and Motion*, which was about human beings and
how they move in their environment, how they add things to themselves,
vehicles of all sorts – a couple of simple bits of board on your feet and you're
skiing on water. I tried to do things that were about space, about the way that
people move in space. It was part of a genuine interest in perception at that
time. I can't say that I was absorbed in Arnheim [Rudolf Arnheim, author
of *Art and Visual Perception*], but I did value greatly a book which came from
America by a man called [James J.] Gibson, *Perception of the Visual World*.
It was a fascinatingly interesting small booklet about visual clues: how people
on trapezes saw the ground and how they related to it. He said that it was very
important to establish the rigging, so that the two trapezes were absolutely level
and were related to a level ground. If the ground wasn't level, then it could be
disaster. Gibson examined all the facts, and it turns out that when accidents
occurred with trapeze artists, it was because the ground wasn't perfectly flat.
So it's not just a question of moving about up there, it's a question of knowing
your relationship to the ground.

How did that influence the work you were producing?

 All sorts of perceptual clues became interesting to me, and I just examined
them in a very thorough, systematic and obviously scientific way. I tried to
understand the experience of moving in a train and looking at a certain point.
Then I felt that everything that I was doing, which was a kind of schematic way

of describing motion, was related to normal perspective. It just became much
more complicated. And then I tried to put objects in – say, a car moving in the
opposite direction to a train. Around this time in the early 1950s there was all
this stuff going on at the Independent Group. But that was also very systematic
and analytical, and related in some ways to those two exhibitions. For example,
the *Man, Machine and Motion* exhibition was in close collaboration with
Reyner Banham, who was thoroughly interested in American automobile
styling, and he wrote very smart, snappy captions for the catalogue annotating
each of the items. There was a great deal of encouragement in the Independent
Group to study further, so we were given the book of the week to read, which
might turn out to be very difficult. It might be on cybernetics, on information
theory or on theory of games, and it got very tough. When Lawrence Alloway
was involved we really scratched our heads over these books, and we were then
expected after two weeks of study to discuss them. It was like a sort of Open
University on a small scale, but there was very little discussion of art.

Why did you think it was best to avoid discussing art?
The things that we discussed were cinema, pop records even, but there was
a whole area of interest which almost required the avoidance of art: there was
something in our make-up which made us do that. I was teaching from 1953
onwards and I tried to avoid talking to my students about art. It was always:
'If you do this something happens.' It was trying to make the mind take over,
and it wasn't necessary to point to art. That would be saying that there is some
stylistic mode that you should adopt, and I always see that as dangerous.
I think the same sort of thing pervaded the Independent Group discussions:
we weren't really interested in artistic styles, but in what was happening in
the world, and I think it paid off.

*Certainly. Within the Independent Group, there was almost an obsession with
things American, wasn't there?*
Yes, that was because Britain was in a very deprived condition after the
war. If you'd been in a factory, you probably would have spent some time
making a lighter out of a bullet and a flint. The most desirable possession
after the war was a real lighter, a Zippo was really macho. That I think was
the attitude with just about everything. You hankered after a Whirlpool
washing machine and you drooled over pages of advertising in *Good
Housekeeping* and *Esquire* for all the snappy clothes. The equivalent here
was *Picture Post*, which is good, straight, documentary journalism, but it
didn't have the glamour of *Life* magazine.

*Although you were 'drooling', what fascinates me about that surprisingly
small 1956 collage,* Just what is it that makes today's homes so different,
so appealing?, *is the element of send-up in it. You are, at one and the same time,
fascinated by and also satirising many of the preoccupations of what came to
be known later on as pop art.*
I don't think sending up is satirising, and I don't think of it as drooling.
I was drooling over the magazines, but I wasn't trying to get across this idea
of drooling over it. I was trying to get somewhere right in the middle between
these two possibilities of glorifying and sending up. Different people from
different backgrounds have accused me of satirising America: the cultural
attaché at the American Embassy came to my house and was really curious to
know why I was so unpleasant about America. English critics would say there
was a mid-Atlantic tone of voice in my work. So it was hard to please everybody.
But part of the ethos of the Independent Group, along with information theory

and theory of games, was non-Aristotelian logic, which I took into my soul
as a fascinating, new, philosophical possibility where you didn't say things were
bad and you didn't say things were good – they were just there. I uphold this
principle all the way through until I come to someone like Margaret Thatcher
and I think: 'She's bad.' You must have some value judgements: I wouldn't
go the whole hog and say everything has to be neutral. But at that time I was
interested in the aesthetic possibility of something which was completely
neutral. And that's the explanation for that work. It was a kind of summary
of the things that we'd all been thinking about, our group's contribution to
This Is Tomorrow.

That's the landmark exhibition at the Whitechapel Art Gallery in 1956.
Yes, which one always sees as the summation and termination of the
Independent Group. Our contribution was not only about pop culture –
Wurlitzer disk players, that sort of thing – but it was also about perception.
This even went back to my 1951 interest in the way we see things. I persist
in being interested in the two strands: you express things in a visual language
which people understand or not. And in that visual language, what are the
images and icons which you're using, what myths are being expressed?

*Of course, it's strange the way in which the grinding processes of art history
get going.* Just what is it that makes today's homes so different, so appealing?
*is often seen as some kind of presentiment, even a begetter of pop art. Whereas
in fact it was very much tied in with that particular exhibition: you wouldn't
have seen it in 1956 as any kind of christening of a new movement, would you?*
Oh no, not at all. In fact I didn't show it in a gallery context until 1964, at the
Hanover Gallery. I tried for eight years to persuade dealers around London
to give me an opportunity to show. I would have shown that picture at any time
between '56 and my next show in '64.

You mean they simply weren't interested?
No, I couldn't persuade the gallery who had given me my first show to come up
to Highgate and take a look at what I was doing. Putting it on the shelf for those
years didn't mean that I wasn't interested in it, and when I put it in the show,
it made sense of the work that I'd done between 1957 and 1962. To go back to
your original question, I felt myself to be in total isolation up until something
like '61, when Lawrence Alloway said, 'there are some interesting kids at the
College', and I learned about the existence of Peter Blake, Allen Jones and David
Hockney in particular. And then somebody arranged an exhibition in a little
gallery on Cork Street or somewhere, which consisted mainly of people from
the Royal College. And I don't know how anyone knew of my existence even,
but I was very pleased that I was invited to contribute.

Did you feel that you belonged in that context?
No, I felt as though I was of the older generation in a way. I was anything
up to ten years older than most of them. I was rather pleased, as I think of it.
I was carried along on David Hockney's golden coat-tails. He wafted in, and
I was somehow given a little reflected shine from this gold suit that he wore
on special occasions.

*Of course, he's always said that he was nothing to do with pop art. In fact,
he made a public statement to that effect at one point in the 1960s, didn't he?*
Well, I've never chosen to deny it, but there have been disclaimers. Paolozzi
made a famous disclaimer: 'I am not responsible for pop art.' I think it was

at the last meeting of the Independent Group, which I didn't attend for some
reason. I don't think I was invited.

*You talked about the British manifestation of pop art. What about its American
manifestation? When did you first become aware of what was going on in New York?*
The first sign of it was an exhibition at the ICA of American painting in the
early 1960s. I think those were probably the first Pollocks to be shown in
London and the first Warhols. And Warhol was a knockout. The end wall of the
Dover Street ICA was covered with thirty or forty of the great early Marilyns.

And it certainly wasn't done under the banner of pop in any way at all?
No, it was just New York, and it was paid for by Peter Watson, one of the original
sponsors of the ICA. He was a wonderful rich young man who paid for *Horizon*
all the way through the war and helped the ICA afterwards. He was motivated
to get this exhibition over, and it was an absolute flop. He was very depressed
about it, because it had been quite a big venture for him to do. A lot of effort
and a great deal of money had been expended, and it sank like a stone as far
as critical work was concerned. But it was a very powerful experience to see.

*Allen Jones has recalled how difficult it was for an art student to actually
find out about Pollock or whoever. When did you first start finding out
about Marcel Duchamp?*
I knew Jasper Johns slightly from a lecture that we did at the ICA – one of
the few lectures there concerned with art – which was a triple talk with three
members of the Independent Group: Anthony Hill, Sandy Wilson and myself.
We had an interest in Duchamp. We didn't know much about it, but we thought
it was worthwhile boning up and each doing a presentation. And I decided
I would find out what was in the *Green Box*, since I couldn't speak French and
couldn't read it. I'm the only monolingual translator in the business, I think. I'm
always thought of as being the translator of the *Green Box*, but really I had to
get somebody to give me the meaning of every word in the thing and then put it
together. But this was quite an important moment for me: I began to work on a
typographic version of the *Green Box*, which was eventually published in 1960.

And how did Duchamp respond?
Well, I wrote to him after the lecture because I'd made a diagram of the *Large
Glass*, and there were people in the audience who purported to know about
Duchamp, one of whom said we were absolutely stupid and Duchamp would
have thought we were crazy. So I sent my diagram, which I'd been working on
for weeks and weeks, to Duchamp with a little note saying: 'Could you tell me
what's wrong with it?' I didn't hear a word from him until almost exactly a year
later, when I got a letter in this familiar handwriting that I'd been poring over
in the *Green Box*. And it said that a professor of art history at Yale called George
Heard Hamilton – no relation – had done a little collection of jottings on the
Green Box and would I collaborate with him on a complete English version.
He didn't mention my chart and never did subsequently. My publication was
reviewed. There were very few reviews of this book but one of them, strangely,
was written by Jasper Johns in a one-issue New York underground newspaper
called *Scrap*. He wrote a beautiful little review, not of the book as much as
of his approach to Duchamp. He ended this piece by saying he was reminded
of a cartoon in *The New Yorker* where two cavemen are sitting there and one
says to the other: 'OK, so he invented fire. Then what did he do?' Most artists
of my generation who I feel close to share this attitude towards Duchamp.
He invented fire.

*You certainly fired me up by curating that revelatory Duchamp exhibition
at the Tate in 1966. It was the first major retrospective survey of his work
to be held anywhere in Europe. And I'll never forget visiting that show,
at the age of nineteen, because it changed my whole notion of what modern
art could be. I guess your profound involvement with Duchamp transformed
everything for you, too.*

I made friendships all over America and Paris – largely through Bill Copley,
who had lots of contacts – but it was always through an enthusiasm for
Duchamp. I met people like Jean Tinguely with Duchamp. I went to America
for the first time because I'd been working with Duchamp, corresponding
practically weekly for years. When I went from New York to Pasadena, I sat
beside Marcel on the plane and we travelled all the way across America and
he pointed out Massachusetts to me three times. He was very interested in
maps, Marcel. And then, when we got to Pasadena, there were all these people
there. Andy Warhol was having a show at Irving Blum's gallery, there was
a magnificent show of Oldenburg at the Dwan Gallery, Billy Al Bengston was
there, and five or six other people were all having shows there. But the arrival
of Duchamp was treated like a feast: it was incredible, like a young occasion.
The kids really made it a riot. The enthusiasm for Duchamp was extraordinary.

And how did Duchamp respond to this?

He loved it. He liked to be fêted, strangely enough. He was thought of as being
very retiring, but I think he enjoyed the admiration that all these young people
had for him.

*What about your own attitude towards Warhol, Lichtenstein, Oldenburg
and the others? How did you react to them when you first saw their work?*

I thought they were wonderful because they, especially Warhol, seemed to
be doing something that I thought was quite impossible. When I made my
suggested list of characteristics of pop art, all these things like glamour, youth,
wit, big business, all these characteristics which could be identified in Elvis
Presley seemed to me to be not incompatible with fine art – you can see it,
Rubens was pretty glamorous. But I thought that records were made for very
temporary consumption: they were transitory and expendable. I thought, that's
not fine art. Popular art is expendable, but fine art relies for its being on the idea
of permanence, and it's preserved by other people who believe in that idea. And
then, when I went to America, I thought: 'He's done it, good for him! He's proved
me wrong!' Warhol made an art designed for a short life. Who would have
thought that people would collect Brillo boxes and that they would end up at
museums? So it wasn't really Andy who made this big leap. He made the big leap
in doing it, but the people who made the biggest leap were the museum officials
who realised that this was a great man, a great artist and the stuff was good.

Were you shocked in any way by the work?

No, I thought it was marvellous. The show in Irving Blum's was the silver
Elvis Presley. It isn't a big gallery, but the first room was just completely covered
with Elvis Presley. He just got this big canvas, painted it with silver paint,
got a silk screen and started pulling his squeegee all the way along with black,
overlapping them sometimes to leave little gaps, but I think it was done in
a very arbitrary kind of way. For the show at Irving Blum's he had one of these
lengths, like a silk-screen-printed textile you buy by the metre, and he just
cut them up and they were put on stretchers, sometimes double Elvis and
sometimes single Elvis. I'd seen the Marilyn Monroe painting, but the first sign
of a freshly made Warhol was in that exhibition. I was just tagging along with

Marcel everywhere. He was treated like royalty, and I was treated not like a
prince exactly, but someone associated with the court. The back room where
the public didn't normally go was full of Liz Taylor paintings, and then in Irving
Blum's office there were the Campbell's soup cans, which were little paintings,
one of every flavour. Irving Blum had sold one and had bought it back, because
he realised that he had broken the set. And when we met him he was preening
himself with the luck he'd had in getting it back. I think Warhol made a
tremendous impact on me at that time, but it was because I thought that it was
so extraordinary that he should have succeeded in this throw-away attitude.
These things looked so casual, and yet they were obviously magnetic presences.

*He made an impact on you, but did he change your art – or, in your knowledge,
that of any other British artists?*

He changed it only in the sense that the first thing I did when I got back home
was a thing called *My Marilyn*. Because there had been lots of Marilyns before,
I called it *My Marilyn* to distinguish it from other people's Marilyns. I also
made the *Epiphany* disc, which was a direct response to California, though
not directly to Warhol's work. Irving Blum took me to Billy Al Bengston's
studio in Venice, California. There's a big place there which is the West Coast
equivalent of Coney Island, and I thought how marvellous it was that it should
be called Pacific Ocean Park: POP. We went to this little joke shop, and there
were statues of hands and every kind of vulgar monstrosity, and among them
a disc which said 'Slip it to Me', which was the only thing I purchased in there.
I just magnified it, but it was really to show my understanding. It could be
thought of as a kind of pop-Duchampian thing, to make an enlargement of a
ready-made. But it also has more to do with the feeling that the kind of imagery
made by the American artists ought to be recognised and established in a work.

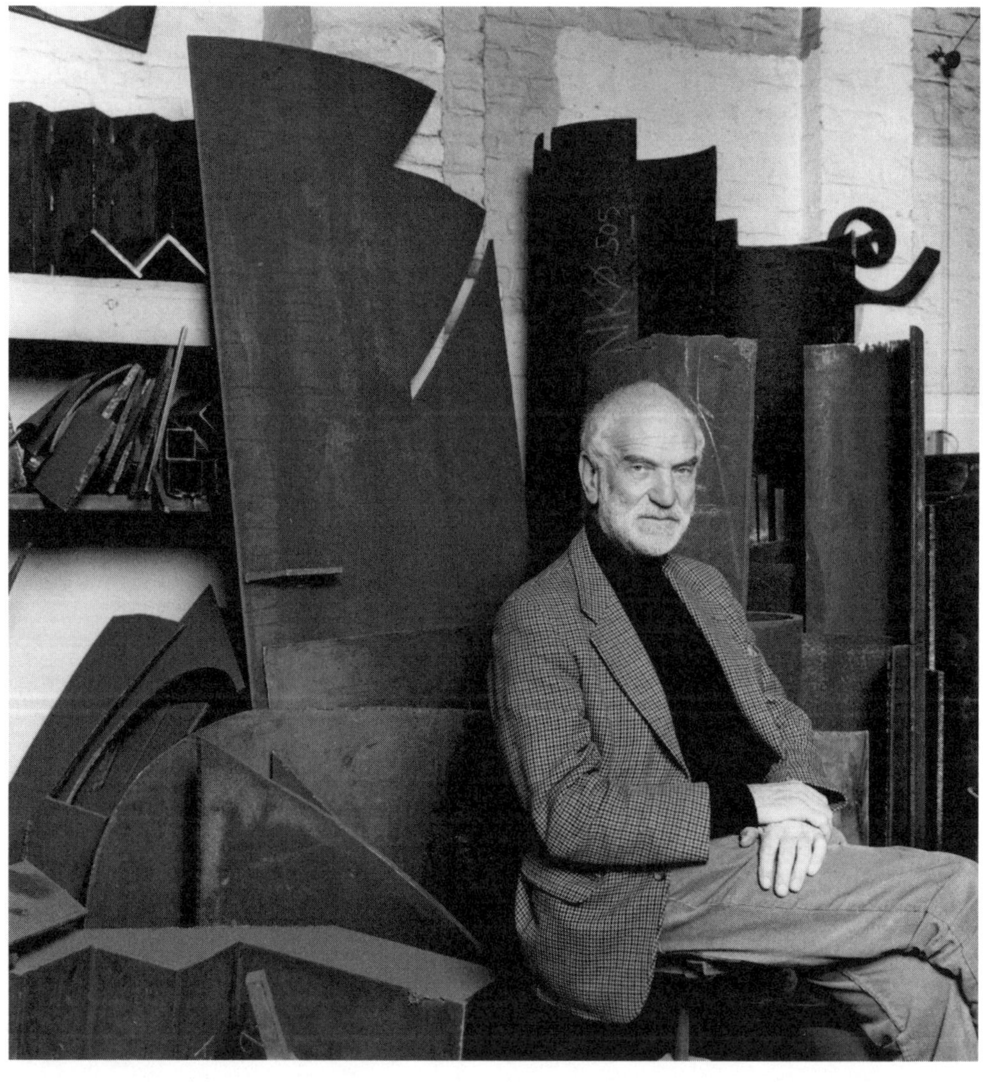

1992

Anthony Caro

'It really cut through all the stuff that was irrelevant. That's not purity – people say it was purity. It was a cutting-through situation, you know, and getting right down to what I felt'

Unlike any previous British sculptor, you were liberated by first-hand contact with American art. During your first trip to the US in 1959 you were greatly impressed by abstract painters like Kenneth Noland and Jules Olitski. Their work helped you to realise how important a role colour could play in your own work, and the critic Clement Greenberg encouraged you to explore new ways of making metal sculpture. You also found a sculptor in the US whose example provided the fundamental catalyst you needed: David Smith. Without in any way aping Smith's achievement, you now saw yourself in the tradition of welded sculpture which Smith had done so much to distinguish. After he died, you purchased the many tons of scrap metal which Smith had been using for his sculpture at Bolton Landing. But Twenty-Four Hours, *which dramatically announced your Damascene conversion to abstraction and welded metal in 1960, does not seem at all overshadowed by Smith's example. The prime quality of the sculpture you went on to make lay in its high-spirited élan and sense of release. No longer bound by your earlier need to represent the human figure, to cast in bronze and to display the outcome on a plinth, you transmitted this fresh confidence into your work with infectious zest.*

The radical sculpture of your maturity seems dramatically removed from an early piece like Man Holding his Foot, *done in 1954 when you were thirty years old. This is the work of an artist who didn't go straight to art school. While being educated at Charterhouse in Surrey, you worked during holidays in the studio of the sculptor Charles Wheeler. Then, after the Second World War erupted, you went to Christ's College, Cambridge, where you took a degree in Engineering. And you attended Farnham School of Art when on leave from serving with the Fleet Air Arm of the Royal Navy. In 1946 you went to the Regent Street Polytechnic to study sculpture for a year. And then, between 1947 and 1952, you studied at the Royal Academy Schools.*

But I'd like to start by asking you about Charles Wheeler, who eventually became the first sculptor to be elected President of the Royal Academy. What was he like? Did you relate to him at all?

He was very nice to me, and he was the one who said: 'You should go first to the Regent Street Polytechnic.' Because he came from Wolverhampton, and that was a kind of decorative school: he made all the sculptures on South Africa House and the Bank of England, and he also made one of the fountains in Trafalgar Square. I always rather threw myself into what I did, and so while being influenced by him, he was the only artist I really knew. I took a trip, when we were starting to be allowed to travel after the war, I went with my sister to Sweden to see those dryads and things – I'm ashamed of it!

You mean you're ashamed of liking them?

Yes, indeed. But we go through times like this, and there we are.

Did you have ambitions at this stage, perhaps, to be a maker of grand public sculpture? You weren't interested in the alternative modernist tradition?

I didn't know anything about it.

Really?

Well, as a matter of fact my great-uncle was a painter, and he stood up on a chair in the Picasso show at the V&A and said: 'It's all rot!' His paintings weren't very good. I did go to that Picasso show, but it was far too out for me. It took a long time for me to get to modern art, because even when I went to the Royal Academy we had different teachers every term, like Maurice Lambert, and it was pretty interesting. We'd have Charoux one term talking about making terracottas, and another term we'd have teaching about ivory carving, and so you picked up a bit from each one of them. You asked me whether I liked Wheeler: well, I liked him personally, but he said to me – and even then I realised it was a terrible thing – he said: 'You should look at the Greeks, because when you want to get a style for yourself, the Greeks are very useful.'

So when did you decide that it might be a good idea to go and work for Henry Moore? Because by 1951, while you were still at the Royal Academy Schools, you actually went to Moore's studio at Much Hadham as his part-time assistant.
Yes, at the Royal Academy Schools they've still got old corridors with those casts of Greek and Renaissance sculpture, and we drew those. But really not much attention was paid to them, and my ambition was to get something upstairs in that dreadful Royal Academy Summer Show! I knew there must be something better and more intelligent and meaningful in art than that – I just knew it. So I said: 'Who's the best? I suppose Henry Moore's the best.' He wasn't famous then, and I went to Henry Moore's studio.

Looking at it with hindsight, I would have thought that you'd be a rebel at the Royal Academy Schools, and stand out against what they were teaching.
No, I was a reluctant rebel. I didn't go there to be rebellious. I went there to try and make art as good as I could, and you just kept being pushed a bit further away from what was happening at the time.

I imagine that the Henry Moore experience, which lasted roughly two years, must have been somewhat ambiguous. On the one hand, he probably taught you a lot. On the other hand, there was something there to rebel against, I guess.
I didn't rebel against that until I was on the point of leaving, or until I left. I was turned on a lot by his work, the way he talked, the way he ran his studio. He let me borrow his books. I was still officially at the Royal Academy, so I would often drive him into London when he had to go to the Tate or the bank or whatever it was. And I would go to the RA Schools and draw. At the end of the day I'd drive him back, and then he'd say: 'Now come on, show me what you've done!' And I would show him the drawings. I never understood drawing at the RA: you were taught like a painter, and it doesn't make any sense to a sculptor because there was no volume. And Henry said: 'Make the light come from the left-hand side, or make it come from your eyes, and then you can accentuate the form in this way – invent the light.' I mean, he'd go through all that with me, and he'd go to a lot of trouble. So I was learning, and he was a kind of parent to me, sculpture-wise, which was wonderful. And then after two years I felt that I was too closely influenced, and it was time to move away. I'd seen a couple of things, I'd looked at a Picasso book and I'd seen a Francis Bacon – the walking Van Gogh ones – and I'd seen some De Koonings. And I said: 'I've got to move away from this and try.' When I went to Henry Moore I'd never seen an African sculpture, never: we were discouraged, you see, so really it wasn't thought anything of.

So Moore opened your eyes.
Absolutely, an enormous eye-opening experience.

And he had a very good library, didn't he?
Yes, he had very nice books, and he'd simply say: 'Take two books at a time. When you're finished we can talk about them.' And we would talk a lot – he was very open with me in those days. He was only about fifty-six and he was very free, you know: 'Who are your favourite painters? Look, you've got to have one picture you've seen today: who do you think is good?' And he was all rather like that.

*I think he must have changed later on, because I've met other people who
worked there in the latter years and he didn't, it seems, talk to them as artists
half so much.*

Well, it depends partly on the people, and he was getting older. He had a lot
more demands on his time and a lot less energy, I suppose. And he changed.

It sounds as if you got him at the right time.

Oh, I was very lucky. Besides, he had one or two old soldiers who went there
and played him up and said, 'I'm not going to do it unless I get more money',
and all that stuff. And in the end he said: 'To hell with that!'

*So if we had slides of the work you were doing at that point, what would
they look like?*

Well, they started off by being very Henry Moore-ish.

Did they?

Yes, and then I began to discover that you can take things and make them into
sculpture. So I dug up a tree-trunk and I made it into a bull's head – angry
animals. At that time it was the geometry of fear: everybody was thinking about
angry cats and cocks and so on, and I remember that I went to a stud farm in
order to see what bulls really looked like. They said: 'Please, you mustn't go in
dressed as you are, you'll have to put on this white coat and then the bull won't
go for you.' They were rather terrifying, these bulls. They moved their heads
very fast and they looked ferocious. But I drew them like that, and came back
and made sculptures of them and that sort of thing. So it was angry animals
first, and I think that was from Picasso, really – that angry period of Picasso.
Then I found it much more difficult to do a man, a person.

By this time were you well acquainted with Paris? Were you going to Paris?

Well, not really, not much.

*When you were interested in Dubuffet, for example, where would you have
seen his work?*

Oh, later. I wasn't sophisticated like Eduardo Paolozzi and Turnbull, who had
spent time in Paris. I didn't. And really, in a way, I didn't want to meet people,
like all the big shots here, Pasmore and Scott. I didn't want to go down to
St Ives and those people. That wasn't where I wanted to be.

That's entirely understandable. Looking at your 1954 sculpture, Man Holding
his Foot, *is there any way in which this derives from a posed figure?*

No, no.

Was it preceded by drawings?

Yes, I did hundreds of drawings at this time, big black ink and pen and brush.
Lots and lots of drawings, men holding a foot, holding bits of meat, they were
all very derivative of Picasso.

*It's interesting to me that, on the whole, the artists who meant most to you
at this time – unless you're talking exclusively about Picasso's sculpture –
are painters. You mentioned Bacon and De Kooning. So is it true to say
that painting, at this stage, meant more to you than sculpture, in terms
of what interested you?*

Later I think it meant more to me than sculpture. But Picasso was very
dominant at that time, and I think more was happening in painting.

Well, Bacon was certainly becoming very prominent by the mid-1950s.
And in a sculpture of yours like Man Taking Off His Shirt, *there's a tremendous*
sense of volume here.

> Yes, ideally I was interested in not what it looked like but what does it feel
> like to be taking your shirt off? What are you trying to do? Are you trying
> to shrink your head and make your head as small as possible, so you can
> get that thing off? Or in *Woman Lying Down*, it's kind of compressed,
> and those breasts and the head, they were picked up on a beach – they
> were stones. I'd go to the beach and bring back lots of stones. I developed
> a fine reputation with the landlady of a little boarding house. She didn't
> know what I was doing!

She took a dim view, I expect. Where was this?

> In Somerset.

Of course, this in a sense relates to Moore, because he always set great store
by what he would pick up on a walk through the countryside. In fact, you can
still see them at his Much Hadham studio, ranged rather neatly on the shelves
– all these little shells, pebbles and stones. Quite small things.

> Quite small, and he's wonderful on a tiny scale. He would pick up chalky stones,
> so they would have a harder piece of stone and then he would add to it and so
> on. And also at Much Hadham, where I was living at this period when I was
> with him, we would find things there and put them on the path where he
> walked, and he'd pick them up and he'd say: 'Look what I've found!' [Laughs.]

But you found, on the whole, rather bigger pieces?

> Well, I'm more comfortable with a slightly bigger scale.

Yes. But what relationship would they have, these found things, to what you
were doing in your sculpture?

> Not so much, but they would be starters of the whole thing, and sometimes
> I did take casts of much bigger stones than that. I took some rock casts, and
> in fact the tide came up and one would have to try and pull them off in time.
> So they were starting points.

Ostensibly, these works of the 1950s look dramatically different from what
you're famous for. But in what way would you say now, looking back, that they
relate to the work of the early 1960s, for example?

> I don't think they do.

Not at all? Not in any way? There's no underlying kinship?

> Not really. They're to do with feeling and getting to know the body. And all that
> is very important in my later work.

Yes, that's right. That hasn't changed, has it?

> No, it's as if I had to know that in order to do my later work. I don't really think
> there's a direct relationship. But if I hadn't known about, if I hadn't examined
> this thing about the body – which seems to me very much what sculpture's
> about, because sculpture, however far it goes towards the visual, is still very
> physical – had I not known about the physicality of the body, and experienced
> it and tried to express it, then I don't think my other sculpture would be as
> physical as it is visual.

And at the time you were doing these pieces in the 1950s, were you conscious,

*within yourself, of dissatisfaction – the kind of dissatisfaction that would
lead on to the 1960s work?*

Not until the end, no. Not until '59.

*By the time you were making your work of the mid-1950s, you were teaching
at St Martin's School of Art. We know a lot about St Martin's in the 1960s, but
what we don't know so much about is St Martin's in the 1950s. What kind of
context did that give you? Was it a stimulating one? Or were you conscious
of having to push it forward yourself?*

No, I loved teaching because I taught myself. The thing about teaching, for me,
was that it was fun and I was learning. It's never fun if you're kind of putting
on a gramophone record and saying the same thing again. But if you're trying
to work something out and learn, and the students are saying to you, 'Just
explain yourself, what do you mean and do you really mean it and how can
you do it?', if students are doing that and challenging you and giving you a hard
time, you can have a good time when you're teaching. Really, it was pragmatic.
I had no theory and no programme. Things would come up that would need
an answer, so we did that.

And did you find that teaching fed your own work?

Absolutely.

It sounds rather like it!

Oh, all the time, all the time.

*Let's push on to the late 1950s. I know that Clement Greenberg came over to
London and visited your studio. Was that an important moment for you?*

1959, I think. Yes, very important indeed, very important indeed. I met Clem
at a party, and he said: 'Well, British sculpture is cracked up to be very good
indeed, but it is no good.' So I said: 'You've no right to say that, because you
haven't seen mine.' That took him back a bit! So in the end, he said: 'Well,
I'll come and see you on Sunday. You've got to come and fetch me' [laughs].
I showed him my stuff and he still said that British sculpture was 'no good',
including mine. But I had this wonderful day with him, and he started going
through a lot of books on art, and talking about what he thought art should
be about, and he said such challenging things. He was really looking afresh
each time, and I began to understand why he was saying things like that.
I was beginning to get a different view of art, and it was very interesting
and very exciting.

*Was he in any way prescriptive with regard to your own work?
Did he try and channel you in any sense?*

Not at all, not at all. When I went to America and I saw him, I said: 'You came at
the right moment. I am fed up with what I'm doing, really. I feel I've got through
it, and I'm trying to find something else.' And he said things like: 'If you want to
change your art, change your habits.'

What did he mean by that?

Well, you had to figure it out – it's like the oracle [laughs].

*What did you think it meant? Apart from brushing your teeth three
times a day!*

For me, it meant that perhaps I'm going to try and find some other material
that's going to be able to do the sort of thing I want to do.

*But did he point you in any direction which you hadn't seen before from the past
– certain kinds of Picasso or certain kinds of Gonzalez, for example?*

No, but he clearly liked cubist Picasso better than any other Picasso. I mean,
good though the whole of Picasso was, I still think cubist Picasso is the
knockout. And I think actually that I've always been terribly interested in work
process, in ways of making art. And I think that I learned as much on that visit
in 1960 from Kenneth Noland, who told me that he made a painting flat on
the table, or flat on the floor – in a way that he couldn't see. He didn't put his
work up and look at it and paint. He painted what he felt and he painted what
he wanted, and he decided at the end to put it up and look at it and that was
it. This was for me quite an eye-opener in terms of a way to work, because then
when I got home I made very big things in my one-car garage studio. And
I couldn't see them! I just had to make what I wanted, and during those first
three years, from '60 to '63, I did actually make one or maybe two which I put
outside. And when I put them outside, I started to make balanced judgements.

Was Twenty-Four Hours *made in the one-car garage at home?*

Yes, it was the first, and it's very Noland in a certain way.

*Yes, it certainly is. Would you say that Noland had more of an impact on you
than David Smith, in a sense?*

Yes, much more, much more.

I find that quite surprising.

Well, Smith was fifteen years older than me, and he wasn't as friendly as Ken.

He was rather difficult, was he?

Yes, he was a funny man. No, I learned a lot from him, too. And actually he
was all right, but he didn't show it, he didn't tell you what he thought that much,
and he was very macho and he was actually terribly kind to my little sons.
He had a really sort of soft heart, and he was very sweet with my wife Sheila,
and very nice with babies. But if a man came anywhere near him, he'd put
on the big 'fee-fi-fo-fum' stuff [laughs].

Even with younger men?

Very much so. I arrived in America with my family in '63 to teach at
Bennington College, Vermont. We had quite a horrendous trip over, lost
our luggage and so on. The children were very young, and it was all terribly
new and strange to us the first time in the States – it was the first time to go
and live there. I was met at Bennington, after this horrendous day we'd had,
by Ken Noland, who said, 'Well, put the children in that hotel and you come
up with me because David [Smith] is waiting for you – he's having dinner at
The Rainbow', which was a little pub. The place was completely empty, except
at this table right in the middle was sitting David and his assistant. He was
a very big man, and he was gnawing a chicken bone. When I walked in,
he stood up and he was stretched as high up as that clock – you know, big!
He wore these big welding boots, and I just felt so shrunk by the time I got
to him, because he seemed to be this giant saying: 'I smell the blood of an
Englishman!' [Laughs.] No, he was all right, he was all right. But there was
a more competitive thing with him than with Henry [Moore], who was like
a daddy. And he did say things to me like: 'Spend all your money on art – have
the best paper, and the best tools.' I know he did that, because his wife didn't
have a washing-up machine or anything like that, and he had everything
[laughs]. Two wives left him, I may say!

*What about the radical change in your working materials? Or maybe this
is what Greenberg meant by 'habits', was it? There was a very dramatic change
in every sense – not only in terms of the language you were using, but also how
you were going about making things.*

Well, I started by going to the scrapyards and got some stuff. And stuck it
together. But I didn't even know that world. I really didn't know how to cut,
or anything. I didn't go to any classes.

So you had to buy your oxyacetylene equipment.

Yes. We didn't use any electrical stuff. Butler did – Reg Butler was a cutter
and an electric welder. We thought he was so extravagant!

And colour is already playing a very major role, isn't it?

Yup. I never really could get colour right. I never was that interested, and
I'm not still. In fact, Sheila was the person for my colour. I'd say: 'What colour
should that be?' And we'd try it, and if it was wrong we'd do another one, till
it was right. I think *Early One Morning* was brown.

So Early One Morning *was brown originally?*

Well, only for a couple of days [laughs].

What inspiration did you take from the well-known folk song of the same title?

You know, it's got nothing to do with the sculpture. It's bright, and it's like 'good
morning', and it says 'yes'. It's absolutely nothing to do with 'that's the red sun',
'that's the view'. Nothing at all, none of that comes into it anywhere. But I have
great difficulty in getting titles, and I sometimes look at songbooks, and I often
look at the names of racehorses [laughs].

*If you had to sum up what abstraction actually gave you at this point in your
career, what would you say it was? Did you feel that in some sense it released
you from all that bodily preoccupation that you had in the 1950s? They look
very exhilarating, these works of the early 1960s. They still have an
extraordinary exuberance about them, which strikes me every time I see them.*

I felt it cut through something: it really cut through all the stuff that was
irrelevant. That's not purity – people say it was purity. It was a cutting-through
situation, you know, and getting right down to what I felt. And I think that
I wanted it that way. I remember saying: 'There have been books that have
gone on from *Ulysses*, and if I'd been a writer I'd have taken that.' I don't need
a story any more. I need this feeling, and I need the words, and that's it –
straight through. And of course the nice thing about Manet is that he cut right
through: feeling, painting, nothing in between. And I think, in a way, our art –
for me, contemporary thinking – dates from Manet.

I guess that, by this time, late Matisse cut-outs may well have been important to you.

Yes, the colour comes straight out of the book [laughs]. But Clem said: 'Nice
sculpture, except for the colour.' He might be right, I don't know.

Is that what he said? Well, I think he was wrong.

Well, you see, colour does define certain things. But perhaps it doesn't need
colour – I don't know.

Month of May *was put on view at the Battersea Open Air Show in 1966.
This annual event was one of the big ways in which you could exhibit your
sculpture in those days.*

It's a terrible pity they don't have them any more. They were so good.

*They were extraordinary. And in 1966 you got your work, with Moore and
Hepworth behind you, in this small area of Battersea Park. It was a kind of
madness in a way, but also every exciting.*

The time before, *Midday* was put in a corner. There was a lot of American art,
and it was as if the Americans were kind of fighting – they were all put in one
area, and all the rest of it was the Europeans. It was like a battle! But I don't like
my sculpture out of doors at all. Not this sort of thing: it's very much an indoor
piece, for a very contained space.

By the time you made Bennington *in 1964, you were getting much more severe,
more stripped down. It's true to say that, around the mid-1960s, you were really
simplifying things and taking them much more down towards the floor level.*

Well, what happened was that when I went to Bennington, one of the nice
things about being with Olitski and Noland and Greenberg and all those people
was that they told the truth. They were close enough to be able to say: 'We like
that, we don't like that and this is why we like it.' One of the things Ken said,
which I took to heart – I don't know whether he was right or wrong – he said:
'Those early sculptures of yours are OK, but you've got four or five sculptures in
one. Why can't you do all four? The way I work is in series.' He'd learned that
from Smith, so he would do several. I'd say: 'Do you think it's right, Ken?' 'It's all
right – do another!' That would be his idea. And so I worked through, in a quite
different way, the stripping down.

One of your pieces, in 1965, is actually called Strip.

Before I left England, I did put up six or nine – nine, I think – H-beams, tilted,
and I was going to make a sculpture and I couldn't. Rauschenberg had said
things like, 'if I take this, and I take this', and he came into the room and it was a
sculpture. I knew that was stupid. But on the other hand, it's a really interesting
idea that two completely separate things can be the same sculpture. How can I
push things apart, pull things apart? In those years it was all to do with
extension, all to do with separation. And how can I try and make those things
join? I had these pieces in the studio for ages, and I couldn't make them work
together. By looking at Matisse, and seeing that Matisse would take several
things – jug, apple, pitcher – then he would divide the picture, the background,
half black and half blue. And that way, they wouldn't just sit on nothing: they
would sit on a background which had enough movement in it not to make it
just sheer decoration. And I thought: 'I can do it with sculpture. If I can make a
wall going across things, then the whole thing will become one thing.' That was
the power, really. And then Michael Fried said to me: 'You're making the floor
part of the sculpture. So you don't have to go up like you did before, because it's
all working in a way to do with the floor.'

This is about as minimal as you get, isn't it?

Yes, probably.

*Looking back on it now, it seems as if you must have decided, having done
something like this, that it was as minimal as you wanted to be, that there
wasn't anywhere you could take that – except, perhaps, to move towards
greater complexity again. Would that be right?*

Yes, except that it wasn't quite like that. Because I had made these things
which were very, very simple, and I decided that I had to clothe them in
a new way.

*By this time you had decided to restrict yourself to one colour only, hadn't
you? And to let your sculpture inhabit the floor, you now became interested
in the idea of the table – the idea, almost, of the plinth. But it's a sort of
subversive relationship with the plinth, isn't it? It's using the plinth or the
table in a new way.*

Well, I'd got so bored with seeing all these. I mean, by that time everybody was
making their work snake across the floor. And I thought: 'I can't go on like that
– I've got to change.' And I also thought: 'Why has sculpture got to be a certain
size? It's very much to do with us, you know – to do with our size. So why
shouldn't I make a small one?' And if you're going to make a small one, you've
got to think freshly about what is a small sculpture. It's not a maquette, it's not
a little building. How do you avoid making it the wrong size? Well, better have
a handle – most things, like cups, have handles, and that relates their size to us.
Going over the edge of the table is important, too. And after a bit, I began to lose
the handles and also lose going over the edge. But the edge was very important.
They sometimes look like a bit like paintings of still lives – I looked at a lot of
Cézanne, a lot of Chardin and a lot of Matisse. Nothing I have done is funny.
No, I hate wit in art.

But you're not a solemn kind of person, are you?

Well, the English do get into all that whimsical stuff. It's a pain in the neck.
Real art isn't about that.

It's a bit of an English curse, in fact.

I think so, yes. And I don't like that. I think one has got to be jolly careful about
trying to find tie-ups – with still lives and things – because by and large the
works are themselves. I can never understand why people can't see abstraction.
They can't seem to grasp that something is more about its abstract qualities,
perhaps, than it is about something else. It's not necessary to put all that extra
stuff on it.

And then you made Prairie. *This, I remember so vividly, was a great excitement
to me. As someone really quite young, in 1967, I came across this sculpture in
that wonderful Kasmin Gallery in New Bond Street – it was a very remarkable
space. You approached it through a long, narrow corridor, and suddenly there
was this extraordinary room at the back. And* Prairie *was just there – nothing
else. It was a one-piece exhibition.*

I think it was. D'you know something? It was incredible, and shows how much
Kas [Kasmin] was in love with this sort of art and how much he would do for
it. I said, 'Kas, I don't see how I can put *Prairie* there on this rubber floor,' which
was up and down.

Yes, it was bumpy.

And he said: 'Don't worry, I'll put a new floor in for you.' And he put an entire
new floor into that gallery just for *Prairie*. It was amazing. He was mad about
art in those days, and I thought he had some lovely shows there. But anyway,
Prairie was all about floating.

All about floating?

It's called *Prairie* because the paint that I used is called Prairie Gold.

*But is there no sense in which this relates to an experience of landscape?
Maybe your experience of the American landscape?*

No, no, no. But I'll say one thing, which is that the last time I came back from

America, I noticed that my way of looking had changed. When I was in America, I was looking at a long way away, and when I came back to London I was looking at my garden [laughs].

Prairie is a very remarkable, beautiful piece – it's one of my favourites.
Thank you. I'll tell you how I did it. You see, the corrugated steel, I started by putting that up on a block of wood. I left it there, and it was sitting there, nagging at me for a few weeks. And then I said: 'Well, of course I'm stupid! It's got those four dents in it, and it needs four poles across.' Then we started laying them across. It was never an idea.

Are you the kind of artist who takes the previous work as a springboard, in terms of reacting against it? Because it seems to me that Trefoil, *which was done a year later in 1968, could well be reacting against* Prairie, *couldn't it?*
Well, not so much. It was all about levels in those days. Also, I remember when I did it I had a studio in London Road, and I built something on a table and I said: 'The table's part of it, so let's take it through the table.'

Incorporating the table in the sculpture?
Sort of, yes.

At the same time you were still using 'the table' as this space – falling off, flying in between, almost weightless in a strange way, even though it's resting on the table.
So they tell me [laughs]. I did once have a sculpture which somebody bought and welded into their gate.

No!
I heard about it, and I wasn't very pleased. I couldn't do anything about it – it wasn't worth making a fuss. Then suddenly, it came up at Sotheby's with an extra bit of gate on it!

By this time you were very well known, and your 1969 Hayward show was an official recognition of that fact. But how did you feel about your relationship with the wider public? Did you still feel that you were misunderstood, or did you think that by this time you were getting through?
I don't think people feel very comfortable with abstract sculpture. And steel sculpture, I don't think people like it very much. I don't think I'm being too paranoid. But I didn't really give a damn. At St Martin's, you know, we were mad. And we were regarded as very mad, and as a hostile, difficult bunch of people. I realise it now, because we had no time for, say, the Royal College and the people there. They weren't bad, but we were intolerant, and so who did we care about? We cared about what the other sculptors thought: about half-a-dozen people in the world. It's very strange. And it was very wonderful and exciting in the 1960s, because I would get a telephone call from Bill Tucker or Phillip King or Mike Bolus saying: 'I've made a new sculpture, come and look at it, see what you think!'

Do you miss that feedback now or do you still get it in a different way? Obviously, this was quite a tightly knit thing you're talking about, wasn't it?
It was lovely. I had it at St Martin's around 1960 to '63, and I had it with Jules Olitski and Kenneth Noland also. And when I made those triangular workshops the same thing happened: we always asked each other what we thought of things. I don't think there's much of it at the moment.

When you get older, you tend to go on your own way. You get a bit more tunnel vision – you can only see what you're interested in.

So maybe you don't need that feedback any more.
Oh, you always need it. And when it happens, it's great.

I'm leaping forward a bit now, in fact a decade, to a piece called Emma Dipper, *which is probably familiar to a lot of us because it belongs to the Tate. I've always imagined, because of that title – this is a very dangerous thing to imagine, I realise [laughs] …*
I'd like to hear what you do imagine …

I've always imagined with this one that it's something to do with a child's movements. And I'm entirely wrong, I suppose.
I'm afraid so [laughs]. All that series was called Emma because I was asked to go to a workshop in Saskatchewan, in a place called Emma Lake, and they had a lot of painters but they hadn't had many sculptors. And I remember before I went – the day before – saying to Sheila: 'I'm going to be miles from anywhere, I haven't thought about this, what am I going to do in terms of steel? I can't go and have any heavy stuff, because they won't have any equipment for lifting.' So she said: 'Why don't you work with a cube and rod?' So I did. And I remember Dorothy Knowles saying to me at Emma Lake: 'What are you going to call these?' And I said: 'Oh, I don't know – Emma This and Emma That.' So this was *Emma Dipper*, and there was a place called A Big Dipper, which was where we all went for a dinner and it was such fun there. It is a kind of Dipper, too!

Absolutely, it is a very evocative title. But you've ruined my interpretation of it!
Oh, I'm so sorry [laughs].

I'll never mention it again [laughs].
I should leave them all in mystery. But I'm not very good at all that – one really should learn to cultivate that as an artist.

Yes, be completely silent and mysterious.
Yes, absolutely.

What I admire about the way you've gone on, as you got older, is the fact that you refused to stay in one place. Having revolutionised British sculpture in the early 1960s, someone in your position might well have felt, 'Well, that's OK,' and be content to reiterate what they'd formulated for the rest of their lives, in a rather cosy way. But what you've done is to be completely intolerant about that whole idea. You've always wanted to try something new. I guess perhaps you're rather a restless kind of person, are you?
No, but I really don't want to be bored. And I can't see any point in turning out more versions of the same. Also, if I make a bad one, I make a bad one: I'm not going to edit and say, 'I didn't do it,' and try and worry about what you did. You make it, you really do your best, and you put it up there, and you make a note of it, you take a photograph of it, and that's it! Now let's go on. Don't agonise and go back and say, 'Oh, I shouldn't have done this,' endlessly.

Looking at this later piece now, it dates from the mid-1980s and it's called The Moroccans. *So someone like me immediately thinks of Matisse.*
Yes, that's right.

*Oh, that's right, is it? Good! [Laughs.] So what made you think of Matisse's
1916 painting* The Moroccans?
> Well, that particular picture has got me going a lot of times. It's marvellous,
> it's wonderful. There was a show in New York not so long ago of Matisse's
> Moroccan pictures. People were getting very enthusiastic about most of the
> show, which wasn't that good. I mean, one or two or three were very good
> pictures, but it's all about that final picture. It's a wonderful picture.

It's a memory picture.
> It goes on bothering you, and actually I think that three or four times I've used
> it. For example, I've used it in a sculpture called *Garland*, which was separated
> by a wire mesh. And I've used it in another one called *The Mosque*. I don't know,
> it keeps on fascinating me. I can't get away from thinking about it, and there
> you are.

I can quite understand that.
> I thought at this time: 'I'll try and make something in terracotta, and I'll use
> this as a starting point.'

Why terracotta?
> I did make some terracotta in another workshop, and I thought I could take
> terracotta a lot further. I still think so: I don't think I'm using it right.

After Olympia *was shown at the Tate only last year, in the Duveen Galleries,
and then in the summer of 1992 it reappeared in the battered grandeur of the
Trajan Markets in Rome. We're talking here about an immense sculpture.*
> What happened was I went to Olympia, and it's totally devastating. I had a
> wonderful trip to Greece, and you're driving back afterwards and start talking,
> and Sheila said: 'You know, you could do that. You could do a sculpture like
> that.' And for a long time I've thought: 'Why do I have to make sculpture a
> certain size? Why can't sculpture, instead of being one thing, why shouldn't
> it be like *War and Peace* and have four or five different themes going through
> it, interlacing and so on?' I happened to have a completely empty studio,
> so I thought: 'Well now, I'm going to take up the whole studio.' I made it in
> Camden Town, that piece, and actually it suffered very much from being made
> in that small studio, because you can't really ... I don't know yet what the right
> viewing distance is. Funnily enough, when it was in Rome it wasn't a bad space.

*I thought Rome was so much better than the Duveen Galleries, yes. It looked
terrific. This was the exhibition you had in the Trajan Markets, part of the
Roman Forum. And it seemed to fit there, partly of course because you're talking
now about a relationship with classicism, aren't you?*
> Maybe, I don't know. Maybe, maybe.

*If somebody had told you in the 1960s that you would now be looking at the
Temple of Zeus at Olympia, would you have been astonished by that? Would
you have believed them?*
> I don't know, I don't know. I don't think about the future and I don't think
> about the past. I'm a very superficial person – I hope I've made that clear
> this afternoon [laughs]. I think about what I'm doing now. I get on with it,
> you know.

But in terms of Olympia, *I'm going to pursue you on this one, I'm sorry.*
> Oh, you are a pain [laughs].

I know I am. In terms of Olympia, *is it to do with the fact that you felt there
was something missing from your work before – some kind of relationship
with the tradition that you fought shy of earlier?*

No, no.

*Is it that only at this stage of your life can you come to terms with all
that classical brief?*

Yes, that's absolutely true. Let's put it in a different way. Everybody, when I was
at the Royal Academy Schools, we all went to Greece and so on. I wouldn't go
– I wouldn't go. I couldn't take it at that time. And it really did take thirty years
until I could take it. Now I've got to go to Greece, that's right. But in my work
I don't think I can say that. My work is always reacting against the last sculpture
I've done. If it's very dry and very cold, let's get a bit more Rubens in there or
something. You look at other art, and you say: 'God, it's so good.' And what you
liked yesterday is very dry, perhaps, or you see this other thing. All sorts of
things like that are going on every time you make a group of work, and you say:
'Yes, but.' So that's how it came about, really. Every time you go to somewhere
like Italy or Greece or India, I'm not turned on necessarily by what I expected
to be turned on by, but by something different. And I think I was most turned
on, in that Greek trip, by the lions and things – the very, very early ones in the
Acropolis Museum.

After Olympia *still looks to me pretty abstract. But of course, the west pediment
of the Temple of Zeus is figurative. So what relationship does this piece of yours
have to the figurative tradition?*

The steel is bent and twisted and contorted in different ways, and gets a little
bit more like figurative things.

So you wouldn't deny the figurative strain in it?

There's a sort of suggestion of figurative, but I can't get as close to the figures
as some people can. Not comfortably. And I don't know what the reasons are.
It often happens, when I'm drawing, I draw the figure and love it, but I leave
the head out. And I don't know why. Now maybe this is some psychological …

Deep waters here.

Deep waters, yes.

This piece is called The Descent from the Cross after Rembrandt,
and it relates, unless I'm mistaken, to The Descent *painted by*
Rembrandt in 1633–4.

Yes, you're right. But it's too close. I'll tell you how that came about. In the
After Olympia the geometry is outside: the way I made it was to put a bit
of string up there and start from that. And you're very conscious of that, of
being held in, even though it's not there. And I thought: 'Why don't I make
the geometry come inside?' So I could be as loose as I like, and take the cross,
which is not held by anything.

*But did that idea come to you before you settled on the Rembrandt, or
afterwards?*

I don't know, but I think it was about the same time.

Was the Rembrandt something you saw in the original or in a book?

I had seen the original, and my first thought was the Rubens *Descent*,
the big one.

---

*We're dealing here with very intense human emotions – the sense not only of
pathos but death. How far would you say that your piece was to do with mortality?*

I don't think it's anything to do with mortality. I wish I could ascribe such
thoughts to it. I just wonder how much the other picture is to do with the
subject matter – the figures and the faces – and how much it's to do with the
pulling and the dropping of the Christ figure, and the holding up of the arm.
It seems to me that it's all to do with pushings and pullings – and that's what
I'm getting turned on by. Death and that? Well, no, that's Rembrandt's depth
of character, it's his incredible depth of feeling and compassion. I don't think
I can really go out and … it's something you've either got or you haven't.

Let's turn to Night Movements, *which was on show last autumn with* After
Olympia *at the Tate. I thought it looked very good there.*

I had a lot of trouble placing it. But it was changed on the last day, and I was
quite happy. But I did do that show wrong. I think that I lost my nerve, putting
that tower in the middle, and it wasn't a very good sculpture. It was lovely for
the children and the warders and people, but it wasn't a very good sculpture.
I should have done the show with three. And if I had done with three, I would
have done better to put the long one in the North Duveen and the short ones
in the South Duveen. I think so, don't you?

Quite possibly.

The North Duveen is a horrible space – it's very hard to cope with.

Night Movements – *what can you say about the starting point for this piece?*

I did think of connecting it up. Then I thought: 'It isn't necessary.' I did have
some connectors in it, along the floor. No, funnily enough, I got a lot of material
and I had those very squashed pieces. We did a workshop in Maastricht, and
when we were there, I went to this rather marvellous scrapyard where they
actually crush motor cars and things. They had very good crushed steel there,
and Pat went back to get me some steel. He got twelve tons of steel – and you
know, you have to take a chance then. He did get these pieces which were
almost cylinders, but very crushed. And I thought: 'Well, we've got jolly good
things here, but I'll never use those, they're no good at all.' And you know, three
or four years after, I used them in *Night Movements*. But trying to get
something close to the monolith – we'd been talking about monoliths and
things – I thought: 'Well, how close to the monolith can I go without it
becoming a lump?'

*It's interesting that you use the word 'crushed', because there's an element in your
Rembrandt piece of some body being crushed. There's certainly something
running through* After Olympia *of battered-ness, it seems to me. There's a kind
of link between these three very different sculptures in that sense, isn't there?*

I suppose, yes, certainly.

It's not something that would have interested you earlier.

Not a bit, not a bit. And in a way, you see, I couldn't. When you think about
the 1960s – Kennedy and, you know, rockets to the moon and the whole thing
– the whole idea of the 1960s was so different. And it's only when you look back,
you say: 'Gosh, the art expresses it.' I mean, the art you were making and the
way you were thinking was to do with that. And the way you were thinking in
the 1980s was to do with something different. I don't really know that we have
very much of our own to say – maybe we're just saying what's around now or
something, maybe we're just saying what's in the air.

And what is in the air?

I don't know.

Can you say something more about this?

I'm getting towards something very much more architectural, very much more held, very much more solid.

Is the Elephant Palace, *a 1989 piece, much more architectural?*

More architectural. You know, I'm interested in going not necessarily entirely this way, but going towards something that says to you that it has an inside. And maybe it's a skin, and maybe you can get in or something. Whereas I was looking at painting a lot before, I'm looking at quite a lot of architecture, too, now. Actually, architects are interesting to talk to. They're more interesting than sculptors, most of them, by and large.

By calling it Elephant Palace, *you're certainly leading the viewer to the meaning of this piece, aren't you? Are you aware of that?*

Not particularly.

It sounds quite specific, Elephant Palace – *in a way that* Month of May *or* Early One Morning *don't. But in the sense that it reflects a vastly increased interest in architecture,* Elephant Palace *is certainly an appropriate title. In fact, you've coined this word 'sculpitecture' – a fusion word.*

Well, that came about because I worked at a workshop with some architects, and I worked with Gehry and we talked about the idea that an architect could work like a sculptor. Architects could pick units and put them and attach them like a sculptor does, instead of making drawings – or as well as making drawings. And we did it together a bit, and when I made something that people could get into, I said: 'It's not really architecture.' I was talking to the wife of an architect, and I felt ashamed of it [laughs]. And I said: 'It's not a sculpture, it's a sculpitecture, it's not a joke.' And you know, it got picked up.

It stuck.

Yes, it stuck. I think that architects could do with being a little less wedded to the right angle, a little looser and so on. And I think sculptors really had better start thinking in a different way – I mean all of us. And I think with ordinary-size sculpture, the whole question of solidity is a problem. The solid, the object, is tied up with the idea of the body, and all that got completely opened out and broken up with cubism. Or rather, not so much broken up but peeled, really, and I don't think you can go back to it. So if you start thinking about something a bit more monolithic, maybe you have to start thinking in terms of skill – which of course is what architecture is anyway. And you don't think of a building as a lump, you think of it as a lump you can get into. And that getting in keeps on being revealed by windows and doors and things. So I'm intrigued by that. But I don't think I've ever actually followed anything to the end. And I'm terribly impressed with, say, Chillida's exhibition, because I think Chillida is a great sculptor. He takes a thing and he presses it every way.

Yes, quite true. His show is on at the Annely Juda Gallery, and it's well worth a visit.

It's not as great a Chillida show as the one at the Hayward, but it's a nice show. And I think you'll see there how he takes an idea and does it in steel, and in terracotta, and in etchings and paper works and so on. I think it's very good, but that's not been the way I work. I think much more that I have something

and I push that idea. Then I'm deflected to something else and I can't
help following it, so I follow that. I'm interested really in pushing the
possibilities of sculpture in every direction that comes along. Because
I think sculpture has been a very constricted art – it got very bad, and it's
suddenly being taken seriously again. So we've got to try and give it a chance
by going every way you can.

Do you think you've got a lot more left to do? It sounds like it.
Oh yes, I hope so. I hope so, I hope so. Yes, I think I'd better start!

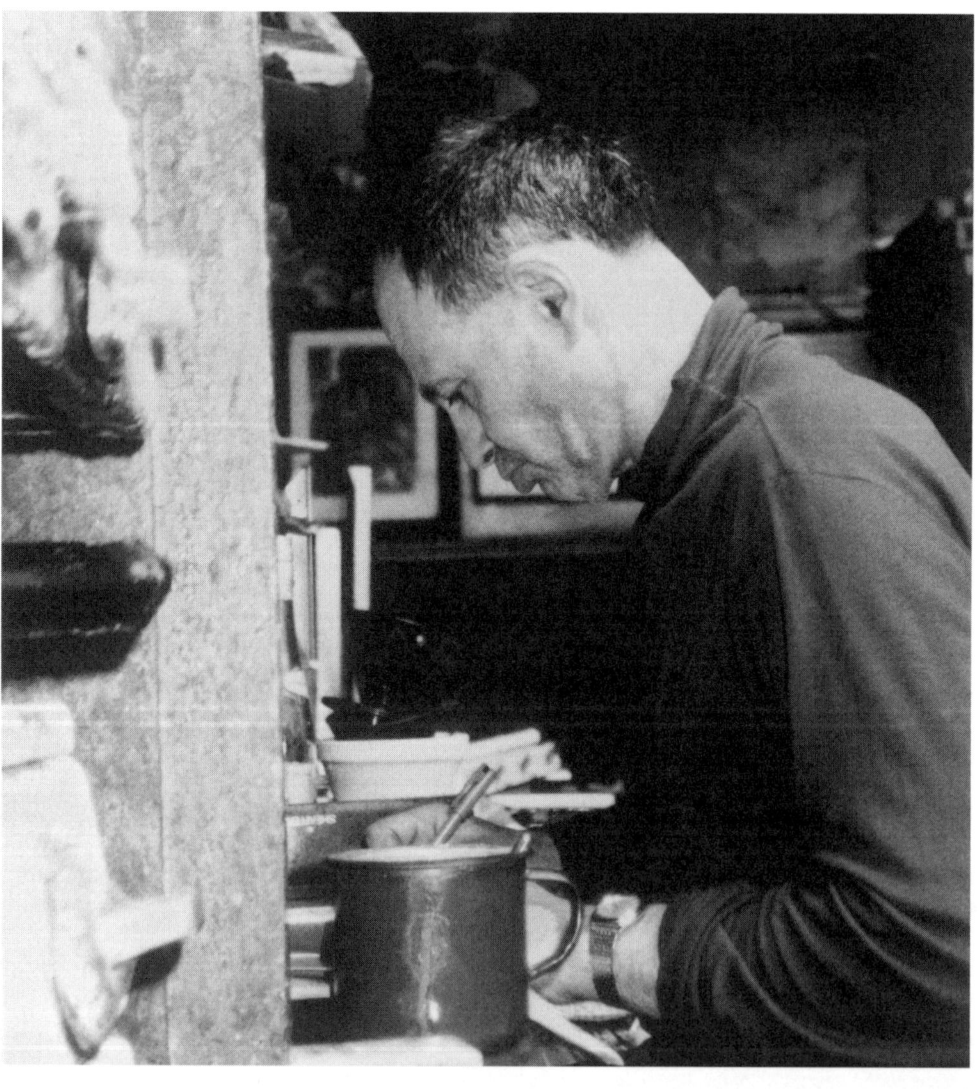

1983

Frank Auerbach

'I think people do start painting because of a sort of anxiety about time. One knows that the experience is going to go, one knows the people are going to disappear, so one tries to pin them down'

For the past three decades, you have concentrated on a deliberately narrow range of subjects. With great single-mindedness, you return time and again to the faces of a few friends and relatives, the streets around your studio in North London, and the terrain of a nearby park.

There have, on occasions, been other subjects – most notably a dramatic series of paintings inspired by building sites elsewhere in the city – when your paint took on something of the gouged and churned quality of the excavated earth itself. But the building-site pictures came to an end some years ago, and you have concentrated since then on the people and places you know best. Even so, your strength as a painter and draughtsman lies in a refusal to take anything for granted. With every new attempt to tackle a figure isolated in the darkness of a room, or the looming facades of buildings in your Camden Town neighbourhood, you study the motif as if for the very first time. Why do you so rarely stray beyond these self-imposed confines?

Because I think it serves as a corrective factor, knowing something well. One has a life, and the people one is involved with seem to me tremendously worth recording. There are these people whom one pays attention to, who will never occur again. I think people do start painting because of a sort of anxiety about time. One knows that the experience is going to go, one knows the people are going to disappear, so one tries to pin them down. One starts a large painting, one has certain arbitrary habits or ambitions, and simply to make a record of this ambition, which finally I suppose would be a sort of decayed memory, isn't sufficient. There has to be a sort of conflict between what one wants and what actually exists. So one goes out and does a drawing, and it's always easier to do a drawing of a place that is close. Also there is a sort of intimacy, excitement and confidence that comes from inhabiting the painting, and knowing exactly where everything is. A sort of magic in conjuring up a real place, a record of it that is somewhere between one's feeling about the facts and the appearance. Well, more than appearance – substance.

But this is rather paradoxical, isn't it? Because when I look at your paintings, even of things that you know extremely well, I am very aware of the fact that you find them very strange and, in a way, mysterious.

Well, it's precisely those things that do seem mysterious. People who use the world as tourists begin to have habits of perception: they move around and have a way of grasping things. Even, for instance, infinitely more powerful painters than me who do portraiture eventually get into certain habits. So that a painter who is as magically, inexplicably gifted as Gainsborough, or an enormously talented painter like Sargent, when they get down to painting a stranger they get into certain habits – simply because the thing has to be done, and they have formed habits of coping with this enormously testing challenge. I respect portraiture: I think it takes an enormously intelligent person simply to make a likeness. But I think that they fall into these habits. Whereas if I paint somebody, what happens is that I paint them once and I do my damnedest to discover something that I hadn't known before and that stands up as a coherent whole. As soon as one has done that, it's a little bit like the feeling when one has finished a crossword puzzle: one has the solution, and at the same time there is a feeling of let-down because there is something about them – simply because one knows them well – that has escaped one. So the stimulus is there immediately to do another one. And actually the whole business of drawing is much more chancy than people think. If you draw outside, whether a line is horizontal or slopes up or down is very much a matter of choice. And unless one has an absolutely set method, which to me would be boring, the possibilities are infinite. Actually, the more one squeezes the lemon, the more one is likely to get out of it something that one hadn't predicted.

You mentioned drawing there. I mean, do you see drawing – which is obviously an extremely important activity to you, and ranges over the whole idea of observation – do you see drawing as a distinct activity or as something which is indivisible from painting, something that merges with the process of painting?

I think of it all as drawing – whether with charcoal or paint. It's a question of trying to throw a lasso to capture the organic fact in a way that doesn't throttle the life out of it, and at the same time makes a coherent theorem – as it were, a geometrical theorem – where everything leads to everything else and is part of a whole. I mean, the further one stretches the preconditions, the further the things are apart, the more different things one notices before it's tied together, the more one is caught in one's net. But finally I think of it all as drawing: colours, drawings. Painting is drawing in slabs rather than edges, but it's all drawing to me.

I can understand what you mean by saying 'it's all drawing'. But at the same time, when I am looking at your painting, I'm very aware, acutely aware, of the substance, of the pigment. It's something that you declare very openly, isn't it?

Well, it is. But I never sat down and decided that what I wanted to do was to slosh a lot of thick paint on. It's my nature and my nurture that comes out in this way. I'm not satisfied with my first attempt. I cover the painting quickly, I can do something that looks like one of my drawings in half an hour, but I find it unsatisfactory. It never seems specific enough for me, it never seems to be new enough. And so I find myself going on with the thing. And as I go on, I find the problem more and more impossible. And because, I suppose, of my temperament, I find myself behaving in an excessive way, in order to solve that problem. And because so much has gone on, because so much paint has been put on to strengthen the canvas, I find I have to put on fairly large quantities of paint in order to make an impression on it over the wet paint, over the scarred canvas. It's an intemperate business, but it isn't to do with a programme. I mean, it may be that people in a domestic situation find themselves telling hard truths when they are in a quarrel, and it may be that I find myself telling truths when I am finally with my back against the wall and don't care any longer what I do. Because I'm aware of manners, I don't want the paintings to look disgusting or excessive. It's simply that I do want them to be alive. And they don't come alive to me in ways that are full of clichés, or they are incomplete or not coherent. And finally it drives one into a state where I find myself behaving like that. And that, in fact, is the unity – not because I chose to don a mantle of a style or have a programme. I think that the unity in any painter's work is because people, when brought to a desperate situation, behave in a certain way. And this is what real style is. It's how one behaves in a crisis.

You've already said that familiarity with people or things gives you a certain valuable sense of freedom. Do you find sometimes that telling the truth, which is clearly one of your major preoccupations, disturbs the person you have been painting? Or is that something you cannot allow yourself to take into account?

I am not aware of their judgement, really. Firstly, the process of painting itself is so painful and goes on for so long. I mean, some people sit for me and I go on doing it and go on doing it. I think they would gradually begin to lose all hope of the thing ever being finished. It's only people's sense of duty and decency, and the feeling that they would let me down, that makes them go on sitting. When finally I get the result that satisfies me – it probably might not look very different from the many results that don't satisfy me – people have got so tired passing any judgement that they no longer do so. I think some of the people whom I painted have probably thought it is a lot of nonsense, and some people thought it had something. I don't think I have ever been aware of either attitude, particularly.

How often do you abandon work, reject it completely?
D'you know, almost never. I think that is obsessive. Very, very occasionally I started a thing and then found that there was something else I would more urgently like to do. I can only think of one sitter who has let me down, and then I substituted another sitter and went on turning the one head into another in the same pose. I never abandon the things. That's perhaps why they look as they do, and it isn't that I have marvellous ideas before I start. I have certain things I want to do which seem to me to be worth doing. I don't know how to do them, and then I go on. I may not know how to do them because they are immensely complicated; I may not know how to do them because they seem so bland, ordinary. In either case, I am very interested to see what will happen if I go on working on them, and so I go on.

Does all your work take an inordinate amount of time, or do some paintings come off very quickly?
A few paintings come off quickly: almost always a second attempt at something that I had worked on for a long time. On the other hand, I think almost all the paintings that I am not ashamed of have gone on for a painfully long time.

Knowing this, when I look at your work I am always tempted to think that what I can see actually on the canvas are layers and layers of work dating back perhaps weeks, perhaps months. But that may not be true, I suppose. I may, in fact, just be seeing the final reworking.
I think it used to be true early on, thirty years ago. I was so unsure of what it was I wanted to do. I felt I would really be throwing the whole painting away if I scraped it all off, so I would always leave some of it on and scrape some of it off, so that the paintings were thicker then, were an accretion – not only over weeks and months but sometimes over years of paint. But as times got on, I have become aware that I can finally only work one way, which is to try to do the whole thing at one go. Many times I have scraped it off, and what you may be seeing is a single layer over a scraped-down canvas, which yet is the result of a long period of working.

Yes, it is certainly true that your most recent pictures are, in a literal way, less thick than your work was in, say, the early 1960s. But I still get a very strong tactile sense from your work – almost, sometimes, a sort of sculptural sense. Have you ever tried to make sculpture?
Only when I had to, for the intermediate examination at St Martin's. I thought about it. But there again, setting up a sculptor's studio is even more like light industry than setting up a painter's studio. I am not organisationally very competent. I could turn what you say into a sort of compliment. There is always the danger, if one is talking about one's own work, that one thinks one is marvellous. And that isn't really what it is about. I am talking about my objectives and not about my stature. But when I see a Matisse painting with its marvellous economy and its marvellous implications of the sculptural, in what are finally more or less flat gestures on a flat canvas, it seems to me that this is distilled experience. And because the thing has been inhabited and worked

through and understood, one makes the marks to conjure up the sense of
something haptic – which actually is, for me, the magic of all painting. From
Cimabue and Giotto right through to Matisse. And because that conjuring trick
is performed, because these flat marks conjure up a solid form, one gets the
feeling of the passage of time. It is as though a flat surface suddenly becomes
three-dimensional and much thicker in space, so that a glimpse might awake a
sense of the passing of time. I don't know – I may have taken the whole
argument too far. But anyway, the evocation of the sculptural I don't think has
to do with thick paint. That's what I might say more economically: because
Matisse does it, too.

*I am equally aware, apart from the sculptural feeling, of the idea of a
declared struggle. You are very conscious that your perception of the
subject changes each time you return to it. And you want to, in some way,
incorporate the fact that your awareness has altered in the painting itself,
so that ultimately what one is presented with is a series of tensions between
different perceptions of the work. Is it important for you to keep that alive
in the picture?*

It's not of conscious importance. I am aware that I have a taste for a
crossword puzzle, again, with corrections and emendations solved. It seems
to me more exciting, rather than done immaculately. It's a taste, though not
a taste I am proud of. I mean, Vermeer and Velázquez and Manet and Matisse
– that is, sheer paint done without any overt struggle, without any irrelevant
accent – actually seems to me the pinnacle of painting. It's what I'm trying
to get towards, but I'm afraid it's a by-product of my way of working. It doesn't
seem totally contemptible. But again, it's not something that I would stand
up and say was preferable to another look of a painting. But I do find in my
work a certain engagement, a certain perhaps rather cheap engagement,
with an overt struggle.

So you see it as a weakness rather than a strength?

I think so, I think so. On the other hand there are certain artists – like
Giacometti or Soutine or Rembrandt, even, and Cézanne – very great artists
where there are also signs of struggle.

*Of course, the whole idea of an overt struggle brings to mind the notion
of expressionism. And the fact that you were born in Berlin – although
you left Germany in your very early years – makes me wonder whether
you feel any kind of affinity with German art. It's not something that
you talk about. The German artists are not those, apart from Dürer,
whom you ever mention.*

I've looked at Dürer a lot lately, and I was really rather surprised to find how
interested I was in those portraits by him in the British Museum. They seemed
to me to be quite astonishing, and the pinnacle of a sort of curious knotty
intellect and impulse which is quite extraordinary. The word 'expressionism'
doesn't thrill me at all. Most of our tastes are conditioned by fashion: most
of what we say, if we are very original, is 90 per cent repetition of what other
people have said and 10 per cent of our own. But the tastes in painting
of painters are genuine, simply because they find themselves returning to
certain painters with a sort of hunger because they need them, because they
find them satisfying and exciting. And I don't find myself returning in that
way to Beckmann and Nolde and Kirchner. There is something, to me, arbitrary
and unclassical – in the sense that the forms are not complete – about those
painters, although I am aware that many of them were very talented, probably

more talented than me. And the painters who are called expressionist that
I respond to greatly – for instance, Soutine and to some extent De Kooning –
simply don't seem to be expressionist painters. Soutine seems to me a very
great craftsman, and I return to him for the way that he follows the form round
in a very thorough way – inhabiting it and pursuing it and really understanding
the plastic form in what seems a very deep and sinewy way that relates him
to Tiepolo as much as it does to expressionist painting. So the idea of
expressionism doesn't seem a thrilling one. And the expressionist painters
whom I admire don't seem to me to be expressionists.

You mentioned Soutine. His drawings are very rare, aren't they?
But there again I think of the drawing in the paint. That seems to make him
a great twentieth-century draughtsman in the way that Braque and Gris,
for instance – who had other qualities, including the very important one
of intensity – don't seem to me to be draughtsmen on the same level at all.
The level, that is, of correcting their ambition by a response to the organic,
supple twists and turns of fact.

*Can I return, then, to the reason why you choose to use charcoal on paper as well
as oil on canvas?*
Ah! There are several very good reasons. For one thing, I make myself out
to be interesting in a way that I don't think I am. I don't like the tremendous
mess I make when I paint. It really seems burdensome in a way that I hadn't
predicted when I entered this business. I think most people's strong impulse
for entering painting is because they don't want to go to work every day, because
the regular job of being in a bank, being behind a counter, seems to them a sort
of prison that they would rather not inhabit – given that they have got one
life-time. So they start painting. Then they find themselves working not only
five days a week from nine to five, but working seven days a week all out. Then
they find themselves running a sort of curious light industry, which actually
is what painting is: one has to provide a space and colours and models. I get
through an enormous amount of colour, and I wash my hands and I wash
my brushes and the day has got a great deal of chores in it. This splashing,
messy business of painting doesn't seem to me to be especially attractive.
It seems much more intelligent to have a piece of black chalk in one's hand,
to have a piece of paper, to be able to make one's points economically. And
I am delighted, occasionally, to be able to do that. After a time, it seems an
impoverished activity and a sort of escape, and one gets back to painting.

But drawing is much quicker, apart from anything else, isn't it?
It is much quicker, although I do go on a long time with the drawings as well,
and rub them out. I therefore use the flexible medium of charcoal, because
the portrait drawings, for instance, do actually take a large number of sittings,
and I rub them out again and again. But it seems to be the more direct, the
more abstracted and therefore slightly quicker way of working. Also not so
much colour, although colour itself is of course an enormous factor. But if
I look at a Manet painting, which is a painting almost without accent, it seems
to be a heavier burden, a greater feat, to have been able to take the whole plane,
the whole surface, the whole mass and to put it down in that way. It simply
seems harder than to capture it by accents, which is finally what drawing
is, isn't it? One catches it by these black accents on white paper, whereas
in painting one takes the whole surface and works the whole surface,
one against another, and it seems to be more difficult. And if it is achieved,
it seems to me more satisfying.

*I would imagine that with drawing you always work from the motif, whereas
sometimes with painting you don't – you work from memory based on an
experience of the motif, is that right?*

No, the business of working from memory has totally atrophied in my case.
I work from drawings. I do two entirely separate sorts of drawings. One is the
drawing instead of a painting, where I have a sitter – or was once able to draw
out of the window – and go on drawing in an effort to find an authoritative
statement: somewhere between my impulse and the fact. And I do another sort
of drawing, which I do almost every day, a drawing for the big picture. That is,
I might go through the gate and look at the studio, I might walk to Primrose
Hill and do a little drawing, quite quickly. At the beginning it might simply be
a notation of where the trees are, many times. At the end it might be an attempt
to find a unity, but I have hundreds of these drawings and I have let out one
out of twenty or thirty which seem to have a little validity in their own right.
But they are really notations, and they act as a mnemonic that almost lost their
virtue the day after I have drawn them. It's simply that I look at them and
remember what it was like to look at the subjects. So I don't work out of my
head. I work either from drawings or from the model. I'd like to be able to work
out of my head as well, but it's atrophied. I used to when I was very young, but
I rely more and more on drawings. The danger with getting older is to make
the business of painting a simpler business, which is how most people fail and
weaken. I try to counteract this simply by taking more notice of the subject.

*Would you ever consider working from photographs, in the way that late
Sickert did, for example?*

I use photographs as well, because they are a corrective. Although they convey
very little information, and therefore I use them only occasionally. But not in
the way Sickert did. Sickert, in fact, made a curious sort of model system of the
business of perceiving the accident by using the squared-up drawing, by
working from it in a very abstracted way. And he was able, late in life, to turn his
enormous vivacity to account – although in a restricted and provincial national
school like the English one – by working from photographs in a very particular
and really very sophisticated way. It has to do with the shapes that the
photograph has of tone, which are often accidental and strange in a quite
extraordinary way. And simply because I wouldn't be able to render up,
somehow press up the sculptural in my imagination from them, I don't think
I could work in that particular way. I have worked from my own photographs,
supplemented by drawings – occasionally when it seemed to me a useful
corrective. I don't think one can have too much information, and photography
is another sort of information.

*Yes, I often feel with the late Sickerts that he used photographs in a way
to keep himself surprised, and I imagine that the element of surprise is
also very important to you, isn't it?*

It's enormously important. I mean, to do something predicted doesn't seem
worth doing at all. To actually stand in front of one's canvas and render
something that has been thought out – I don't know whether anybody does
it, but it seems to me to take all the fun out of doing it. The element of surprise
is enormously important, and of course the thing that really surprises one is
to have done something that one hadn't foreseen and that seems true. To have
done something that one hadn't foreseen – by itself – would simply seem to be
a gesture. And I can't even see how that would be interesting. But to have done
something that one hadn't foreseen, but at the same time actually seems true
to a specific fact, seems to me to be very exciting.

*You came to England when you were very young, as I've mentioned already.
And yet you are German-born. Do you feel English in your identity or do you
feel European?*

I think, like every emigrant, I feel passionately English. One of the things
I am conscious of, when painting London, is how little London has been
painted, and what a curious, touching city it is. One walks around Paris and
one sees these landmarks that have been recorded by great artists. I hardly
travel at all. And because of the emigrant's anxiety, I actually hate to leave the
place that I am at. What you'd call my repetition of subjects may have to do with
it. I hate leaving my studio, I hate leaving the district, I hate leaving London.
I don't think I've spent four weeks abroad since I was seven, because I hate
travelling so much. My status as a foreigner is curious, in the sense that I was
actually a born-again Englishman. I came just before my eighth birthday, and
I didn't see again anybody that I had seen before I was eight. And I haven't seen
again a place that I saw before I was eight. It was a total break. I was sent over
by myself. I didn't see my parents again, so I haven't brought any cultural
luggage with me at all.

*Do you have a sense of loss – not only what is obviously a very tragic sense of loss
to do with your family, but also a loss almost of roots, national roots?*

No. I don't. I feel my national roots are of the length of experience I have had
here. There may be all sorts of patterns of behaviour that are dictated by a sense
of loss, but I was actually, I think, happier here: I went to a co-educational
school and I had, I think, been very uncomfortable in the sort of middle-class
life that I had in Berlin as a child. Of course I was surrounded there by anxiety
and unease, personal as well as to do with a very threatening situation, and
I came to a co-educational school. I had come from a place where I was taken
for a walk by a nanny in the park by myself, and lived a life that even then –
though I have very few memories – seemed to me to be constricting and
inhibiting, and I felt uncomfortable in it. I came to England and went straight
to a school where girls and boys ran around in a sort of wild piece of country –
a progressive school. And although I was locked in a shed on my first afternoon
in England, I immediately felt a lot happier. My strangeness has more to do, in
a sense, with being at that school for nine years, in a very particular and curious
community, rather than to do with being abroad.

*In terms of formative influences, your name is often linked with David
Bomberg, whose classes you began attending at the Borough Polytechnic
in London towards the end of the 1940s. How long did you study there?*

I studied for longer than anybody else. I entered the class in January 1947
and stayed until it closed. I never joined any of the groups: I was there before
members of the family began to stalk around, I was there after the members
of the group had left.

Was it actually your first experience of being taught art?

We were not taught art at school at all. Because it was the war and because
it was a strange school, the teachers were far too qualified to teach us. So from
the gardener – who was a pianist and a pupil of Schnabel – and the stoker, who
had been a director of a town theatre in Germany when he was twenty-three,
I probably learned more than from anybody else. But art was taught by people
who were totally unqualified, and I was fairly innocent when I came to London.
I had no proficiency at all, although it was a very sophisticated school and I had
read a lot of books about modern art, and I knew about Klee and so on. Then
I went to the Hampstead Garden Suburb Institute, because that was the only

place that would take me. And then I got into St Martin's, but there were
two terms before I could go at seventeen. So I went to the Borough Polytechnic,
and I happened by chance to find Bomberg teaching there. When I went to
other art schools I kept going to his evening classes, because I felt that it was
somehow valuable.

How would you define that value? What do you think the value consisted of?
He was enormously courageous and enormously serious in a way that very
few painters are. He had no gift at all for prevarication or for fitting in. He had
a deep instinct as to how a painting should go. The link is tenuous, but his art
teaching was not like verbal teaching, there was an element in it of something
like teaching ballet: certain things are transmitted that don't have to be fully
articulated, and there was a line stretching back from Bomberg to Sickert to
Degas to Ingres to David, which had a deeper understanding of how drawings
are made. It left some of its traces on what he had to say. His pedagogic method
seems to me now not to have had to do with teaching people how to paint
pictures or how to be artists, but to do with trying to instil a sense of the quality
of form. He never talked about subject (subject seems to me central to the
whole business of painting); he didn't talk about certain things which I think
he took for granted, which had to do with rendering the specifics of a scene,
because it was so deeply in him that he never felt it necessary to articulate it.
What happened was that people would draw, and as soon as they seemed to
be drawing in a way that was bitty or affected or mannered, or using a cliché
learnt from art, he would refer people back to the model and say to them:
'Look, there are these grand possibilities about this disposition of masses
which you are betraying.' I am putting this in my own way, of course, in a partial
way. He would suggest a total destruction of what the students were doing, and
they would destroy it and go on. Probably at some point of destruction, at some
point where they were not in the least aware of having done a picture, he might
stop suddenly and say: 'There is some quality in this form.' There would be
these pieces of paper and these paintings which I think had very little of the
sense of achievement, of the responsible achievement by the artist, but which
bore within them a hint of something very grand and noble and profound in
painting. They would carry in them somehow a language, hints of a language,
of a greater depth and of a greater freedom and of a greater courage than most
of the achieved art that was being created in other places in England.

It sounds as if his classes were very much an inspiration to you.
They were very much an inspiration, but also an inspiration in the sense that
I very early on found myself taking a certain stance against, as well as for, his
teaching. I think it was very much – something that I have had much less
experience of – the way people react to parents. I had other teachers, who
seemed to me to be valuable and lively. There is so much poorly rewarded real
spirit and real devotion in art schools. I had a number of teachers who meant
quite a lot to me, and from whom I learnt a lot. But I think that, on the whole,
in my time as a student he was far more important to me than anybody else.

*Can you remember the precise time when you felt that you'd really begun to
define what you now see as your identity as a painter?*
Yes, I can. I can remember it almost to the minute. I'd been a student for five
years. At Bomberg's classes I'd worked more or less in the way that he had
taught within the atmosphere of the class – although I always felt slightly
detached from the other people who were working there, and I think I had
slightly different aims and needs. In St Martin's I drew quite often in a different

way, which I also felt to be necessary – a way where I could follow every path of my thoughts, in which I was responsible in a far less abandoned way for what I was doing. And I was aware of the conflict between these two approaches. I'd left St Martin's and I'd failed my army medical, and I was supposed to go to the Royal College of Art. By that time, I was fairly resistant to institutions. The business of not going into the army, which I had managed to avoid, was something of a crisis for me. And I felt under considerable pressure, not wanting to be a student for ever. I somehow had to be my own man, and I had a summer working at Battersea Fun Fair for two days a week and getting really rather well paid. It was something like £6 for two days a week, and I could live on it. I did a building site in Earl's Court Road, this was in Walham Green. I went and drew it, and I went on with the painting in a fairly controlled way. It was fairly prismatic in colour: there were yellows and reds, and they stood for space. I made these things every day, and I went back and did drawings. I preserved little bits of the painting which I thought would help it. Then I went to the Royal College, and on my first day there was some sort of talk, and I was given a few tubes of colour. I felt offended by the art school, went home and in anger repainted my picture. It was, in fact, the picture that is now called *Earl's Court Building Site* – the first composition in there. And when I had done it, I recognised that somehow I had cut through my habits. I had made some shapes that seemed to conjure up a coherent, plastic fact, and I felt I had done my own painting. I didn't know whether I would ever be able to do it again, but I knew what it felt like. I had done a nude during the summer, too, in four sittings, of someone with whom I was deeply involved. It also seemed to me to be a painting which had proceeded in a very similar way. But because it hadn't gone on for so long, and I hadn't done so many drawings, I wasn't quite as conscious that I had broken through the sound barrier that, in a way, reversed the habit in order to make a painting. But the business of finishing a painting was a very radical change, and a much more extreme gesture than I normally do in order to get the thing finished. And in order to finish a painting since then, I have really found myself in a similar situation every time.

We are really talking about, I suppose, at least thirty years ago, aren't we?
    Yes, it seems like yesterday.

And yet, looking back over those years, it seems to me that although your work has become much more subtle, extended, eloquent and assured, one of its most striking aspects is the extraordinary sense of unbroken continuity. Unlike so many artists in the twentieth century, who had to grapple with very specific styles and then break away from them, refute them and start all over again, you never seem to have been afflicted by that problem.
    No, it's true. I think it's partly because of what you talk about as my 'foreignness', and partly because I started a sort of grown-up life when I was sixteen – I was living more or less as an adult at seventeen. I actually remember saying at college: 'We are now laying the foundations on which we will build for the rest of our lives.' I was treated with great leniency at college, I worked, I painted at home all the time, and I was aware of the fact that being a student was, in a sense, a privilege. One had all one's time to paint. And I felt that if I wasn't courageous then – as courageous as I could possibly be, not caring what the things looked like, driving myself to every possible extreme – I would never have the chance to be quite as courageous again. So I tried to do things that were certainly beyond my grasp. And because of that, it may be that I have never found it easy. I have never been able to stand back and say:

'Well, I've done this – what shall I do next?' It's always been sufficiently difficult
to keep me engaged. And if I have changed, it hasn't been by a conscious change
of direction, but simply by changing biologically.

*And there have been various distinct episodes in your life, like the time when
you did those variations after Titian. But they seem to be very much the
exception in a career which has concentrated on the portraits, the urban views
and the paintings of Primrose Hill, all of which were present in your recent
exhibition at the Marlborough Gallery in London.*

Well, the copies of Titian were provoked, in a sense, although I had done a copy
of Rembrandt before which was my own idea. Somebody commissioned the
copies of Titian. When I have got even slightly fed up with painted portraits,
I always wanted to paint people for a challenge, as it seemed to me when
I started again. But there have been changes. I painted building sites for years,
and I stopped about twenty years ago. Nobody seems to have specially noticed.
I painted the scenes around Mornington Crescent – I did sixteen of them – and
I stopped doing them. I have been painting Primrose Hill, simply because that
bit of country has such different rhythms and it's the nearest bit of country. But
I only started the studios eight or nine years ago. There have been phases, in the
sense of chunks of subjects that I have exhausted, or that seemed to me to have
become habits, and I have turned to others.

*The copies after Titian immediately make me realise that what is missing from
your work, with very few exceptions, is large figure compositions. Is this
something that you would like to do?*

I would very much like to do it. I did four paintings of people walking up
and down steps recently. And I am just doing a painting of a sitting room with
a large person in it. I have always thought of the things which people call
landscapes as 'compositions', but I haven't done as many as I would like. I would
like to do more. It's partly that I paint specific scenes, and I would have to make
drawings of specific people to fit into them, which I think is perfectly possible
– Manet, for instance, must have done that. I mean, these people are not people
in pictures. They are portraits, and yet they are sitting in cafes or representing
Nana or whatever. I would like to do that. I will try.

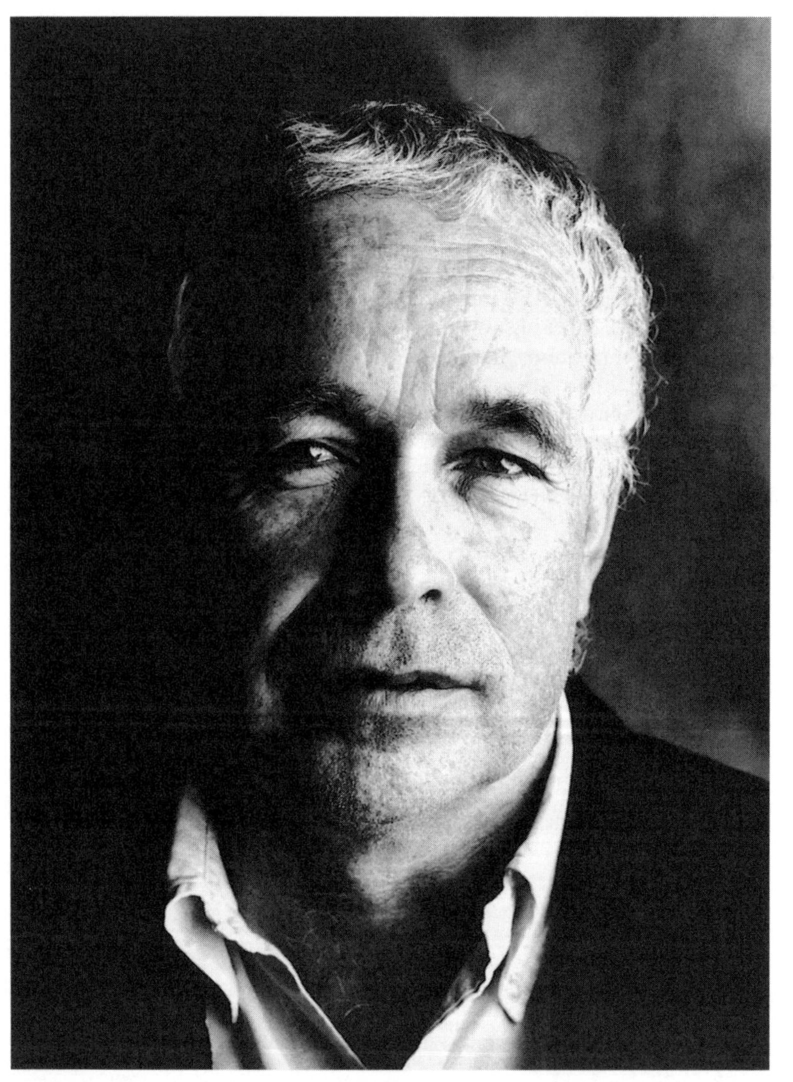

1984

Howard Hodgkin

'I don't care about mortality in the slightest, but I certainly want to beat time. I certainly want to defy time… the point being that really they should be like memorials, that's what paintings were'

*However far you may seem to depart from representation, you have never been
an abstract painter. Your images are always attached with umbilical firmness
to particular memories, but you don't try to reconstruct them in a literal way.
The occasions are summoned back to life freighted with retrospective emotion,
as all acts of remembrance must inevitably be. Experience, not diary-like
description, is what counts.*

*Over the decades you have developed and enriched your art, learning
above all how to loosen up and explore a more uninhibited, frankly sensuous
vision. The preoccupation with memory is still there, and you have often
favoured the device of a containing frame through which people and places
from the past can be summoned and given new meaning. But the emphasis
is increasingly placed on the artist's own emotional autobiography. Many
of your current paintings are far less specifically attached to locations than
before, and more bound up with the drama of a mood. Your vocabulary of
mark-making has grown more supple and eloquent in recent years. You move,
at will, from tight, urgent thrusts of the brush to the most liquid sweeps of
pigment. They carry much of the work's potent emotional charge, and always
conjure up the physical actions which brought them into being.*

*But I'd like to begin by taking you right back to a crucial early
moment. In 1949, when you were only sixteen years old, you painted a small
gouache called* Memoirs *which already seems to contain, in essence, many
of your mature preoccupations. It's about your memory of friends in a room,
the objects in that room, and everything seems to have been flattened, distorted
and even sliced off, like the head of a lady lying on the sofa. Do you see that as
a prophetic painting yourself?*

> Yes. When I painted it, I knew that was what I would always be concerned
> with. It took me a very long time to paint – not as long as painting a picture
> takes me now. But I had a feeling, when I did finally complete it, that
> I would probably spend the rest of my life as a painter trying to do that
> again. This may sound like hindsight, but it's a historical fact that I felt like
> that at the time. And it was a sort of talisman for a long time, when I went
> through the English art-school system and learnt to draw from the model
> and paint landscapes and still lives and so on. This picture was a reminder
> of what was to come.

*The curious thing is that, although it does announce your future preoccupations
with such clarity, you seem to have taken quite a long time to arrive at your
mature style. I mean, it wasn't a simple process of building on what you had
defined in* Memoirs, *was it?*

> Not at all. And the physical side of *Memoirs* I rejected at the time completely.
> I made a deliberate decision – which I think was mistaken now – to put myself
> through an art-school education. The style in which *Memoirs* is painted was
> really artificially mature-looking. It's very stereotyped and very stylised; and
> I think it's only the intensity of feeling which it contains that stops one seeing
> immediately what an impossible position that would have been for me, to
> continue using such an arbitrary language. I mean, the language was arbitrary
> because I knew no other. But you are right: it took me a long time to get back
> to the intensity I achieved in that picture. I wanted to get there from another
> direction. I wanted to be able to use paint as a substance. I wanted to be
> a painterly painter, because I wanted more possibilities.

*Do you resent the fact that the art education you put yourself through didn't give
you what you wanted?*

> I resented it profoundly. And in fact the older I get, it's becoming a sort

of paranoid 'bee in my bonnet' about how pointless and useless that sort
of art-school education is.

What in particular did you object to?

The fact that one was not given a language, which is what one should have been
given. And particularly life drawing, where people were expected with an empty
piece of paper and a piece of charcoal to sit in front of a naked person and
produce something that had significance or meaning. There is no possibility
that could happen without them being taught first how to draw – in the sense
of how to make marks which meant something in themselves.

*But by the end of the 1950s you were embarking on a series of paintings to
do with friends of yours, very often artists and their wives at home together.
It's extraordinary, the way in which you incorporate within these paintings
comments on the stylistic identities of the artists you are portraying – and yet
at the same time you seem able to assert your own identity as well. It's a bit of
a tightrope, isn't it? Did you enjoy that?*

Yes, at the time I did enjoy it enormously. It was great fun to make often loving
tributes to the work of another painter – but also, perhaps, to make slight digs
at it as well, particularly in the way that it related to what they were like as
people. It was great fun to put into somebody's interior – where it usually wasn't
in real life – an example of their own work hanging above their heads while they
were sitting on the sofa. I enjoy doing things like that. They didn't always.

*Yes, it's difficult to tell sometimes where affection shades into satire in
these paintings.*

Yes, I find that difficult to tell as well. There is certainly a lot of satire. It was also
an attempt, I think, to make a space for myself, because the kind of painting
I was doing at the time was hardly taken seriously by anybody but myself, and
I felt that I was being slightly 'tolerated' by my abstract-painting friends.

*Why didn't they take you seriously? Did they see you as somehow far too
idiosyncratic, whimsical or wayward?*

I think idiosyncratic in particular. I remember Lawrence Alloway being sent,
as a friendly gesture by one of my friends, to look at my pictures. And he said:
'I think you are too slow. I think you might one day perhaps find something to
paint that would interest other people, but I probably won't be around to see it.'

What sort of effect did comments like that have on you?

Well, they were hardly encouraging. But they did make me feel, in an old-
fashioned boarding-school way, 'try harder'.

*They are difficult paintings to bring off, because you are setting yourself up
against other artists' personalities in a lot of these pictures. It seems like an
almost impossible aim to set yourself.*

It was an impossibly difficult aim in some ways, but I wish I could explain how
necessary it was. It was really an attempt to make a space for myself within the
context of all these other painters.

What do you mean by that?

By fighting it out, to some extent, with this one and that one. By perhaps
making little nudges in their direction and pushing them around a little. I felt
very inferior to them, because they were always saying they painted ten pictures
in a weekend, and they could paint very large pictures very easily. My painting

came very slowly, and it wasn't that I didn't believe in it. I felt inferior in a sort
of professional sense, and certainly thought they wouldn't take me seriously
as an artist. It was a very long time before they did.

*Yes, it's curious really, because in many respects I suppose your work
at that period fought against the prevailing conventions. It wasn't extreme
abstraction, it didn't really seem to be concerned with pop art, and it
certainly didn't want to achieve the gigantic scale that a lot of artists were
working on at that time. Yet I can also see that you were acutely aware
not only of the work of your artist friends, but also of work going on
elsewhere, over in New York. You had obviously been looking, for example,
at painters like Frank Stella.*

Oh yes, I was a great admirer of Frank Stella's and I did eventually get to know
him. It's very difficult to say this without sounding arrogant in a false way:
I knew what I wanted to do from the time – as you rightly suggested – that
I painted *Memoirs*, but I had to establish a place for it that was not part of
a school or a movement.

You don't like to belong?

I don't see how any artist can.

*But some artists, particularly at the beginning of their careers, are quite happy
to go along with being identified as a member of a movement.*

Yes, I wouldn't have minded that particularly, and there was a brief moment
when I was thought to be a pop artist. But I think that, because artists now
get no help from outside, really they have to do it all themselves. And I was
determined somehow to do this within the context of what was going on.
But that is different to joining it, or joining in.

*Even so, you were aware of that context. And I think you were also very aware
– right from the start and probably more than a lot of artists – of art history.
It seems to me that you are a painter who feeds off the past just as you feed
off the present.*

Yes, I like you saying that, I think that's absolutely true. But I cannot
understand how any painter or sculptor now could work without being
aware of art history, because an awareness of art history is part of being
alive now. I like to explain what I mean by an analogy. When somebody
went to see the great designer Eileen Gray, in her apartment in Paris which
was full of work she had designed herself, she was asked why there was
an enormous bronze-age pot on a lacquer stand and why she had installed
the eighteenth-century French panelling that filled the room. She said:
'Oh, you don't understand. It wouldn't be modern otherwise.' And this feeling
which we have for all sorts of reasons, that all art history is ours, I don't think
you could ignore.

*Yes, one of the things I like about your work is the freedom you have established
to roam around, almost at will, within this incredible legacy that we've all been
given from the past.*

And which is one of the amazing things about living now and working
as a painter, which wouldn't have existed fifty years ago.

Do you feed off reproductions a lot, or do you prefer to go and see the real thing?

I always want to go to the real thing. Reproductions for me don't mean
anything, except as a reference.

That makes sense, because I remember when you contributed to The Artist's
Eye *exhibition at the National Gallery, you made what I thought was a very
good point: trying to emphasise where these paintings had come from, what
kind of particular niches and spaces they had originally filled. You wanted,
in a way, to restore to them their identity, which they may be in danger of losing
through reproductions.*

        I wanted to restore their physical identity, which is, of course, to me of
paramount importance. And the best thing I did by far at that exhibition was
putting the Tiepolo ceiling painting flat on the ceiling, where the whole identity
of the picture in physical terms is completely altered – and is real, for once.
When you looked up at it, you could see it at last.

*Trying to evoke the experience which one of your paintings gives me, I have to
say that it consists of a whole host of influences and references, all jostling round
within the picture. Not in an uncomfortable way: one of the qualities of your
paintings is that they seem very direct and unforced. But that complexity is still
there, and it embraces Matisse, Léger, Vuillard, Indian miniatures and many
other things. Would you be prepared to single out, among all these, one influence
which is more important than any others?*

        No, I think it's usually much easier for other people to see where artists'
influences come from. But the influence of Matisse – not as a painter, but
rather how he lived as an artist – was of tremendous importance to me in
my early twenties.

Could you be more specific?

        The relationship of one work to another, the way his career unfolded.
I don't mean his career in worldly terms, I mean how he organised his years
as a painter of pictures was deeply moving to me and impressive. It was far
more important than how the appearance of his work affected me, which
I don't think it did very much. But he as a moral force, he as a person who
made his decisions about how to proceed year after year and sometimes
taking tremendous risks – that meant, and still does mean, an enormous
amount to me. I couldn't understand how my colleagues, people at the same
age as myself, would paint enormous quantities of pictures which really
contained, in terms of how I saw Matisse, one beginning of an idea. And
far from resolving this idea or even using it or making it into something,
they would spread it thin, unresolved and unconstructed over yards and
yards of canvas. I couldn't understand this.

You are really talking about concentration, aren't you?

        Concentration, and somehow a sort of moral investment. I mean more than
concentration: commitment. And that meant an enormous amount to me,
the commitment of Matisse.

How did your preoccupation with India come about?

        As a child, I was shown some Indian miniatures, and I thought that they were
very beautiful and another world. They were accessible but somehow different.
They were a microcosm of the whole world. It had nothing to do with our own
ideas about how the world is constructed in terms of appearance, and yet they
were completely legible and understandable.

*Of course, when you were first shown them, they must have still been
slightly belittled.*

        They still are. Few people take them seriously even now.

Was your fascination with Indian painting reinforced when you visited India?
No, when I first visited India, I rather forgot about Indian painting and started
looking at India itself.

It's a preoccupation which has endured, hasn't it?
Oh, certainly – partly because it's somewhere else, rather in the same way that
I liked the Indian miniatures. They were a relief from always looking at Western
art made with a Western sensibility, and going to India – where of course
everyone speaks English – is just that bit different. Also, eventually the
extraordinary correspondence comes when you are looking at a lake with
flowers sticking out of the water, and you realise that this stereotyped pattern
along the edge of so many Indian pictures – flowers sticking out of the water –
is identical. Because I assure you, it is exactly the same, and it's a totally
different form of representation. These moments are quite impressive.
But the way everything is put together is entirely different to here.

*What impressed you most about Indian miniature painting? Was it the
suggestion that reality, or the experience that you value most, could be
approached in a more oblique way than the tradition of English art would have
led you to suppose?*
I would change that to 'a more direct way'. I'd also change it to 'the tradition
of Western art', because great Indian painting does try and do something which
is quite as ambitious as anything one finds in great Italian Renaissance painting
– but with much less stylistic paraphernalia. And they do really try and show
man in the world with his feelings both material and sublime – as well as the
natural world, all in one go, and that is quite ambitious. So they usually fail,
but when they come near success, they are very remarkable.

On a spiritual level, do you feel close to Indian art?
No, I can't really say that I do, partly because I don't know anything about
the spiritual content of Indian art in any way that I can talk about. It may
be something I feel.

You never particularly studied Indian religion.
Not at all. And the iconography of the pictures I collect is something
I deliberately turn away from – so that I can see the pictures better.

*Sometimes, writers on your work may be in danger of overemphasising the
Indian element. When I think about the way your paintings are put together
and the way you handle pigment, that doesn't seem to me to owe anything to
Indian art at all. I am thinking really now about the rawness, the directness,
the way in which each of your pictures makes me very aware of how you paint,
how you handle the stuff. That's not an Indian characteristic.*
Not at all. And in fact the only sensible remark that any writer has ever made
about that was: perhaps they were the answer to Indian painting, the other
side of the coin, so much the opposite. Because all you have just said is virtually
the complete opposite of how an Indian painter of miniatures would proceed.
But there is one great similarity, one real parallel – and that is they can use
anything in the same picture. They can use modelling and flat pattern,
expressionism in terms of emotive brush-strokes, the smoothest possible
paint, fragments of architecture, fragments of pattern, flesh which is described
as simply flat areas of pink and can turn into the most elaborate three-
dimensional modelling, still in the same figure. That is something I think that
I share, or have been affected by. Because when I am painting, I would like to

feel that I can do anything I like within the context of the situation I am in –
so that anything can be used, anything is useful as a means of expression.
Anything physical or stylistic you can just pick up and use. That is surprisingly
the freedom that Indian artists do have, even though they work within such
a very strict tempo, such a very strict process.

I have a feeling that you may often be very surprised by the end result …
Of my own pictures?

*… of a painting that you are doing. Looking at them, I am very conscious of
the fact that changes of mind have occurred, that earlier statements have been
covered over, but not in a way to disguise them. I mean, you are very open about
that. One of the characteristics of your work is that you declare cancellations
and second thoughts, leave them there, existing in a state of pictorial tension
on the surface. So does that mean that your starting point is often completely
disguised by the time you have finished?*
I would have said covered over rather than disguised, but you are quite right
in suggesting that I am surprised by the end result. To me, a picture is really
finished when, in theory at least, it's as far away from me as it would be from
anyone else. So that the emotion – which is often extremely intense, the subject
of the picture, the situation – becomes so completely turned into an object,
a thing, in other words a painting, that I look at it as a painting that is being
transformed. And I should be able to look at it with the same surprise and
interest as anyone else.

*The marvellous thing to me is that the sensuous delight you have in paint as a
physical substance never becomes pursued as an activity for its own sake – even
though you are concerned with the autonomy of the picture. At the end of the day
I am very aware that a Hodgkin picture has its starting point in some really
very specific memory – of people, of places, even of works of art.*
Yes, they are all combined. But they couldn't be more specific. The subjects
are sometimes one moment. Somebody might be suddenly lifting their hand
or saying something appalling – and that would be enough.

*When that event happens, does it occur to you instantaneously that it might make
the subject of a picture, or is it something that occurs to you in recollection later on?*
I have had, over the years, to fight back the appallingly falsifying – in every
direction – feeling of 'oh, that would make good copy', as it were. Both
artistically and in life that would be disastrous. No, usually it would happen
quite a long time afterwards, the feeling that this would be a painting.

*And is there some sort of constant value attached to those memories, something
you can identify, some sort of common theme running through them – or are
they all very disparate?*
Well, as time goes by, they become remarkably disparate. And they are not just
two or three people in a room, as they were at one time. I've painted landscapes,
I've even painted still lives.

Yes, the figure seems to be becoming less important in your recent paintings.
Well, it's making a comeback, in a rather more legible manner than in the past.
The content of my pictures has become more diverse, but the nature of it has
not changed. The landscapes I paint have figures in them. Maybe I am with
somebody looking at the landscape. I have often painted myself as a spectator
in a picture, as a sort of lay figure.

---

*It seems to me that although the locations you paint are often very far-flung,
the people you start off wanting to depict in some way must be incredibly
different from each other. I would have a guess and say that ultimately you
want to celebrate things, to affirm something which you value, something
which you cherish.*

Yes, I would. I am very touched that you say that. I think that's exactly right.

Why is celebration so important to you?

Celebration means that in the end – it's an extraordinary optimistic thing,
and perhaps rather fatuous, finally – but I remember reading in Muriel Spark's
last novel – this is naturally only a paraphrase – but she said that for the artist
time is always regained. The past can always be brought back. Everything
can become beautiful or charming if you want it to. So it's really a kind of selfish
optimism on my part that makes me want to celebrate everything, and also
a feeling of economy – that no miserable emotion should be wasted when it
could be turned into a sort of piece of knitting, which is a picture, that you get
at the other end.

*Are you saying that you want to beat time in some way? And perhaps even
beat mortality?*

No, I don't care about mortality in the slightest, but I certainly want to beat
time. I certainly want to defy time. And in the first writing I ever did, which
was about classical art when I was thirteen or fourteen, I remember saying
that these pictures should be like 'war memorials'. Why I said 'war memorials'
I don't know, but the point being that really they should be like memorials,
that's what paintings were. I was talking about paintings by Poussin and Ingres.

*Does it pain you that the experiences you do value, and try to recreate in
your work, are all inevitably transitory, that they have all passed, that they
can't be regained?*

No, because they have been regained, they can be regained. I've put them
into pictures.

*Yes, I know you have done that, but in a way are you trying to compensate
for the fact that the event itself has been transitory?*

No, because to me it's there. It's never gone once one has brought it back.
No, I am not filled with sadness about what has gone.

*You've travelled to Naples and made a series of paintings about your Neapolitan
experience in recent years.*

Yes. I can't remember how many paintings there are, but surprisingly I was
actually in Naples for only four days. The circumstances of my being there were
that I went with a great friend of mine from New York, who came to London
and said to me: 'Would you like to go to Rome?' This was without warning.
So I said, 'Certainly,' and went to Rome where we had an extraordinary time.
We spent all our time looking at works of art. And then he said: 'I've never
been to Naples.' So off we went. The pictures are not just about feelings between
him and myself, but about two people looking at Naples and feeling an
extraordinary mixture of having been there before, of passionate involvement
in the painting and the architecture which you can see in Naples. My friend,
who is a dedicated art historian, was also passionate about antiquity. But
our experiences were of the most banal sort if written down and described.
We would go to the Capodimonte, look at the pictures and become almost
transfigured by the experience of looking at them. And then we would go away

and get drunk and look at the view of the bay. But all the time I realised that
the sediment was sort of rising very, very fast. There was one occasion when
I knew. I said to him, as we were going back, I knew that I was going to paint
lots of pictures of Naples, and he said: 'How ridiculous! Why? What about,
what about?' And then, when years later he saw the pictures, he was not at
all surprised. He said: 'I should have realised then.'

*Your Neapolitan pictures, so far as the titles are concerned, seem to be more
about places you visited like the public gardens than works of art you had
encountered there.*

Well, I think I would have found it almost impossible to paint a picture about
looking at the collections in Capodimonte. But these kind of feelings that one
had looking at works of art, or feelings of all sorts, feed what you feel when you
look at the sunset over the Bay of Naples, for example. Or the largest painting,
probably up to now the biggest painting I have ever painted at all, was a view
of what we saw sitting and having dinner by the sea one evening. I think that
the temerity to feel I could even attempt a picture of such a transient little
subject, such an evanescent scene, on a panel more than 6 feet square, was
for me a great challenge and a great risk. But the confidence came from seeing
these enormous Neapolitan pictures.

*Did it make you want to paint larger, did it make you feel that perhaps in the
future you would like to experiment with an increase in scale?*

Yes, I think it did. I think that's why I was able to paint this one.

*Presumably one of the reasons why your painting has been relatively modest
in scale – although I don't want to exaggerate, I mean, you don't paint
miniatures – but presumably one of the reasons is that you are dealing with
very intimate personal experiences that don't lend themselves to that kind
of exclamatory, large-scale declaration?*

Yes, that is absolutely true. But there is also another reason: the subject has to
be physically contained. And so I was painting pictures which were the scale
of that illusionism which I use as a pictorial language. Now illusionism doesn't
work on a large scale, because you cannot make the spectator stand in one place
very easily if you are painting an enormous picture. You have to use a different
kind of illusionism, which is far more architectural and far less intense.
And I think that was the reason, the most important reason, why my pictures
are comparatively small.

*I have often wondered what kind of influence your father Eliot Hodgkin might
have had on you, because he was an eminent horticulturalist. There is
something about your work which does remind me – not always when you
are painting landscapes necessarily, but to do with the whole way you approach
a painting – of the notion of tending some kind of garden, the whole idea
of nurturing, even perhaps of planting out and pruning. And certainly your
willingness, especially in the more recent work, to let things bloom in a sort
of exotic way. Am I being entirely fanciful?*

No, you are not. It's a thought that had never occurred to me before. I can only
agree. My father was a man I was very close to, who, probably because of his
passion for works of art and for looking at them, had more effect on me as a
child than anyone else. But he also had an attitude to his garden which is very
similar to what you say – except that he never felt he could make it all succeed
as a work of art. There were too many warring forces. No doubt in that sense
you are right as well, because I thought, 'Well, perhaps I will be able to,' because

my pictures are filled with different kinds of things which all have to be finally resolved. Usually, by a last-minute anxious improvisation, I painted out half the picture. I've painted out most of five or six years' work with one stroke. That, my father with his garden, he could never quite do, however much he knew it was necessary.

Did he ever live to see your mature work?
Unfortunately not.

Do you think he would have understood it?
I think he would have understood it all too well. He probably would have understood the subject matter in a way which I would have found slightly uncomfortable.

Why?
Because the actual subject matter of my pictures is not something I want to share with anybody.

That is interesting. So you don't really want people to go too far into the origins of the painting. I mean, what you were saying earlier about the picture having a life of its own, an autonomous existence – that's almost like a guarantee that people can't probe too far into the autobiographical origins, is it?
It's that, but also the autobiographical element, if it was known, would come between the spectator and the picture.

You mean the autobiography would be irrelevant?
I hope that it's become irrelevant when the picture is finished.

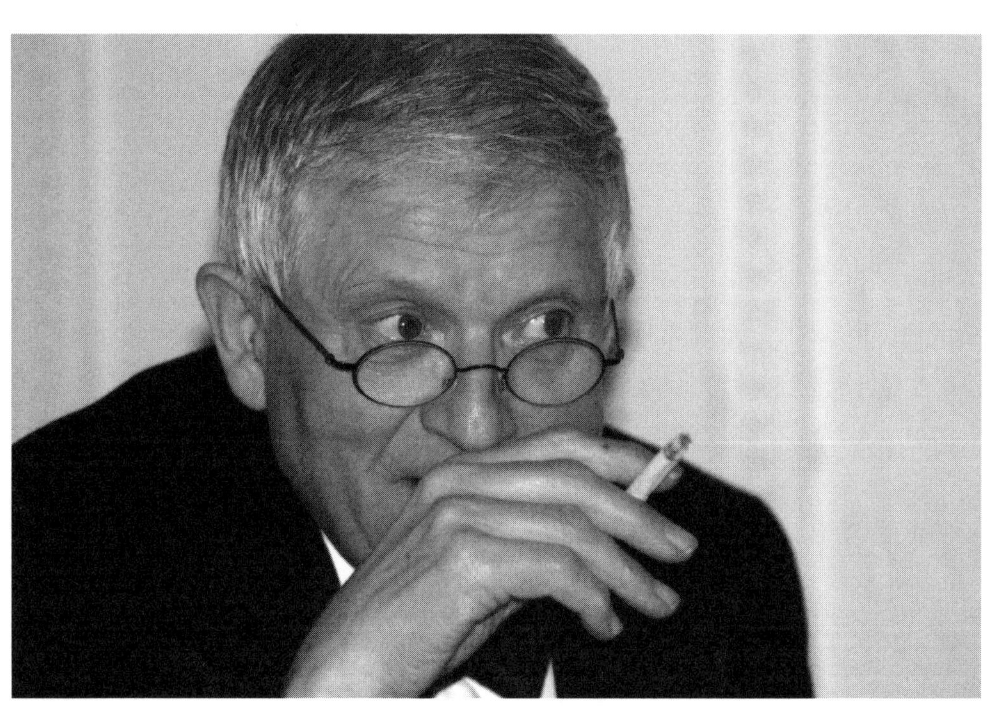

1984

David Hockney

'I shy away from violence,
am not attracted to it
in any way. Yet I know
that people like it,
people are attracted to
it, there is beauty there.
But I cannot grasp it'

Your brilliant recent series of opera designs have proved how enormously stimulating it can be for artists to take their work out of the gallery and onto the stage. One of these excursions, for a triple bill at the Metropolitan Opera in New York, unleashed a remarkable torrent of energy which then flowed back into your subsequent paintings. The venture turned out to have two-way rewards. It raised the often banal standard of opera design to a new level of visual literacy, and provided your other work with the imaginative release it needed. Your two previous opera projects – Stravinsky's The Rake's Progress *in 1975 and Mozart's* The Magic Flute *in 1978 – likewise enabled you to move outside the problems you were encountering in your own painting. Designing for the stage reminded you that there were alternatives to the careful, almost photographic naturalism you had pursued in the early 1970s. You felt stifled by the painstaking style adopted for large double portraits like* Mr and Mrs Clark and Percy. *However appealing and sensitively judged such pictures may have been, they repressed too much of the exuberance which earlier prompted you to juggle with different idioms, keeping all your options so open and alive.*

Glyndebourne's invitation to design The Rake's Progress *must have reminded you immediately of the major print sequence, with the same title, which you made back in the early 1960s. The opera project unlocked an imaginative door leading back to the freedom and vitality of your precocious beginnings as an artist, when you threw anything and everything into a stylish confection mixing together satire, obscenity and sheer high spirits. Looking back over the last twenty years, one of the things that strikes me immediately is the surprisingly wide range of idioms you have employed. Has it always been important to you, claiming the right to adopt a lot of styles?*

Yes. I mean, how wide-ranging they really are I don't know. For instance, very early on I showed some pictures at the Young Contemporaries and I deliberately gave a name to each style and claimed I was being versatile. But looking back, I don't think they were very different styles, and I suspect now there is less than I think. There are more connections between one and another than I thought. But I liked the idea of being able to use any style you wanted. Partly because suddenly it's easier to look at things, for instance books. Art books increased, and even as a student you could have a kind of library and look at things without going to a museum necessarily. So this is bound to affect art in a way. It will do. Because you are aware of all the styles, they become a part of you. And if you then realise what a certain style can do, you find in the end your own way of treating it will slowly come out. But it might take time. There was a point when I realised that, in a sense, you could use any style because in the end it will look like yours. There is no way it can't. For instance, I have made a copy of a Matisse that I saw in a friend's house, I was staying there and I copied it with crayons on a piece of paper.

When was this?

A few years ago. I pinned it up on a wall and I'm going to keep it there for years, because I know one day, although it looks like the Matisse, it cannot totally look like the Matisse, it must look like my copy of it. But how long it takes for this to appear interests me, really. It does take time. It's just the way we see things. When I lived in Paris there was a show at the Louvre, it was called *Fakes* – copies and things. And nineteenth-century copies of Rembrandt oddly enough looked like the nineteenth century, even though they were meant to be faithful copies. They naturally looked at it a bit differently, just as we would now look at it differently. You see, I don't think you can escape your time.

*But I have a feeling, looking at your early work, that in a way you were trying
to escape from the idea of an artist having one style. You seemed to be almost
frightened of becoming stuck within one sort of rigid handwriting. Is that true?*

Yes. And partly, of course, you had this marvellous example of Picasso. I mean,
he would move from one to the other in the same day.

*You were very impressed by the big 1960 Picasso exhibition at the Tate,
weren't you?*

Oh yes, every Picasso exhibition I've been impressed by. I've never seen a rotten
one. The one in New York was marvellous, because they arranged the pictures
consecutively, as much as they could, and there was a marvellous example in
the middle of the cubist rooms. He is still really involved with analytical cubism,
but suddenly goes back to Barcelona and there is a painting of a girl with a
perfectly normal-looking face. Obviously, he just thought she's rather pretty
or something, and he painted her in another way. Of course, all the other
cubists thought this was terrible. It was like when he gave up the style and
they thought this was terrible, but he just ignored them. He didn't bother,
and I think I see why, really.

*The one style you have never adopted is abstraction. You have always shied
away from it, haven't you? And that was the prevalent avant-garde style
when you were a student.*

So did Picasso. He too never really painted abstract pictures, ever. That was
very clear in the New York show, and it becomes clearer to us now when we
look back. I assume he thought it was a bit of a cul-de-sac, and therefore not
that interesting. Because everything he does really begins with something real.
And in a way, everything I do begins with something real. To me, abstraction
is too internal, in the end. I see its achievement, of course. It's marvellous,
but I think in a sense it will settle down till it's kind of a branch of painting,
like landscape painting.

*But when you started your career, to be a figurative artist was to be old-
fashioned, wasn't it?*

Yes, in fact that was the word you would have used. But my problem was,
I couldn't. I did a few: there was a period at the Royal College of Art when
I made some kind of abstract pictures, but I just couldn't go on. I thought:
I am not really dealing with myself. You know, in a way all painting is abstract
– it's older than people think. There has always been art where you weren't
allowed to make representations, like in Islamic art where you were not allowed
to make a representation of a human being. Consequently, the artists did
develop a beautiful ornamental art that is abstract. I mean, it's from nature
really, but so is all abstract art, and it's very beautiful and ornamental. Oddly
enough Kandinsky, in his *Concerning the Spiritual in Art*, is talking about
abstraction, laying it down, the idea, and then pointing out that there is one
flaw in all this, that for him it could degenerate into ornament. He didn't like
it, although there is nothing wrong with ornament to me. After all, there is
wonderful ornamental art. But it's interesting that he would think that. It's true
of a lot of abstract art that people might say is not ornamental when it actually
is. Nothing wrong with that, but I think a lot of the claims made for it were
a little exaggerated. I can remember even Clement Greenberg saying that
ornament would never come back to architecture. And the moment he said it,
I thought: 'It's bound to one day.' It could not just disappear. Just as portraiture
can't disappear. I mean, the most interesting thing we see in the world
is another person. And the way into the other person, spiritually anyway,

is through the face and the eyes. So of course we are going to be interested
in them, and artists are going to deal with it always in some way. It seemed to
me a naive idea to think it could disappear. It was, temporarily, a rather serious
absence for a while: serious artists did not deal with it too much. But they did
really. And I think the gap won't look like a gap in the future. Because we will
find that people were always doing it, really.

*It seems to me that, with very few exceptions, your work has always been
based on autobiography of one kind or another. Either yourself and your friends
in your immediate surroundings, or in a slightly wider sense the places that
you have encountered on your travelling, which is a kind of incessant activity
with you, isn't it?*
I travel too much, I think, now. Yes, but all artists must deal with that, in a
way. They deal with their own experience. How can you deal with something
else? I mean, even if you are dealing with something else, it has to be filtered
through your own experience or feelings. In that sense, it's always
autobiographical. Rothko is autobiographical in that way. He is dealing with
some aspects of his life.

*Yes, but in your art it's franker, it's much more overt. It's almost possible to see
the whole of your work up till now as a kind of dramatisation of your life.*
Yes, I suppose. And it will go on that way, I would assume. For me, anyway,
it would be hard not to. In the end, however, you react to something way
outside yourself, I tend to draw the same people over and over again.
Because the great advantage is that you do not bother whether it's like
them or not – you always think it will be. You realise that there are many faces,
in a sense. The drawings don't all look the same, there is another aspect to
them. Whereas if you were drawing people you didn't know, different people
all the time, you tend sometimes to think: you must make it look like them.
So you think: what do they really look like? And you don't really know for
a while. It would take me quite a while to find out, and I've never done a
commissioned portrait. It wouldn't really interest me. The problems would
be the kind I wouldn't want to bother with too much. So I choose the people.
In the end, everybody lives in a small world. How many people can you really
know intimately?

*The portraits gradually became larger and larger. I'm thinking of the series
that began with the double portrait of Christopher Isherwood and his friend,
and then developed through to the painting now in the Tate, of Ossie Clark
with Celia. But these portraits did bring on, perhaps crisis is too strong a word,
but something of a problem in your work, didn't they?*
Well, the problem was naturalism, in a way. It wasn't that they were portraits,
it was that after I had painted Ossie and Celia, there was a double portrait that
is often reproduced but no one has ever seen – a portrait of George Lawson and
Wayne Sleep. I destroyed it later, but I spent a long, long time on it and I finally
gave it up because I thought I was doing something that has gone really wrong.
The way of looking is wrong, and I completed abandoned it, went off to live in
Paris and spent a year or two just drawing. I hardly did any painting. I thought:
'I'll draw, I'll learn to draw better.'

So what do you think had gone wrong?
It was trying to deal with something real, with your friends. But it was about
perceptions that had gone wrong. In the end, what I didn't realise at the time
– I realise it much clearer now – was frankly I began to paint pictures in a way

we never see, we do not see that way. It dawned on me there after a while,
but I didn't quite understand what it was about. Also, at that period I took
a lot of photographs, a lot – quite seriously. I pretended that it wasn't, but
I thought about them and then I would go off it and think: 'This is crazy, these
photographs. They are not very real, either.' That was always my problem, and
it took quite a few years for me to figure out what was wrong.

Was it in California that photography first came to influence your work?
Because it seems to me that the series of swimming pools – A Bigger Splash,
for example – are influenced by a photographic way of seeing.
> Well, that particular one does, but the other swimming pools don't. In this
> sense: I took photographs of some water, and in the photograph you have
> one serious problem. If you photograph moving water, it looks rigid when
> you look at the picture. These dancing lines are suddenly rigid, and it's not
> very real. I would look at the photograph thinking: 'It's not what you see when
> you are there.' Now, some of the pool paintings had very vigorous lines that did
> dance about, and when you look at them they do seem to move. They were
> not based on photographs at all, they were based on simply looking and then
> painting it. From memory I mean, trying to think: 'Why is it so delightful, this
> water moving about? How do I represent it?'

Some of them are actually like ironic references to abstract painters' spirals.
> Yes, Dubuffet – that occurred to me. In a way, that's what water looks like in a
> swimming pool. The more you look, the more you realise there's many ways to
> do it. It's rather a fascinating thing. Never mind the reflections, you don't even
> have to get to that. I think *A Bigger Splash* is the only one where it's frozen, in
> the sense of the splash you never see. You never see the splash stopped. And that
> was done because I was amused by the photograph of the splash and I thought:
> 'Well, it would be nice to paint it slowly.'

But with the portraits, there are photographs astonishingly close to the final
painting. I'm thinking of the Geldzahler portrait, for example, which is quite
close, isn't it?
> Well, there is no photograph that looks like the composition in the end,
> although there are of the figures. But the Ossie and Celia one, there are
> photographs that look very, very close to the composition.

And at times you have actually executed paintings based almost entirely
on a photograph.
> Yes, there were about four paintings where I did that. Although then I gave
> up. I thought: 'This is really terrible.' Then I thought the photographs were
> better than the paintings! I mean, there is a certain fascination all the time.
> I go on and off photography. But it's really about a way of looking and what
> you really see.

Actually, I find it in a way surprising that you are attracted to photography.
Because a lot of artists who have your kind of commitment to drawing,
and sitting down and recording in terms of line your response to something
observed, are vehemently against the camera, aren't they? But you don't
share that particular prejudice.
> Well, I do notice, for instance, that I've either got a small camera in my
> pocket and I'm taking photographs all the time, or I carry a sketchbook
> all the time, and I draw all the time. It's one or the other. Now, I've got
> many sketchbooks, but …

*But what is it about drawing that doesn't satisfy you, so that you have to take
photographs?*

Drawing always satisfies me. It's photography that I get unsatisfied with after a
while. After all, a great number of the photographs are just taken as anybody else
would. You go on holiday or, if people come, or it's some new place, you just take
snaps in that way. But I always go off it after a while. I think: 'It is just not good
enough, it's not about the experience of looking, not about seeing.' It makes you
think about photography a lot. Then I go back to painting and think: 'Painting
just doesn't have these problems.' It doesn't have the problem of time. Any
painting, however good or bad it is, has got layered time in it, therefore giving
you another dimension, in a way. It's more interesting, and therefore it's more
real. The photograph doesn't do this, unless it is a still life or somebody sitting
so still that you assumed they went on after the camera shutter was closed.

*It seems to me now that you are more in control of the different compartments
of your work. I mean, you still take photographs: you recently held exhibitions
of photography, in fact. But the work you are doing now, the painting, is really
quite far away from photography.*

The very recent ones, yes. But after doing those polaroid photographs, I realised
you could push this. It was something quite fascinating, and I was going to push
the ideas back into painting, where they come from originally. And to my
amazement, strange things happened and that is really exciting me. I couldn't
quite believe what you could do with it. Suddenly, I've made portraits of people
with four hands and three legs and things. But you don't quite notice, and they're
a lot more alive. Then I realised that Picasso, of course, has always done this.
His way of seeing is true. I discovered it in doing the polaroids, in the sense that
people finish up with three noses. But it's not that they have three noses – it's that
you look at it three times. That's what it is. Therefore it doesn't worry you: you
don't think they have three noses, and then it dawns on you that it's just a look
– three looks at it. I got very fascinated with it. The idea had come from painting,
anyway. At first I expected everything to be Picasso-esque. I thought: 'That's
what will have to happen, and I shall not bother about it. I shall just push and
push.' But it's amazing that they are not actually that Picasso-esque.

Well, Picasso never really took photographs, did he?

No, he didn't, because he always thought they were dead, they weren't lively
enough. But oddly, the curator of the Beaubourg who did the photographic
show, when he'd seen the polaroids I had done, he said: 'It's amazing, the
only time Picasso ever picked up a camera, he just pointed it everywhere taking
pictures, saying: "This is the only thing to do with it."' In the end, of course,
that's what I had done. And when you do that, it's amazing: you get these
perceptions of space you've never quite seen in photographs. Things happen.
You don't worry whether somebody has four or five legs, it doesn't seem to affect
how you see. And you are aware that time has just done it. I mean, it delighted
me. I suddenly thought: 'This is really exciting and rather a new perception,
for me anyway, of what you can do.' And it seemed truer. So now I've done
a few portraits while the people just sit there. So you don't have to sit still
– do whatever you want. I've to paint a bit faster, but I am amazed at what
happened. Everybody thinks they were very like the people, even though
they are not really one face.

*I said earlier that your art was essentially autobiographical. But of course,
the great exception to this is your illustrative work, the series of etchings in
particular and also the stage designing. Do you find that this is an essential*

*part of your work, something you can't do without? Or do you regard it as,
at most, a distraction from the serious business of painting?*

No, I view all my work in a way as real. It's not a distraction. Of course,
I've been able to choose what I did in the theatre: I don't make my living
doing theatre work. In England they will pay you very little for doing it,
and you finish by losing money. So you subsidise it. But it also makes you
look at things in a different way. For the first time I've thought of doing some
sculpture, because working at the New York Met, that vast stage you have
to fill, suddenly you think of space filling in another way. I'm having a show
in America of all this theatre work, and instead of taking things from the
theatre I'm going to remake them as sculptures. I've thought of Ravel's garden:
it's all going to be with lights and things floating. But I wouldn't have thought
of that without working in the theatre.

*Didn't stage designing also help you when you felt a bit stuck with the
naturalism in your painting?*

Well, yes, because the first one I did was in 1974 when I had been stuck, I think,
really stuck. And I had just been drawing. I thought: 'If you get stuck, just draw
– that's what I do.' And I did *The Rake's Progress* for Glyndebourne. First of all,
it was fun to look through Hogarth and link it all up. I grew to love the music.
I love music anyway, and trying to think of visual equivalents for it I found
quite exciting. Suddenly, you don't think naturalistically at all – you then think
in another way.

Are you saying that it takes you out of yourself?

It doesn't completely, of course. But I interpreted Hogarth in my way, I suppose.
It wasn't literal copies of Hogarth at all. I redid it in a way. Working in the
theatre is very different from painting. It's full of compromises. You are working
with a lot of people, there are deadlines, you're forced to have it finished
by a certain day – which in painting, after all, you don't. Because whatever
you've done, the show goes on at a certain time, and I rather like that, actually.
I liked, suddenly, this change from being alone in a studio, where you're only
compromising with yourself. I mean, it was marvellous, serious theatre. If you
like music, then opera is the last extravagant theatre left. They don't use artists
enough. Then later, when I did the French triple bill for the Met, I really loved
that. The Ravel piece I thought was the best thing I did in the theatre. The work
totally inspired me: Colette's words, the little story that kindness is our only
hope in the end, that destruction is self-destructive. I agree with it, I think
it is true. And the music at first I thought was charming, but after listening
to it about eight times I realised it was far more than charming. Charm was
a disguise, actually, and it's sublime. I think it's a very, very marvellous piece
of twentieth-century music. It's only forty-five minutes long, anybody can listen
to it. But actually I was inspired there, truly by this music, and by Colette's little
story. And it took off – it lifts you up a bit.

*If I have to generalise about your work, in terms of the attitudes that it seems
to convey, sometimes there seems to be a moment of sadness, of melancholy,
perhaps even of lassitude. But on the whole you want to celebrate. You don't
actually express anger, you don't express despair, you don't really express
horror. Would you say this is true?*

Yes, I would say it's true, I think. I'm perfectly aware of certain things I would
avoid. There are certain things that I've always found very difficult even to
understand. I know perfectly well that you could find beauty anywhere, even
in violence, but I find it hard to accept that. I shy away from violence, am not

attracted to it in any way. Yet I know that people like it, people are attracted
to it, there is beauty there. But I cannot grasp it. People are often hypocritical
about violence, pretending they don't like it, but a lot of people are attracted
to it. I do not in life need to be thumped in the arm to be told I am alive. It's not
necessary: the very act of looking and feeling is sufficient. Some people need
physical vigour in that way. It's not in any work I do – very, very rarely. I mean,
there is sadness, there is loneliness at times. But anger certainly is not. It's just
a certain view of life you take. I try to make the best of any situation, thinking:
'Well, there must be something here.' I love certain things about artists – like
Van Gogh, for instance, he had this ability to paint anything. I love that. If you
locked him in the cheapest motel room in Arizona, with hardly anything in
it, for a week, he could still come out with twenty paintings – of the hole in
the carpet or the corner or something. I love that he could find in it something
that is actually marvellous because you are alive: I think that's wonderful.
He is celebrating in that way. I must admit I sympathise with that, because
I think it's true – you can.

*One way of celebrating, so far as you are concerned, is to illustrate writers and
especially poets, I believe, that you particularly admire. You are very responsive
to literature, aren't you?*

Yes, usually when that happens, it happens suddenly, I find. I just read
something and it's not as though it brews a long time. I just react. Wallace
Stevens's poem, 'The Man with the Blue Guitar', I first read in the summer
of 1976. I thought it was absolutely wonderful. Didn't quite understand it,
but the ambiguities seemed right to me. I mean, it is as though they are 'clear'.
I read it a number of times, and then I thought it was so good, what he was
about, really. At first I tried to make paintings from it. I made a few and I threw
them all away, I cut them up. I just couldn't quite do it. So I moved into a
smaller scale and made etchings from them. They were not totally illustrative
of the poem, they were just dealing with the ideas in the poem more.
I remember how excited I was suddenly. There is one thing I keep meaning
to illustrate. I'm always saying I am going to do it and I start – Flaubert's story
of *The Simple Heart*. At one time I made some etchings of it. You know, the
story of the servant girl and the parrot, a beautiful story. I react and think:
'Oh, you could make marvellous images as images here.' I see it as I see things.
And in a way, in the theatre it's like that, it's close. The theatre has replaced it
for me in the last few years, in that it's very similar – referring back to Colette's
little story and Ravel's music. I felt that, in the end, it was a privilege to be able
to try and put this on the stage. It's wonderful to be asked. If I had come across
it on my own, I would have been dying to do it for somebody else.

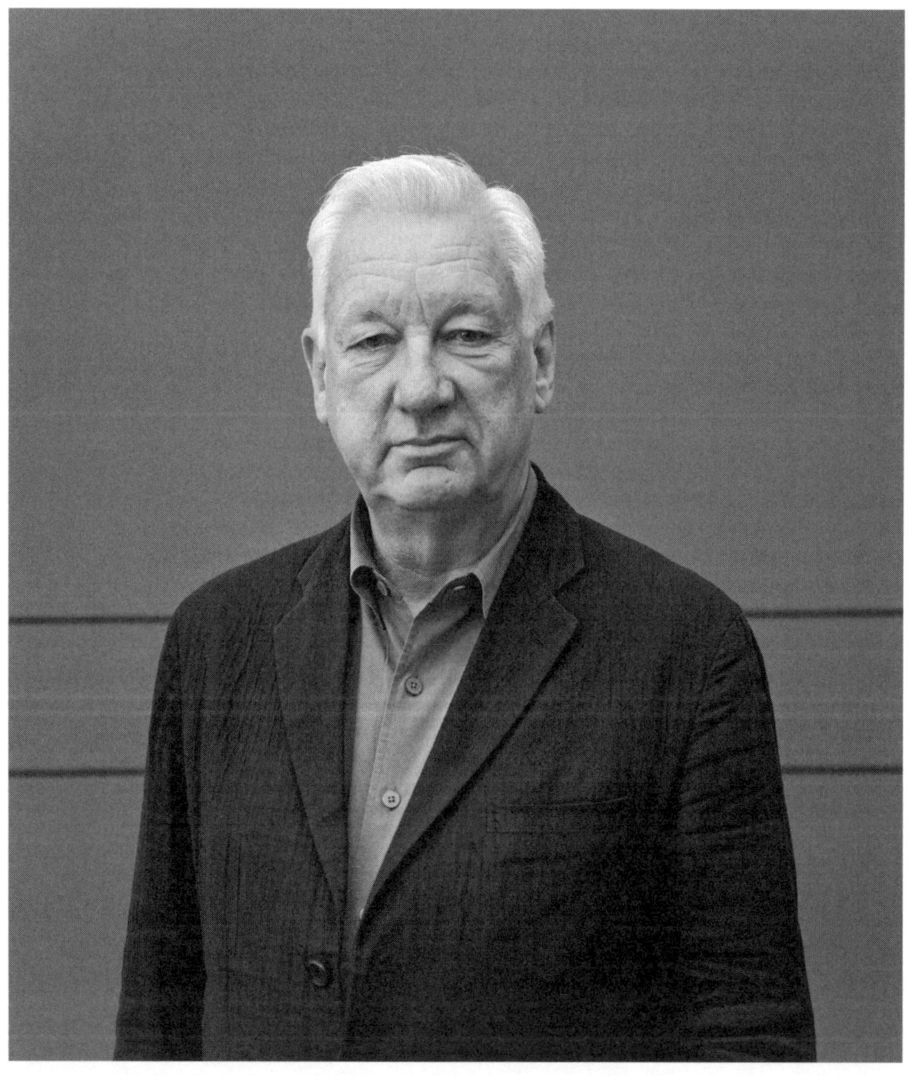

Michael Craig-Martin

'I was very conscious
of the fact that, in a lot
of art that used real
objects, the one thing
the artist got rid of was
usage. In Duchamp's
urinal, you're not
supposed to have
a pee in the urinal'

Although now ranked among the most respected British artists of recent decades, you were born in Dublin and grew up in the US before moving to England. Here you became a leading first-generation conceptual artist. Your most seminal and controversial early work was An Oak Tree, *where an unadorned glass of water rested on a glass shelf near a text containing an auto-interview with the artist. Here, when asked to describe the work, you claimed: 'What I've done is change a glass of water into a full-grown oak tree without altering the accidents of the glass of water.' As the interview proceeds, the questions prove that you realise how outrageous this bald assertion may appear. You seem to be arguing with yourself, voicing two contrasted sides of your character. But you remain firm throughout, and when the questioner accuses you of perpetuating 'the emperor's new clothes', your rebuttal is disarming. 'With the emperor's new clothes', you say, 'people claimed to see something which wasn't there because they felt they should. I would be very surprised if anyone told me they saw an oak tree.' The reply sums up the matter-of-fact way in which you have always presented your adroit and subversive work.*

By the end of the 1970s you had created your signature vocabulary of everyday objects, depicted with crisp outlines in a variety of different forms and media, from neon pieces, paintings and sculpture to large-scale wall drawings and highly coloured wall-painting installations as well as site-specific environments.

While I was working on the new book about your work, we talked at length about your career. Going through what an artist has actually done, a writer is bound to make discoveries and have his knowledge of the work enlarged in all kinds of ways. Not just enlarged, but also modified and sometimes even confounded by what turns out to be the truth. So it was a fascinating exercise, made much easier by the fact that you are forthcoming and articulate. I'd like to start this evening by asking you a question which bears upon your life as well as your art. You've lived in England now for around forty years, but you've never quite felt settled here, have you?

Well, in a sense I've never quite felt settled anywhere. I was born in Dublin and though I never lived in Ireland, I spent a lot of time there particularly as a child – I have a strong sense of being Irish. I grew up in the United States and I left when I was twenty-five. Wherever you're educated forms your basic cultural make-up. It is interesting to me now that, when I came to England in the mid-1960s, the sense of being somebody who went from one country to another to live was not a very usual thing to do, or didn't seem like it. Today, at least half the population of the earth seems to live in a country that's other than the one they started in. And so it seems like a model for something. I have a funny position in Britain, because in a way I've become an insider on everything in the English art world, and at the same time I feel a sense of distance. But that sense of distance is also very useful when you're trying to gain a sense of a place, and a sense of what's going on. You always have a bit of space between you and it, which is quite useful and which other people may not have. The reality is I feel completely at home here – I am in the modern sense a true Londoner.

It wasn't part of your game plan – when you graduated from Yale, where you studied art – to come to England. This happened because somebody offered you a job.

Well, when I was leaving Yale I needed a job teaching to survive – I was married and had a three-year-old child. And I couldn't get a job in America in any city that I wished actually to live in. The only place where it seemed possible to work was in Iowa or Missouri. And then I got offered a job in Britain, and that seemed much more attractive, even though it wasn't London. Of course I did make absolutely the right decision, because I had friends who took those

jobs in Iowa and Missouri, and they are still in Iowa and Missouri and I'm
not. And I'm very, very grateful I didn't.

*You were also lucky that you went to Yale to study art at the particular time that
you did. It was a very good moment to end up there.*

I think a lot of things in life, and certainly in art, have to do with good luck and
timing. I didn't even know there was an art school at Yale when I first went.
And I asked, and they said: 'Oh, we have an art school here.' And the second
I saw it, I was in love with the place – it was my absolute idea of what an art
school should be like. Then it turned out to be a very important moment in the
school, and there were very, very interesting students, and I realised afterwards
– when I came to England – that my generation of artists in Britain were
bitterly disappointed in their own education. They felt they'd learned very little,
they'd learned the wrong things, that it had been shallow and useless to them.
Only a handful of them felt that they had a useful education, whereas I was very
conscious that I had really loved my education. I was very fortunate, it was a
very good school to go to, and I was there at the right moment.

*There was one man at Yale – although you never met him, because he left just before
you went there – who still dominated the scene there in terms of the thinking. And
that was Josef Albers. To you, Albers has been part of your life for a long time.*

It's difficult to explain any more about Albers and the influence that he had.
He had been at the Bauhaus, he then left the Bauhaus when the Nazis were
taking over in Germany, and he went to Black Mountain College in America
which was the most radical educational institution for the arts. And then from
there he ended up as a Professor at Yale, which was – given his background –
quite an amazing thing to have happened to him. And he was a truly gifted
educationalist. He worked out a system of teaching – it's generally out of favour
now, but because it was so coherent and so intelligent, it was extremely useful if
you were a student. You could put everything together, and all the bits you were
doing made sense. It made a lot of demands on you in a very creative way. And
because I was taught by artists who had been his students and assistants, I was
so close to the heart of his teaching. Although it wasn't him, I got the real Albers
education. To be honest, all the things I do now – with drawing and colour –
I learned at Yale. I just do what I learned, though it took me about thirty-five
years to figure out how to use it. But in the end, that's what I go back to and use.

*Can you say any more about that – about how you think of colour and how it
might relate to what you learned then?*

Well, Albers believed that colour was a matter of perception not taste. He wasn't
interested in taste, and he wasn't interested in theories of colour, the symbolism
of colours or the representational use of colour. He was most interested in the
perceptual aspect of colour – the way in which colours work in relation to each
other. Everything had to do with relationships. All of his teaching had to do
with the way one thing affected another thing. And with colour it was to do with
how colours interact with each other. His book, which he produced after years
of teaching, was called *The Interaction of Colour*, and that's really what
engaged him. So all of my sense of using colours has to do with how are they
interacting, how do I get things to happen. Essentially the idea is that you can't
use a colour in isolation, and you can't think a colour – you can only perceive
a colour. And so the whole system is based on individual perception.

*And, of course, he's European. He's not American, although he spent a lot of time
in America during the latter part of his career. And we mustn't forget that while*

you were at Yale, you were again very fortunate to be in that particular place, at that particular time, because in New York all sorts of extraordinary things were happening. Young artists were emerging there in the early 1960s, and redefining things in ways that the good old abstract expressionists would never have dreamed of.

It was an extremely interesting moment, because Albers was a geometric formalist himself, and obviously one could also see him as a proto-minimalist. But in American art schools it was still the period of abstract expressionism, and many of the people who were teaching me in the studio were second-generation abstract expressionists – they weren't the generation of De Kooning, the really great people, but the people who came after and were trying to extend the language, which essentially they were failing at. And then, in the midst of this uneasy situation about where art was going, suddenly you started to have pop art and cool, hard-edge abstraction, and then that was quite quickly followed by op art, and that was followed by minimalism – and all of these things emerged in a period of about six years. During that whole period when I was a student, Yale is ninety miles from New York City so every couple of weeks we went and looked at the galleries. In those days it was much easier, because there were only ten galleries, so you could go and do it – the five galleries that you wanted to see. So I was in a very fortunate position. I saw all of the great early shows of Andy Warhol, Jasper Johns, Rauschenberg, Judd, Robert Morris, Carl Andre. And that's a powerful thing to have when you're a student.

Very much so. At Yale you did a lot of painting, a lot of drawing, but sculpture became a major issue for you during those years, partly because you'd seen all this extraordinary stuff in New York by the minimalists. And one of the great surprises for me, when I was writing the book, was the discovery of your very early film piece, which now very appropriately belongs to the Irish Museum of Modern Art. You've never done a film piece since then. You did it for your graduation at Yale, and for it you travelled over to a very remote part of Ireland. Almost as soon as you had submitted it for your graduation, it vanished. And it only reappeared many years later, when your daughter discovered it in one of those proverbial family attics somewhere. It was a revelation to me, because here was the young Craig-Martin on his own in Ireland, with a camera which you'd never used before, not knowing very much about film – let alone film theory – but training your lens on the most ordinary, everyday things around you. Can you say a bit more about what you were trying to do with the film?

I liked this place in Ireland: it was extremely beautiful to a certain way of looking. There were almost no trees, because it's so windblown.

Yes, you're very aware of the sea there.

Very aware – you're right on the edge of the sea, and the weather is coming off the Atlantic very powerfully. The place is full of stones, and all the fields have been marked out by taking the stones from the fields and making walls. But the fields are still full of stones, because there are so many stones you can never get rid of them. They had no woods, so they didn't make gates: when they wanted to get the animals, they just took down a bit of wall. So in many ways a very bleak place, but strangely beautiful. And one of the things I liked about it, I already had an interest in things that were not hierarchical and not dramatic. So it struck me as one of the least dramatic landscapes it was possible to find. And there was almost nothing of more interest than anything else. Everything was equally interesting, or uninteresting, depending on how you looked at it. So it was a certain kind of blandness about the place that I was very attracted to, and that's why I went and filmed there. When I got there to film, I realised that I had no idea what I was doing. I didn't have a plan, I had nothing. I just had the camera, and I'd never used the camera before I got it to do the film. And I can remember that one of the first things that really struck me was – I went to shoot my first shot, and suddenly I thought: 'How long is a shot? How long do you hold the button?' I had no idea, and I'm in a field all by myself wondering how long. So I did a couple of tests, and then I thought: 'Fifteen or twenty seconds feels about right.' So then I shot every single shot for fifteen or twenty seconds, because I couldn't think of any reason why one shot would be long and one shot would be short. When I came to edit the film, I had no idea if any of it was going to come out, and 90 per cent of it did. So I used virtually every shot, and every shot fully, so in the edited film there's a very strange rhythm, and that rhythm comes from the fact that every shot is the same length. And every shot is very, very still. None of which was planned, and it was all just accepting whatever happened.

It is a very beautiful film. I watched it again over in your exhibition at Dublin, where you can sit on a bench and quietly contemplate it. The film is very meditative, and you just travel around this landscape. You're very aware of the walls made up of individual stones, which almost become ready-made sculpture. And you're very aware of moments that bear directly on what you're doing nowadays. Like there's one extraordinary shot of a window sill with very, very ordinary household objects just grouped on it, and I thought: 'Oh yes, that's absolutely one of his very first still lifes.' I'm also very aware, even though there are hardly any people in this film, of people. They're not there much, but every now and again they pop up. A woman pops up walking in a field. There's a wonderful postman who cycles over a bridge, and then right at the end there's this huge surprise: little children appear and grin at you over a wall, rather alarmingly next to a crucifix. Religion comes into this film as well, every now and again. And that made me realise quite how much, even when the landscape is empty, you're conscious of human use, human existence. This, I think, is absolutely central to one's experience of your work today. When you're painting these objects, I'm terribly aware that they are objects of use, that they belong in somebody's home, that they say something about people, about their owners. Are you conscious of all that, looking back on the film?

I'm very conscious, when I see the film, that here I am in this bleak landscape, but there's hardly a shot which is of real landscape. There's always something in it that somebody has made. There's a road, there's a wall, there's a house, there's a chimney with a bit of smoke coming out, washing on a line, there's always a sign of some human activity, even though they are empty of people. And that is very like my later work. In other ways it's not, because it's a black-and-white film and there are no modern objects, the ready-made objects that I've come to use. But you're right that one of the things that interested me, really early on, was the difference between what was an art object and what wasn't an art object. And why some objects are art objects, and some objects aren't. The thing that defines most objects that we make is usage. So what it's going to be for determines what size it is, what it's made out of, how it looks, how much it costs – all those things are taken into account. All of it is based on the question of usage, and so I just got interested in this question in relation to art. Which is also the question: what is the use of art? What is it for? I was very conscious of the fact that, in a lot of art that used real objects, the one thing the artist got rid of was usage. In Duchamp's urinal, you're not supposed to have a pee in the urinal. In his *Bottle Rack*, you're not supposed to put bottles on it. It's been removed from that thing that it was meant to do, and that's partly how it's taken on this other thing of being seen as art. So I tried to play with this question of usage and tried to maintain it.

*By the time you'd finished your Yale course, you were impossible to pin down as
an artist, really. You were doing all kinds of different things, and I guess that's
one of the reasons why you ended up in England, because they accepted you,
whereas other institutions wouldn't. But even in England – even in the Bath
Academy of Art, at Corsham in Wiltshire – they were puzzled, they couldn't quite
define you, they didn't know what kind of artist you were.*

No, but something was immediately apparent to me when I came to Britain.
America is a deeply conservative place by nature – the fact that there are
neo-cons now, all that was there in America when I was a child. And Yale itself
was a very conservative institution, very conservative school, the students were
really quite conservative. When I came to England, the thing that struck me
was how incredibly easy people were with radical proposals, a radical idea, a
different material. Americans thought about whether it was really appropriate
to do this, and wondered about these questions in a slightly puritanical way.
And it seemed to me almost immediately that British art students were much
more comfortable with this. Of course, we are talking about the end of the
1960s, and there's the whole turmoil of questioning of authority which took
place everywhere in the western world. But this was very much so in Britain,
and all of those authoritarian things that had held Britain together, all were
thrown up for grabs. And it's one of the reasons why art education became
so interesting at that time, because there became an extraordinary freedom
about what you could do educationally, in a way that certainly isn't true today
– and to be honest, I can't imagine will ever happen again in the history of
mankind. It was a kind of moment of madness, when you could try anything.

*And when you were at Corsham, it was happening, wasn't it? In quite a few art
schools, up and down the land, students were rebelling to the point where they
were taking over the institution and getting rid of their teachers. And that
travelled down to Wiltshire for a while.*

Yes, it did happen in the Bath Academy. Because I was only about twenty-six
or twenty-seven, and because I was foreign, they assumed that I had stirred
it up! But the reality was that one of the things that was very striking about
the student revolution was how embarrassed were the people teaching them.
We felt embarrassed, because the students were asking for things that really
we should have asked for. They were making demands that we should have
made, and they humiliated us, in a sense, by doing it. I have to say, in the
years afterwards I often thought that the people who were most affected
by the student revolutions of the late 1960s were not the student generation
that initiated them. It was the generation just a bit older than themselves,
who were their teachers. We were really affected by that!

That's very interesting.

And I think the younger people who did it, they took it for granted and put
it aside more easily. We've never forgotten it, people of my age, we've never
forgotten what happened.

*When you came to live in London in 1968, and started teaching here and there,
as well as working very hard in the studio, that was a good time to arrive in the
capital city, too. Because there was a new generation emerging that had very little
time for what their seniors had achieved. In particular there was a generation
at St Martin's School of Art – people like Richard Long, Bruce McLean, Barry
Flanagan and Gilbert & George, and even older artists were there like John
Latham, stirring it up like mad. Suddenly, what we now think of as conceptual
art just changed everything – it changed everything utterly, to quote an Irish poet.*

It was very extraordinary: just at the turn of the decade, from the 1960s to
the 1970s. You think of England in the 1960s as Swinging London, pop art,
mini-skirts, Vidal Sassoon, all that bubbly kind of world, very youthful and
cheerful and optimistic. And suddenly, all that was gone, it was just dated and
disappeared and became unsustainable quite quickly by the end of the 1960s.
Then this other generation took over who thought about the world completely
differently, and I remember quite clearly in the early 1970s that there were
artists of the older generation who were really in a panic about themselves
and their own practice, because the upheaval that was implied in the change
of values between the 1960s and the 1970s seemed so great. It's summed up
in the idea that 'painting is dead', but actually there were many other aspects
to it, because there was also an aspect of sculpture being dead, too. So there
was art that changed the whole idea of what art might be.

*Absolutely. I started writing as a professional art critic right at the end of the
1960s: I got my job on the* Evening Standard *unbelievably when I was twenty-
two. So I was pitched into all this. And I was very aware, right from the word
go, that the senior generation – people I'd thought of as being quite radical and
avant-garde, like Anthony Caro, who had done their own revolutions not long
before – that whole generation felt threatened. The whole notion that art should
be either painting or sculpture was fundamentally questioned, wasn't it? And
everything was opening up, everything was fanning out, nothing really seemed
impossible. It was a question of what young artists actually wanted to do. And
all kinds of things which art now benefits from, all kinds of new materials and
ways of working, sprang out of that moment.*

There's one thing that it's hard to recapture a sense of, but at the time the thing
that was so exciting and interesting was that nobody had any idea what they
were doing – nobody had any idea of where it was going. There was no pattern:
nobody had ever quite done this before. There were these new materials, but
what did it mean? Everything felt very much up for grabs. Now all of these
things that were initiated at that time have settled down into various formats
of art. To me, it's a little bit like pop groups, they're all the same, there's four
people on stage. But there was a time when there wasn't that format – people
just stumbled along doing what they were doing, trying to find something
without knowing quite what they were looking for.

*And you were using all kinds of materials – sculpture at one point, things that
didn't quite work, boxes that didn't quite open, didn't quite fit. The sculpture
of frustration, you could almost call it. But you were also experimenting with
mirrors. You did an extraordinary installation at the Tate in 1972, where visitors
walked in and found themselves in a series of booths which they moved through.
Each one had a mirror, and you looked in it confidently expecting to see your own
reflection there, and you saw somebody else's face. Somebody you'd never seen
before, somebody who was elsewhere, but you didn't know where or who. That was
very disorientating. You also used words underneath mirrors, so that you looked
at yourself in the mirror and then read something underneath which seemed
to question your own existence. And then, most notoriously and hotly debated,
in 1974 people walked into the Rowan Gallery – which is a great loss, really, one
of the most beautiful galleries in London, just off Bond Street, large, white and
luminous – and they walked around. It was supposed to be your solo show, but
a lot of them couldn't find the art. They thought the gallery was entirely empty.
And so quite a lot of anger was generated by this show. But they were wrong: there
was one wall which had on it, quite high up, a very simple piece – a glass shelf,
with a glass of water resting on it. But you complicated this whole thing by calling*

it An Oak Tree. *And there was an accompanying pamphlet, like an auto-interview: you were actually questioning and answering yourself. The questioner was saying, in effect: 'How dare you expect people to come into the gallery and look at a glass of water on a glass shelf and imagine that it's an oak tree?' You constructed this fascinating theoretical debate about it, with a wonderful sense of irony. But it was an extreme moment in your career, wasn't it?*

I'd started off making constructions, and they became the box pieces that you were describing, and then I started to use objects that I could buy. And I used things like milk bottles which I thought were really interesting because, at the time, everybody had milk bottles and it was a very strange object because it had no value at all. They were outside everybody's house and you could just go and take them, and when you had finished with them you put them out and you got new ones. So they seemed very interesting to me in terms of their status as objects. And gradually, I felt that I was trying to find something that interested people a lot at the time, which was about the nature of art itself. The question about what is art and what isn't art, how do you define it, how do you recognise it when you see it? And I had the idea – because I'd also by that point been attacked a lot in the press – of trying to make a work that was invulnerable, so that I couldn't be accused of failing. Because the proof that I had failed would be the same as the proof that I had succeeded. If nothing visible happened at all, I couldn't be told it didn't do it. So that was really my thought, and the only way to do it was to make it entirely on the basis of claim. So that's really the genesis of the *Oak Tree*. I realised the minute I thought of it – I started to work it out quite quickly – that I had done something very special. I knew that instantly.

Yes, and with hindsight we can look back to that glass of water and relate it very clearly to the kinds of paintings that you have done since then. But we can also trace it back to Marcel Duchamp, to those ready-mades, to that act of buying something, putting it on view, calling it something else and asking for a transformation to take place. And more than that: I was fascinated to think about it in terms of transubstantiation as well – religion – Catholicism. Let's talk about that for a moment, because it was a very important part of your childhood, growing up in Washington DC but still very much educated according to an Irish Catholic pattern, it's true to say, isn't it?

It's true to say, yes.

So you come out of quite a few years of Catholicism, and you know a lot about it.

Well, in the 1950s, if you were a Catholic you inevitably knew a lot about Catholicism – I can't believe how much I know, and I'm staggered about how little young people know these days. I suppose I was immersed in the way that kids were at the time – although I have to say I was at university in New York, before I went to Yale, and there was one Sunday morning when I decided not to go to mass. And I never went back: it just stopped, just like that, overnight, it just ended. It was funny, because I went to all Catholic schools and I grew up in a neighbourhood that was entirely Jewish, so I always had Jewish friends and Catholic friends, and I never really met a Protestant until I went to Yale. Because I had no way of meeting anyone who was Protestant – a very American phenomenon, I think.

In 1974, when you'd held this extraordinary solo show with the one thing in it just sitting on the shelf, were you very aware of the fact that it was a question of where to go from there?

Yes, it became quite a crisis to me. Because it was such an extreme statement, I didn't really know how to proceed. I thought: 'OK, I'm going to be the artist of extreme statements.' But the problem was I couldn't think of a statement that was as extreme as the one I'd already done. And I thought: 'I can't say the next one is an apple tree, or the next one is a something else tree.' So I thought it was such a dilemma, and I realised that I'd done something that was so fundamental that the best thing to do was to abandon that as a course of action. And that was when I decided that, since I'd created a kind of Ground Zero for myself, what I should do is reconstruct things for myself. So then I started to do drawing, which I hadn't done for years, as a way of trying to rebuild the fundamentals of art from this position. The thing that interested me, at the time, was that visual representations of things were a kind of no-no in the avant-garde art world, unless one used the new medium of photography. And to make something by hand, like a drawing, to do it in a representational way was considered very dubious. But what I felt was that all the people who did make representational paintings approached the question of representation taking for granted the possibility of doing it. So that they started from the assumption you could do it and then they did what they did. They were never interested in the question, whereas I was interested in something more like a philosophical question about the nature of being able to do that at all. And so I thought: 'Well, what would happen if you took my way of thinking and you applied it to something as traditional as drawing pictures of things?'

What you ended up drawing, and building up as a vocabulary of forms, a lexicon of images, does have a lot to do with the glass of water on the shelf. They were very ordinary objects, and the glass on the shelf was like something we find every morning when we go into the bathroom and open the cabinet door: there it is. And all the stuff that you were drawing, during the 1970s, was of that ilk, wasn't it?

You don't know why you're interested in things as an artist. I can tell you reasons for things, but I don't really understand exactly why I felt certain compulsions. And I had the idea, when I started to draw objects – well, at first I didn't want to have to draw them, I wanted to use found images, just like I'd used found objects, real objects. I thought images of these objects were everywhere, and I would just take them. Then I went looking for them, and I suddenly discovered I couldn't find them, and the simple drawings of objects that did exist – in small ads, for instance – were much more 'expressive' in their abbreviation than I had thought. They weren't neutral. So I started to draw them myself, because I couldn't find them. And then I realised that the characteristic I was looking for was – I wanted to have a drawing as ordinary as the thing I was drawing. I wanted the drawing to be like a ready-made. I had to make ready-made drawings – which is, of course, a contradiction in terms! It was just so that I could have drawings as neutral as the things I had been using when I was using the real thing. I discovered that what makes images so exciting in contrast to the objects themselves is that they're so flexible – you can do so many different things with them. And then, in the odd way of life, I've ended up spending years and years and years playing with these same things, and every time I think I've exhausted them, somehow a door opens and there's something else I can try.

Absolutely. And the upshot was that in the late 1970s you had another show at the Rowan Gallery. It was equally memorable, because we came in and were confronted by those linear images. Taped onto the wall and immense, they contained not just a single glass of water but several objects almost fused together through lines, to the point where we had to try and work out exactly what was represented there. We were very aware of the act of depiction, and of the artist asking himself fundamental questions: 'What is depiction? How

*do we depict? How do we actually put a line around something? How do we
define? How do we recognise anything, anyway?' All those kinds of questions.*

Well, yes, I still thought of myself as essentially making sculpture, and what
intrigued me about the wall drawings was that I thought of them as sculptures,
because they seemed to have a kind of sculptural presence. They clearly weren't
paintings. But they were interesting, because they seemed like sculptures that
had no mass – they had presence but no mass. And that seemed like a very
intriguing prospect. So this led me to an interest in the kind of linguistics of
images: all the objects I've done, everything I've ever drawn, is drawn in a way
that's like naming something. On the one hand, it's the central interest in what
I do, and on the other hand, it's of no interest to me at all. It's like I always think
with Josef Albers: his famous works are called *Homage to the Square* – but the
thing that was of least interest to Albers was the square. It's everything else in
the picture that interests him. And it's strange that what artists use as the thing
that identifies you is, very often, just the hanger for the things that interest
you – it's all the other things that happen in works of art that interest artists.
It's not the objects: it's everything I've done to them that's interested me.
I'm not interested in consumerism, I'm not interested in all the other things
that people sometimes think that I might be interested in, but don't interest me.

*In those big tape drawings, although the objects that you were defining were
inanimate, I'm very often aware of something almost like movement. There's
one called* Modern Dance, *a huge frieze-like collection of these ordinary objects
that seem to be participating in a choreographed performance, which is very
affecting when we are confronted by it on a large scale. And gradually, during
the 1980s, you introduced other elements, too. Rather more sculptural elements,
in a way: steel, things like that, but also colour. So it was almost as if you were
adding, to these things that could be called drawings, sculpture on the one hand
and painting on the other. All in one.*

I saw myself as putting all these bits back together again. I feel like
I disintegrated them all, and they start off as wall drawings, they're constructed
out of steel, then they become installations and they become paintings.
And so in a way I go back to the earliest thing of painting. But then there's
all sorts of new things that are possible with new techniques and computers.
So you can spin it out even further. I'm interested in the idea that all these
things can interrelate. I like the idea that I could use an image on a postage
stamp that's really tiny, and then do something on the Euston Road that's
gigantic, and they're just exactly the same image – there's no difference, really.
So these things can have such different meanings depending on what you do
with them. And it's the depending on what you do with them that interests me.

*And all this time, during the 1980s, you were teaching at Goldsmith's. There was
a very remarkable generation coming up there – well, more than one generation.
But certainly the one that has become celebrated – and I use that word advisedly
– is the so-called Freeze generation who mounted that extraordinary show
in Docklands towards the end of the 1980s. It's remarkable to me, looking back
on what you did as an artist then, that you had enough time to do it. Because
you must have had your hands full with the Goldsmith's lot as well.*

Well, like many artists, particularly of my generation in Britain, I spent much
of my life involved in teaching. During the 1970s I was teaching at Goldsmith's
three days a week. So I had the rest of the time for my own work, essentially,
and everything else in life. I got used to working six or seven days a week.
In the early 1980s, for the first time I started to sell work – that was when
I started to make the metal constructions. Always my idea had been that

I only teach in order to live, and suddenly I started to have an income that didn't need teaching. As I made more money, I reduced the teaching. Every time I could, I took out a day. And by the end of the 1980s I was only teaching one day a week. It was actually the period when I did the least teaching, and I only saw five or six students a week. But I did see the same people every week, maybe between five and ten people, over the course of a year, and then there'd be two or three years and there was overlapping. It was in this period that my teaching seemed to have its greatest impact: when I was doing the least, and seeing a very concentrated number of people. Though I get so much credit, I'm not the only person who taught all those people, of course, and I'm not the only person responsible. There were certainly other very important factors involved. But I was very conscious of the fact that all of them had been my students for quite long periods of time, and I'd often been the person who interconnected them, because I saw that as critical. When I came to England in 1966 I was red-hot from America – I was so in tune with what was going on at that moment, I'd spent five or six years in the heat of this thing that was happening. I came to England, and in a sense it was a terrible mistake. I lost my connectedness to the things that were my own cultural context. I was engaged in a big context there, and when I came to England it was a different context, and nobody knew the context I had come from and I then found myself floundering – trying to keep connected to the American context that I'm increasingly detached from, and trying at the same time to engage with and use my new British context. But it took me a long time. One of the things I understood from that was how important that sense of context, larger than yourself as an individual, is for an artist at a fundamental level. So always my idea of teaching was to try to help the students have a way of having some kind of interconnectedness. And the only generation where it really did happen in an intense way was with those students at Goldsmith's in the late 1980s, because they did all know each other, they were all connected with each other, they'd all been through classes and seminars and tutorials together. And Damien Hirst did a very clever thing. He took all of those people and he put them into an exhibition and – well, the rest is history, because he just sensed the thing that was available to him at that moment. And those people today, they're all still friends. But they created a context for each other that enabled them to be artists, and to grow in the way that they did. I felt that that's what I had come from, and in a sense I had lost some of that, so it was part of my interest to try to put back for them what I thought was lost to me.

That's very interesting. I think it leads on, in a curious way, to what happened next in your own work, which is very much to do, in the early 1990s, with discovering that there was a whole new world out there, really, for you to make work in – the existing interiors of buildings, essentially, that could somehow be invaded by the vocabulary of forms that you'd built up. It began rather out of the blue, really, in Rome, didn't it?

Yes. When I was doing the wall drawings, they existed as slides and I would go to some place and project the slide and do the drawing. In a small sense, each place I did it was site-specific, because you would decide where it would go, how big it would be – those decisions would be made at each location. But in fact none of the works were developed in order to be suitable to a particular place. And when I was asked to do a show at the British School in Rome, which had this gallery, it wasn't a very important show but it was a very interesting room. The building was designed by Lutyens, and there was a great stone fireplace and French windows going out into what had obviously been a tennis court – a rather grand room. And the minute you walked into the

room, you knew that it had never been intended to be an art gallery, and that
it had probably had four or five different lives before it became an art gallery.
That layering of lives, and the fact that it wasn't a white box, interested me.
And so for the first time I made a work for a specific place, and I painted all
the walls in the gallery. I'd never done that before. I added images, but essentially
I painted the walls. And it was just a revelation to me – a complete revelation.
I suddenly realised that I had missed out on something I should have been doing
a long time before: using the specifics of a place to help myself know what to
do, and to use that as a way of making something that was special to a place.
From that point on, I've never done a single installation that was not site-
specific, or that did not use colour.

*You've always been interested in architecture. It may not have been very evident
from your work before then, especially in the 1960s and 1970s, but it was
certainly an interest of yours. And it occurs to me that, of course, at Yale there
was the whole Bauhaus thing going on, which was to do with art and
architecture as well.*

That was another curious thing about coming to Britain. Not only was there
a modernist building boom in America, but it was happening most potently
at Yale: while I was there, there were new buildings by Saarinen, Rudolph,
Philip Johnson and Marcel Breuer, Skidmore Owings and Merrill. There
were incredible modern buildings being built, and I was very interested
in contemporary architecture.

And Philip Johnson actually bought one of your early works.

He did, yes. But when I came to Britain there was very, very little architecture
being done, and most of it wasn't very interesting. There was almost no
architecture of the character or quality that I had been interested in as a
student. I had studied the history of architecture when I was a student at Yale.
It was the most brilliant course: between 300 and 500 students attended every
lecture because it was so extraordinarily interesting and well done by Vincent
Scully – he was the historian who taught it. Then ironically during the 1990s,
I was appointed an artist trustee at the Tate, and I had this backlog of unused
knowledge about architecture when Tate Modern was being planned. It was as
though I had been sitting on this information for thirty years that was completely
worthless, and suddenly it was really helpful – it was helpful to me, it was helpful
to the planning committee that I was on. Amazing how you store up things and
then use them later. As an artist I've always been very interested in the possibility
of making works that are very large, architectural in scale. No matter how large
an artwork is, it is absolutely tiny in comparison with architecture. So if you
want to make something big, you have to do it in conjunction with architecture.
You sometimes need to bully them into letting you do immense things – things
on an entirely different scale than is possible any other way.

*And what's amazing to me, looking at what you've done with buildings over
the last fifteen years, is the sheer range of it. Certain artists just prefer to work
in rather purist spaces, and nothing else. Whereas you've worked in just about
every kind of space I could possibly imagine. At one extreme, a German museum
already filled with sacred objects from the past, like statues of the Virgin, and you
were able to add your own images to the installation that existed there already.
So you're not frightened of something already very freighted. But to go to another
extreme, you have more recently worked with the architects responsible for the
conversion of Tate Modern, Herzog & De Meuron, on a new building: the Laban
Dance Centre. And you're equally happy in both these kinds of contexts, are you?*

Or would you say that you prefer one, essentially, to the other?

I can't say I prefer one to the other. But what I like is the difference between the possibilities of things. And a wonderful thing happened for me: as I became known for doing things in architectural spaces, I have been asked to do lots of things that would never have happened if I hadn't had that interest. So I get offered the most amazing places to do things. I'm much more interested in a place that has a very particular character, and then try to excavate that character. I do some things which change the space, but my idea is always to reveal the space that already exists. I don't alter the architecture – that doesn't interest me at all. Nor does simply adding decoration.

But it's still your language of forms that is applied to these buildings,
even though you're very aware of the history they contain.

Well, the images take on different meanings depending on the context of the places where you use them. I've always found them so wonderfully flexible.

You're also prepared to take risks, because you were invited to do an installation
at the Museum of Modern Art in New York, and you had the audacity to
incorporate in your piece on the walls several key works from MOMA's own
collection, including a Picasso cubist sculpture and the de Chirico painting
of a classical head with a rubber glove. This was a pretty daring thing to do
– you must have guessed that it might upset somebody.

It upset quite a few people. I got attacked at great length – nine pages of attack – by Frank Stella. I've never actually read the attack: I thought I'd better not read it. I've never spoken to him about it, and I didn't want to remind him that he had actually been a tutor of mine at Yale at one point! I didn't think he'd really want to know that [laughs]. I've done a lot of things that made me very uneasy. And I've always tried to counter one thing with another. If you do a luxury project – a bank lobby – it's always good to have a hospital atrium that you're working on at the same time.

But you're not frightened of assailing the viewer sometimes, with often quite
violent installations. There was one in particular called The Eye of the Storm,
at the Gagosian Gallery in New York, where the viewer was actually confronted
with the alarming prospect of an electric fan that seemed to be sending all the
other objects shooting across space – some of them quite aggressive objects, too,
with blades and opened-up safety-pins and things that, if they ended up attached
to your body or lodged in your eye, you'd know about it, wouldn't you? In that
case, the pictorial aggression was very much in response to what had happened
to New York only a year before, in 9/11. On the other hand, some of your big
site-specific pieces are very distilled, calm, purist and lyrical. That's one of the
things I like about your work – I never know what's coming next. You're not a
predictable artist, even though the language you've used is very much your own.

Thanks. It's a great compliment to think of not being predictable. I feel upset sometimes when I feel some people think of everything I do as having a very similar emotional impact. A great many of the things I've done over the past fifteen years have been abroad. And only the people who were in these places ever saw the things that I've done. Many of them are now reproduced in the book, so they do exist as records even though they were temporary things. I was very conscious, going through your book on my work, that I'm the only person who has ever seen all my work. It's a very strange feeling.

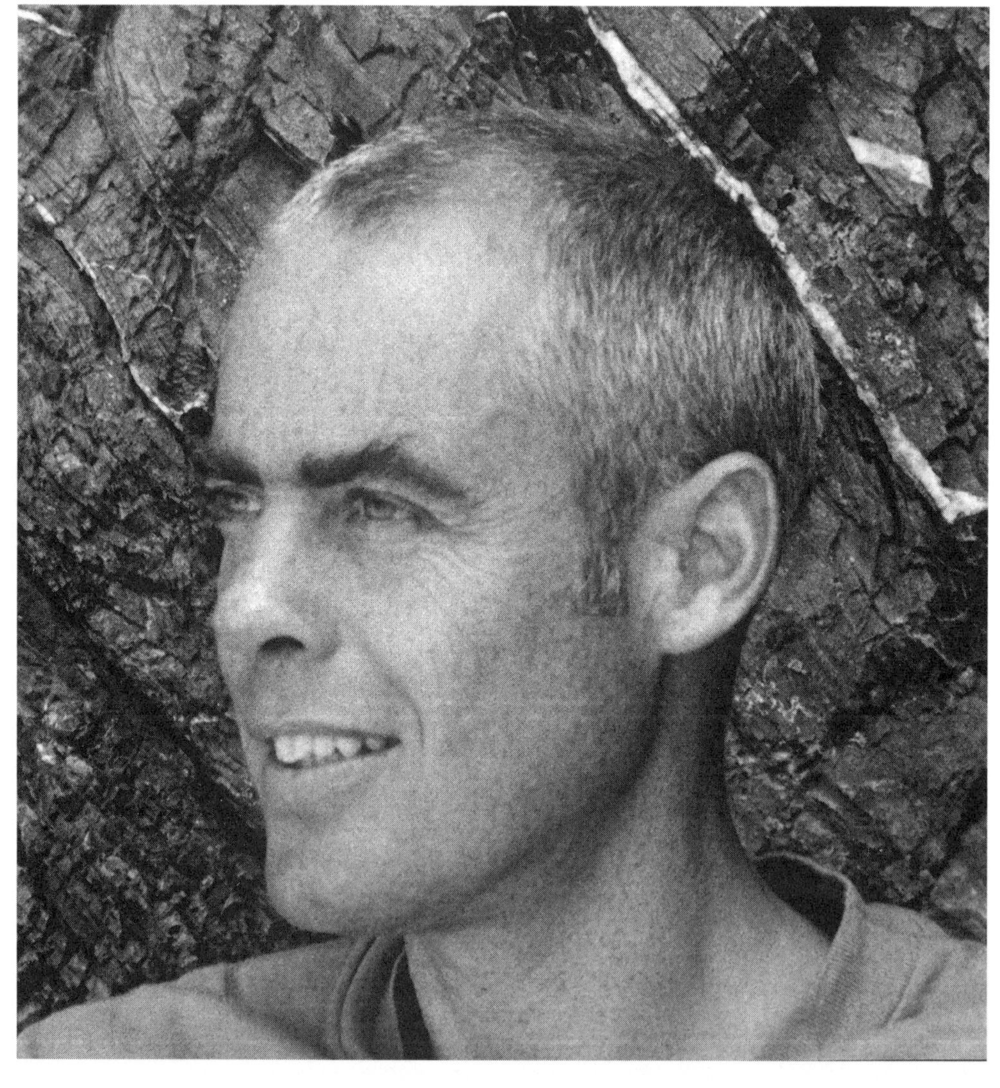

1988

Richard Long

'A sculpture in a landscape, when it really happens well in a good way, is like a celebration of the place and my feelings of me being there and having the right idea at the right time and everything coming together'

*For more than twenty years you have been dealing with the natural world
in the most direct way possible: moving outdoors and taking both your
inspiration and materials from the countryside itself. The sticks and stones
used in your open-air pieces are found on site. You see your work as practical,
simple and vigorous rather than a romantic interpretation of nature.
In a work called* A Line Made by Walking – England 1967, *you didn't
even pick up any of the materials available in the field. You walked across
it instead, treading the grass until a straight track was clearly visible in
the photograph you took of the work.*

*Circles and lines are the hallmark of your art, and they convey
in a very clear, single-minded way your preoccupation with movement,
distance and time. So do words, which refer very concisely to the objects
and natural features you pass. Your exhibitions demonstrate that you
know exactly how to handle gallery space with the spare lucidity which
characterises your outdoor work. But of course, remote country is a very
different arena from a gallery. So how do you go about recreating the
outdoor experience indoors?*

In the way that the photographs and texts feed the imagination. The sculptures
that you can see directly in the gallery feed the senses, and also the mud works
which are made directly on the wall. I like to present art in a very concrete way
in a gallery, as well as presenting images from remote places. I think also the
photographs have the function that I can make a piece of work, for example,
in a canyon in Mexico, by pouring water down a rock face to make a water
drawing, and then record that idea and bring it back into the world of art.
Photographs are useful for recording a work which may only last for the time
that the water drawing dries in the sunshine.

Do you find it easier to work outdoors than in a gallery context?

I enjoy both ways of working, and for me it is necessary to use both possibilities.
I think if I only worked outdoors it could perhaps be seen as romantic escapism.

*Do you ever wish that the gallery visitor could actually see your work
in the landscape?*

All the places where I make my work, such as the Highlands or on
Dartmoor, are free public places where anyone can go. So it is quite possible
that people can go to the locations of my walks and often the information
is provided, as in the map works. It is not my intention that they should
actually repeat the walks, because not only do they belong to a certain place,
but they also belong to a certain time. You can never repeat the time but
certainly people can go to the places of my walks. Also, it is not true to think
that my landscape sculptures are never seen. They are sometimes seen
by local people in the country, occasionally as I make them, or discovered
by chance by people who might not recognise them as art but who would
nevertheless see them. I am sort of interested in all the different contexts
that work can be put into the world and then also received back by different
people in different circumstances.

*But it's surely significant that you would never, by choice, make your work
outdoors with people looking on while you were doing it.*

No, it is never a performance. It is usually a very private, quiet activity.
I am happy to make it in solitude. I think part of the energy in my work is that
I have the opportunity to make art in amazing, beautiful landscapes which
are very strong and powerful. Somehow part of the power and the energy
comes from being alone in that place. The simplicity and feeling of being alone

is actually part of the work. So it would be quite inappropriate to have a load
of people visiting it at a particular site, as that would change the whole nature
of the place. So I think that is another way my photographs work. They present
the idea that art can be made in solitude or in very remote places, or lasts
for very few minutes, or be seen by very few people, or be seen by people from
a different culture.

How much of the year on average do you spend walking, would you say?
It is difficult to say. I have never measured it, but probably not more than half.
I don't consider myself a nomad, and I am not a person who is endlessly
wandering. I like to go to places for a certain reason, following a certain idea,
and to do a piece of work which lasts for a certain amount of time. Then when
I have finished that work I always like to come home. So it is a necessary part
of my life to be quiet at home in Bristol. That is also part of the way I like to live.
I think if I was travelling all the time I would not have the right type of energy
to start making a big walk. It is necessary to have an appetite. Often a good walk
comes after spending a month or so in Bristol, just answering letters and doing
paperwork. Then I have a good appetite to go out into the landscape.

*Since you also spend a lot of time holding exhibitions all over the world, you
must be a highly organised person.*
Well, I think to be a professional full-time artist it is necessary to be very
organised. I think, like a lot of artists, the most organised thing you see
about me is my work. So probably the work is more organised than my life.

How do you decide where to take the next walk?
Oh, for a variety of reasons. I like the idea that it is possible to go around to
the other side of the world almost on a hunch. I may have a feeling or an idea
that some place might be interesting, or I may never have been there before,
or know nothing about it. That is a good enough reason to find out what that
place is like.

So you don't necessarily research a place before you go there?
Well, it depends. There are certain walks close to home, like a piece I did
this summer in Scotland where I had a particular idea about making a walk
in the Highlands. Because you can get good maps in Britain, it was possible
to plan the walk by looking at maps; I could know the place in advance. So then,
it was just a question of going to the place and carrying out the walk. In other
places, like the Hoggar Mountains in the Sahara where I went this year, it is
not possible to get good maps. So you have a completely different way of going
about walking. The way I found my way in the Sahara was just by following the
places where I could get water, without using a map. So some walks are with
maps and some without.

Do you ever get lost?
There are different ways of getting lost, but not fundamentally lost. Sometimes
just for a couple of hours here and there in a mist. In the early days, when I used
to make straight walks across Dartmoor, one of the things I used to like about
walking in a straight line was that, apart from the intellectual beauty of a
straight line, it is the most practical way to cross a moor. No matter what the
weather is doing, and it can be a very thick mist, because I am following a
compass line I can do that walk in any conditions and not get lost. So walking
by compass in straight lines, apart from anything else, is a very practical part
of my work. I think basically all my work is very practical. The only reason

I could do the walk in the Sahara was that I had the amazing good luck that before I went there, there happened to be some freak storms that left pools of water in the mountains. Those storms determined that I could walk there, and where I could find water determined the shape of the walk. So, in fact, how it turned out was that the water lasted for six days. Each day the little pools of water were drying up and disappearing into the ground. So at the end of the six days the water had disappeared, and that is when the walk ended. So it had a nice kind of practical logic about it.

What do you actually think about when you are on your own and walking, mile after mile, in often quite deserted territory?
Well, you can think about everything. I think all I can say is that somehow having the rhythmic relaxation of walking many hours each day puts me into a state of mind which frees the imagination. Quite often I get ideas for new works by doing a walk. In other words, one walk leads to another.

So you never feel lonely?
Oh, no. It never occurs to me to feel lonely. I just think I am very lucky to have these pockets of freedom and silence, escaping from the normal chaos of everyday life in the art world. It is like another dimension I can have in my life.

Do you find some landscapes are more conducive to work than others?
Oh, yes. I would say that, for a start, the British landscape is interesting. It is my home landscape, and I find it very rich, even the footpaths and lanes of the West Country, and then the moorlands and the Highlands. The moorlands in Britain are interesting – it is a very particular type of landscape. Ireland is another country which I feel very sympathetic to. I have very strong feelings about it, because basically, in the west, it is my type of landscape, a sort of stony, wet desert, also with a lot of nice people and a lot of humour and beautiful music. So that is another interesting country. I would also say that Bolivia is again another big, stony desert. I think in a strange way that landscapes like the tundra, like Alaska for example, it's almost like being on Dartmoor but it is much bigger. So in a way I often feel at home in places like Lapland or Alaska, because their boggy, windy, flattish kind of landscape is sort of familiar to me. I think there are certain things that are fairly universal. Footpaths interest me a lot, and you could almost say that the footpath going up Ben Nevis is more or less the same as all the great footpaths in Nepal. It is just that in Nepal the views on either side are bigger and higher and the precipices on each side are much bigger, but basically a footpath is a footpath and it is probably the same in China as in Scotland. It is just one stone after another. It is like a walk, just one footstep after another no matter where it is. So I am interested in homing in on the universal similarities between things, but also on the great differences between places, because each place on the earth is absolutely unique, and no stone is like another stone in that respect. I am all for using that as well.

Do you mind bad weather, or extremes of heat or cold?
Oh, no. I think being a sort of typical British walker, being used to the pouring rain, I'm not bothered about getting wet, and I utterly love all the different types of weather. I just take the world as I find it really. I suppose that I would say that I have been in cold, wet, temperate climates more than very hot climates. But that is more to do with the fact that to make walks alone and to be independent I always have to be near water. So, apart from this last strange occasion in the Sahara, I would not go to a place where it was so dry that I couldn't find water, as I cannot carry water with me.

How do you decide when to stop walking and make a work?

Well, when I come to an incredible place I don't have to make that decision.
I have an instantaneous feeling that this is the place and here are the stones
and I just get on with it.

Then it is absolutely a question of taking your cue from the place that you find?

Oh, yes. But that is not to say that certain sculptures can't be pre-planned.
Again, it is a combination of things. For instance, in Ladakh, in the
mountains of Kashmir, on the last trip I made there, by walking on the
footpaths after a few days I had the idea to make actual walking lines on
the footpath. That is an example of having an idea after a few days of being
on the walk. The actual walking and the footpaths give me the idea to make
the work. When I was by some strange circumstances in Alaska, I happened
to find myself on the Arctic Circle, and it seemed just the perfect opportunity
and place for me to make a circle. Sometimes it might happen that I have
the idea to make a circle or something and then the actual place will prevent
that – like in Africa, I was going to make a circle of stones on a high
mountain in Malawi and then, when I got there, I couldn't find any stones
because there was no ice and snow to break the rock up. So I kept the idea
of a circle and changed the material to burnt cacti which were lying around,
that had been burnt in lightning storms. That is just to show how I can keep
one half of the idea and then change the other half because of the
circumstances of the place. I am an opportunist; I just take advantage
of the places and situations I find myself in.

There is still a contrast, though, between what you describe as the opportunism
of responding to a particular place that you didn't previously know about, and
the unwavering constancy of the language that you always favour – the lines
and the circles.

Yes, it is always like a balance – a harmony of complementary ideas. You could
say that my work is also a balance between the patterns of nature and the
formalism of human, abstract ideas like lines and circles. It is where my human
characteristics meet the natural forces and patterns of the human world,
and that is really the kind of subject of my work.

Since they play such an important role in the form assumed by your work, can
you say something more about why you favour lines and circles as such?

Well, I have to say that the first time I used a circle I had no idea why I used it.
It seemed like a good idea at the time, but having made it, it looked great and
seemed a very strong and powerful image, and I have used it ever since. There
are a lot of things theoretical and intellectual to say about lines and circles,
but I think the very fact that they are images that don't belong to me and,
in fact, are shared by everyone because they have existed throughout history,
actually makes them more powerful than if I was inventing my own
idiosyncratic, particular Richard Long-type images. I think it cuts out a lot
of personal unwanted aesthetic paraphernalia.

They give you freedom, in other words.

Yes, that is right. In fact, they actually allow me to home in on other things,
so the circles stay the same in the different places I make them around the
world but the places change. It means that the viewer of my work is noticing
that there are circles, but he is also seeing that the places are changing and
the materials are changing. I think, anyway, a circle is such an open system
and that it can be a vehicle for perhaps any idea under the sun. It is a freedom,

as you say. I can make a circle of words, I can make a circle of stones,
I can make a circle of mud with my hands on a wall, I can walk in a circle
for one hundred miles. It is a completely adaptable image and form
and system.

Yes, you can make full circles, empty circles, circles with upright stones,
circles with horizontal stones.
And it is also an image that everyone recognises. So people don't actually have
to fathom out what they are looking at.

You are aiming then, in essence, at universality.
Yes, but I think nature is universal. It is no coincidence that there are parallels
between my work and work from certain people of other cultures and societies,
as nature, which is the source of my work, is universal. We all live in different
cultures but we all share the same nature of the world. We all share the same air,
the same water and everything.

When I see lines in your work, they often remind me of the fact that duration
is involved, that walking is fundamental and that a journey is being
undertaken. You have always been strikingly preoccupied with movement,
distance and time.
Yes, time is the fourth dimension in my work, and I am interested in using
it in a very particular way. So I have made walks about pace, walks about time
only, and also certain geometries, for example, walking between a hundred
Tors on Dartmoor in a hundred hours, or walking a thousand miles in a
thousand hours. So it is possible to use time almost in a very classical way,
as a very formal, geometric thing.

Why is walking so central a part of your work? Does the act of walking make
you experience time more vividly than you would do in normal life?
Yes, I think it does. Like art itself, it is like a focus. It gets rid of a lot of things
and you can actually concentrate. So getting myself into these solitary days
of repetitive walking or in empty landscapes is just a certain way of emptying
out or simplifying my life, just for those few days or weeks, into a fairly simple
but concentrated activity which, as you say, is really quite different from the
way that people normally live their lives, which is very complicated. So my art
is a simplification. Also, a walk is a great vehicle for very particular ideas, about
colours, trees, time, anything I choose.

Does time pass more slowly for you during a walk or more quickly?
Ah, well, it plays funny tricks doesn't it, time. It is both. I would say it is very
curious that if I am doing a long walk, at the beginning the number of days
ahead seem a lot, and it seems like a long way to the end of the walk! After
about three-quarters of the way through, it seems that the completed days
have just flashed by, so time is completely subjective, or relative. There is
no real time.

While you are making the work in the landscape, what state of mind do
you like to be in, or do you find yourself in?
Well, usually I am happy and relaxed. I would say that the way I make my
work is from the things that give me pleasure and the materials that I like
using – my work doesn't come from a kind of angst or discontent. A sculpture
in a landscape, when it really happens well in a good way, is like a celebration
of the place and my feelings of me being there and having the right idea at

the right time and everything coming together in a good way. For me that
is the perfect way to make a good work. But I can be happy like that in
a gallery making a big mud work on a wall or something. Part of the
pleasure actually comes from the physical side of things. It is very important
for me to make my work, you know, the actual physical making – standing
the stones up, the long walking, the physical toil, the sweating and the getting
tired, or the getting covered in mud in a gallery throwing mud around in a
circle. I would say that as well as my work being about ideas, it is also about
that physical enjoyment.

*Do you think that in order perhaps to engage your mind and your imagination
fully you have to involve the whole of your body as well?*
Oh, yes. The work is the expression of both the intellect and the body, they
are absolutely complementary. It is no good just having a good idea, it is also
necessary for me to make it, and also not have somebody else make it – for
me to do it myself, because my work is my own footsteps, it is only what I can
do, so the handprints in the gallery are my hands and the stones that I turn
up on the mountainside are the stones that I can physically handle myself at
that place. And I have found that place by walking to it. My work is a portrait
of myself in the world, my own personal journey through it and the materials
that I find along the way.

*Watching the film that Philip Haas made about your work, I was struck by the
amount of physical exertion involved in making some of these big stone pieces.*
Well, it is not hard work because I enjoy it, but anyway it is work.

And you must feel fairly tired afterwards.
Yes, but it is a nice kind of tiredness.

And then you take a photograph of the work. How do you go about that?
Well, normally I just step back and point the camera and try and get it in
focus. Even though it is necessary to get a good photograph, the photographs
should be as simple as possible so that when people look at the photograph
they are not dazzled by wide-angled lenses or special effects. Because my art
is very simple and straightforward, I think the photographs have got to be
fairly simple and straightforward, so that the feeling of the work somehow
accurately comes through. That is why most of the photographs are taken
from my eye level. Usually, after I have made the work, I kind of walk
around it and somehow find the best place to take the photograph. A line
usually has the characteristic of pointing out of or beyond itself, maybe
to the horizon, so often the alignment of the viewer, the line and something
a long way off is important. Circles are different, they are more enclosed,
more of a stopping place.

*Let me end by asking probably the most important and difficult question which
arises from your work. Why do you think that you do go out to these remote
places again and again? Is it bound up with establishing and developing
an increasingly close relationship with nature?*
I have no idea really. I have never had any ideology or fixed ideas. I think all
that has happened is that my first landscape works were made in and around
Bristol. My first turf works were actually made in my parents' front garden.
As I have got older and I have had the wherewithal to extend my arena of
making work, it has just got wider and wider, so that finally I have made
works in different countries and landscapes around the world.

But I want to press you a bit further on this. What do you think you gain from
this closeness with the natural world?

I think it is just the choice that I have made for myself. I do the things that
have a deep meaning for me. I have the most sublime or profound feelings
when I am walking, or touching natural materials in natural places. That
is what I've decided to do and that is what I am showing you in my art.

Since so much of the finest art produced in this country has revolved around
an intense response to landscape, do you feel close to any British tradition
in this wish to commune with nature?

No, not particularly. Just by being English, in my childhood having my
grandparents living on Dartmoor, in Devon, or going on cycling holidays with
my father when I was a boy. I think all those things were much more important
than this so-called tradition of English landscape art. I realise there was a sort
of romantic movement as a result of the industrial revolution. I suppose if
you have to put some historical or political slant on my work, I hope it does
tie up in some ways with the Green philosophy, 'small is beautiful', and of seeing
the world as one place, and using its raw materials with respect. I like to see
art as being a return to the senses.

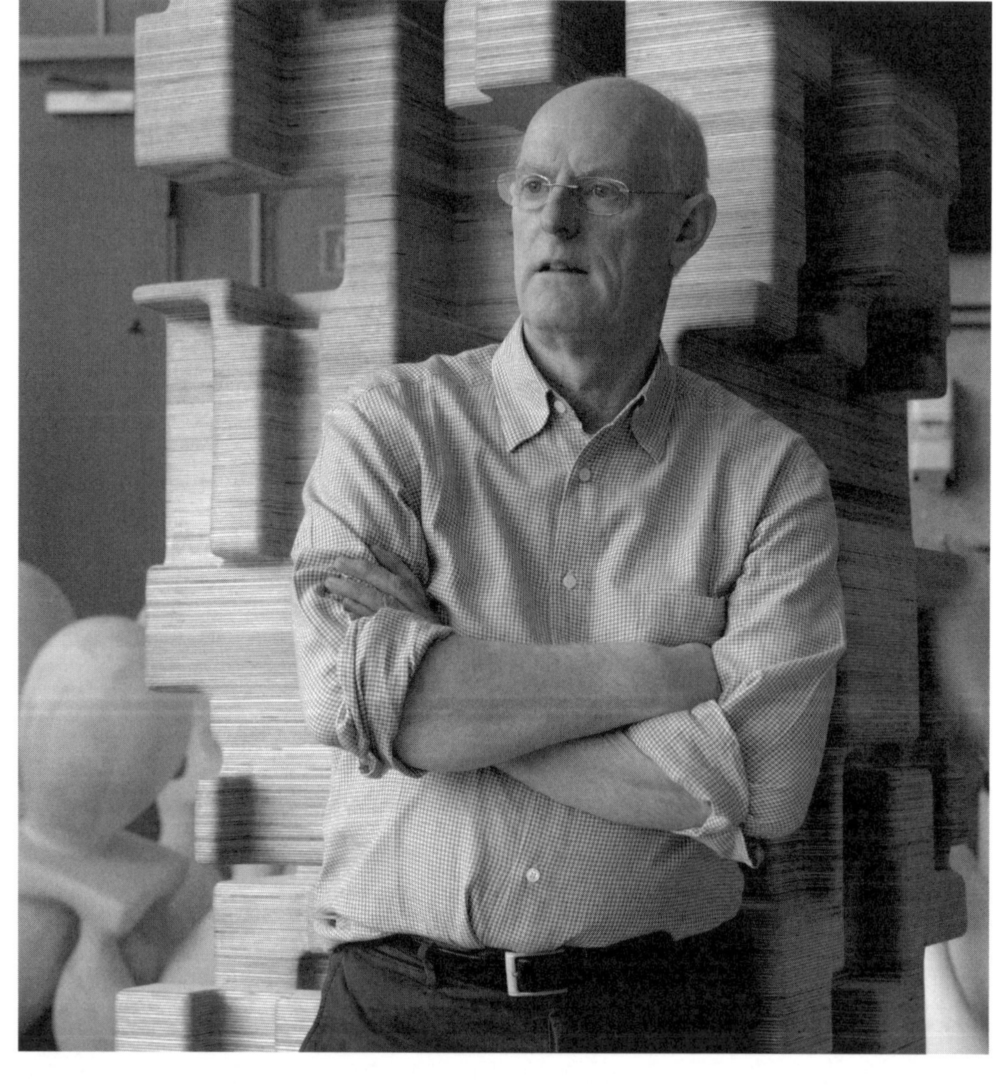

Tony Cragg

'What a tiny little meaningless speck of organic stuff we are in all this mass, in the sea of time. So one is being constantly torn between the picture of oneself as something very, very important, and infinitesimally unimportant'

*You have played a prolific and inventive part in revitalising British sculpture.
Working first with plastic and other discarded materials scavenged from
beaches or the streets of Wuppertal where you decided to settle in the late 1970s,
you discovered how to turn even the most ordinary and unregarded objects
into powerful, often provocative forms. Since winning the Turner Prize in 1988,
your preoccupations have remained consistent with the young artist whose
emergence excited so much interest. But there is no sense, looking at your current
output, of someone standing still. On the contrary, you seem incessantly on
the move. So maybe you're getting tired by now of being described as the sculptor
who introduced plastic detritus into his work. Do you think, in retrospect,
that too much attention has been paid to this aspect of your work?*

I find it very difficult to answer, because that material had two functions for
me. One as a material that was almost the lowest of the low at that time: it was
definitely part of the intention on my part to make work that didn't have a
naturalistic, pastoral feeling about it. And later on, I used it as a kind of drawing
method. It's difficult. I've now probably made sixteen works using plastic.
I would like to say that it was, in the balance of things, a little bit overrated.

Do you remember how you came upon that material in the first place?

I do, yes. The first time I used the material was in 1970, when I was a student
in the first year at Wimbledon and made some work on a beach. I didn't know
how to use it, but I really started looking at the things on the beach, swept up
from the waves, and there was a lot a plastic in that. I couldn't get over the kind
of pop feeling of it. I kept seeing it – yes, in a pop way. It took a long time to
change that kind of feeling for me.

*But in the pop context, plastic objects would have been seen as an exemplar
of a streamlined consumer-society boom.*

Yes.

And presumably the plastic you found on the beach was very different, wasn't it?

Yes, it was different. That was the strange thing: it was what you have just
described, and the fact of it being out there, churned around in the waves.
So it wasn't exactly pop, but it was the correlation of my interests.

*Was it something that you expected to find on the beach, or did you go there with
no preconceptions about what you would do there?*

It was quite a good, healthy student activity. I can't remember enough, but there
were days when you might do nothing for a day, or you might make ten works
or twenty works a day. Even if they were just crap paintings of the sand, it didn't
matter. They were very fast and kind of experimental periods of time.

*And why did you come round, after that, to incorporating plastic in your work
– or, in fact, using it as your work? You used the word 'pastoral' just now, as
something you wanted to get away from. Was it to do with that?*

Yes, partly that. Because there was a certain time, in the middle of the 1970s,
when I suddenly had the feeling that there was a great reduction. Minimal
art, land art and conceptual art, all those interesting things that had happened,
they started to tidy themselves up, I thought. There were certain things
I wanted to challenge and push for myself. What I found very useful and
important, in terms of minimal art, was the reduction of things. But it became
a very strong overt geometry in the middle 1970s, so I really wanted to find a
way round that geometry, and find how to introduce a more organic language,
how to get back into other forms. Parallel to that was another tendency at that

time: an over-romanticising aspect of natural materials, and how wonderful
is a stone or a branch. Art schools were full of branches, and when you walked
around you wondered how there were any trees left. Leaves and twigs and
branches and birds' nests and all that sort of thing! Looking at the stream
of that, I just felt there was something wrong. It was dictating itself, in a sense.

*Did you feel that there was an excessive concentration on 'the land' in sculpture,
as opposed to urban society? Was that part of your complaint?*

Yes, very much so. And I also thought it was a cop-out, because the things
I think about and believe in are not 'returning to a pastoral kind of condition',
or whatever. It is not a question of me turning the clock back. And it's also
not a question of glorifying that which we have so far achieved. It's more a sort
of dynamic question-and-answer situation, where one has to improve on what
has been done so far. I don't think there is a retrogressive way of dealing with
it. One has to go through the problem.

*When you started working with plastic, can you remember what the experience
was like? Did you actually have misgivings, did you wonder whether it would
lead anywhere?*

Lead anywhere? I knew, in the instant I had it in my hand, that it was leading
somewhere, because it just tingled – the whole thing! The colour excited me,
and when I really started to look at the forms, they excited me. So it was
already leading somewhere. Whether anybody else would feel that or recognise
anything about it, I can't say. In those terms, I don't know. But it was leading
somewhere from the minute that I started to wallow in it.

And where did you get the material from?

It took ages and ages to find, walking around in Wuppertal, picking stuff off
the street. You actually don't find very much plastic lying around the street in
a German town.

*So you didn't pick it in the belief that this material was everywhere and
all around us. It was something that was actually hard to locate.*

It is hard to find anyway, and even now. Now I know I can go down to the
banks of the River Rhine and get some: there are deposits of it, but not very
much. It's a bit seasonal as well, but there isn't a great deal of it around. It's
a very specialist material – and it will be, in time, also very specialist, because
it won't be there for ever.

*And how far did you refine this material? Certainly you sorted and arranged it,
but did you actually clean it up in any way?*

No, never. There was one work where somebody wanted it cleaned up, and
we thought about it. But we didn't do it. But we told them we did! [Laughs.]

*Let's concentrate on one particular piece for a moment: a well-known work in
this country, since it belongs to the Tate. It's called* Britain Seen from the North,
*a very large wall-work which consists of a map of Britain tilted in a horizontal
direction, and a figure who seems to be looking at it slightly askance, maybe.
Of course, this entire image of the UK is composed of plastic detritus, and the
figure is as well. I want to ask whether you see it – as I do – working almost on
two levels. I mean, one level is to do with the image of Britain seemingly filled
with this material, which is a very disturbing idea. And the other level is to
do with the fact that it forces you to look at this material in a new way: to see
it not as just rubbish, not as polluted waste matter, but as something with*

*a surprising beauty of its own, and even a kind of delicacy. To me, both
these meanings are there, and they make it a profoundly ambiguous work.
Do you see it that way?*

> The work is read and commented on as a political statement – as the situation
> of Britain as seen from the North. Which is fair enough: I'd say that was in
> the work. I've become very suspicious of 'levels of meaning', unless someone
> actually says what kind of meaning. So I'll try and say what it is. When I made
> the work, I was aware that it had a vibrant political quality, possibly – plus the
> fact that I really believe that the materials aren't rubbish. It's not just plastic:
> there are lots of other things in there. I don't believe it helps, all this straight
> classification. To classify it as rubbish is a great disservice to our own culture,
> in a sense. I actually do like it: I am very, very interested in it. That's not an irony
> – I do find it very beautiful, I really do. But there is also another thing. When
> I was making the work, I remember thinking: how do I know, when standing
> on this territory, that it is that shape? And why is it this way up and not that
> way up? I mean, I know what Britain is like because I have seen a map of it.
> I have only ever experienced the topography of this territory. And there was,
> for me, an analogy to other things. It isn't just a geographical problem: to get
> a perspective on things, to get a view of a whole territory by some very strange,
> artificial means. Because the only thing I am really capable of seeing and
> perceiving is some much closer topographical thing. But parallel to this is
> something that interests me a lot: non-visual, non-perceivable things – cell
> structures and also, on a very big scale, star constellations. I mean, we just
> assume that this is Britain, and that we know what this territory looks like.

So that figure looking at the map is actually you?

> Yes, it is.

*And is it also – because of where the figure is, separated from the image of the
UK – to do with your feeling of detachment, perhaps, as someone who has lived
in West Germany for over a decade now?*

> Yes, at the time I hadn't lived there that long, but yes, I think it was a
> declarational detachment, with a certain sort of distance. Yes, reflective.
> I am not able to discuss that very well, but there is a thing about being an
> 'exile'. That word always infers that one is forced into exile. But there is
> a strange feeling about being outside the cultural context one has grown
> up in: automatically there is a reflective quality to thinking about that.

Why is it that you prefer to live in Germany rather than in this country?

> The fact is that I live in Germany, in Wuppertal, because my wife was born and
> raised in Wuppertal and I have children there. I find it very easy to work there.
> I enjoyed finding a studio, and I have spent over ten years putting the roots
> down there. It's not a question of preference: sometimes I would really love
> to be back in England, and regret that I don't spend more time here.

*It's strange, isn't it? Because you are seen, of course, as a British sculptor
essentially, and you are often discussed in terms of the context of sculpture
in Britain during the 1980s. It seems to me that we have witnessed in this
country a very exciting flowering of sculpture during that period from an
emergent generation, of which you are a very prominent member. I want to
ask you whether you see it that way yourself, or whether – living in Germany
as you do – you see yourself as part of a much broader international context.*

> A little bit of both, because when I started making exhibitions, at the end
> of the 1970s, there was not really the feeling of a new generation of sculptors

coming up. So I tended to exhibit in groups, other very influential groups at
that time, of Italian painters like Clemente and Paladino, or German artists
like Baselitz, Lüpertz, Penck, Immendorff. So that has obviously given me
a sense of being aware of what is going on over borders. But then I still regard
myself – still – as very British. I am a British sculptor. So it is a duality there.
I am very, very interested in what is happening in Britain in sculpture. There
are many good artists.

*And you show in a gallery, the Lisson Gallery, which happens to have quite
a large crop of those sculptors. Do you find it stimulating to see their work,
and to feel yourself – in part, at least – as one of that generation?*

That is difficult. There is not really very much intellectual, cultural, artistic kind
of atmosphere in which things are being discussed.

*Let me talk about more recent work, because you have branched out
enormously in your use of materials since those early days. I was aware,
in your 1987 Hayward Gallery show, of a great variety of materials, and
a great variety of ways of approaching and making work. As I moved from
one section of the exhibition to another, it seemed as though a different kind
of mood prevailed very often. It gave me a sort of sharp feeling. I felt that
very much at the Venice Biennale, too: each area of the exhibition had its
own particular character. Is that something you enjoy doing, moving from
one area of concern to another?*

Well, I enjoy doing it, but it is also dictated very much by what I regard as the
central concern in the work. I don't have a clear choice in it, anyway. In order
to cover the ground that I have allotted to myself, or try to deal with it, I am
constantly having to go into this or that or the other area, and it is a broad front.
Rather than making a linear kind of conduction in terms of the work, it's very
much more like an attempt to make criss-cross references, almost like a volume
of references. And that is how I see both the exhibitions you have described,
at the Hayward and the Biennale. When the exhibitions were finished, nobody
had seen them – that is the kind of sense that I wanted. I can almost emerge in
a world of my own. I don't mean in a diminutive little world of my own, but one
where all the parts are there: I know where the mountains are, I know where
the valleys are, where the forests are, where the clouds are, in terms of
materials. And that, I think, is what I am trying to do.

*Can I close in once more on a particular work from the Hayward show, a piece
called* Echo *where the materials you use are a bit of wood, a pipe, a concrete ring
and a gas metal canister. I am very interested to talk about this in terms of what
you were saying before about landscape, because in a sense when you look at*
Echo, *this enormous piece of sculpture, it does bring landscape forms to mind.
What actually inspired it, what was the starting point for it?*

Well, this is a very concrete and specific moment. It was a drive from Lyon
to Turin, going up through the Alps – not the tunnel through Mont Blanc,
but going round Mont Blanc. And at some point I was driving along and there
was this really beautiful, very high, desolate valley in the mountains. I stopped
the car for a while and went down to a fast-flowing river. I was looking at the
landscape, and there were about four or five points in the landscape where
you could still see – other than the road which I was driving along – where
somebody had tried to build something up in that mountain, like the remains
of a ski lift. So when my eye travelled around that whole horizon and vista, these
man-made bits caught the eye. There was no way of avoiding them: very clear,
visible signs of intervention. In terms of percentage, they had got much more

than their fair share of attention. And that interested me: the way one recognises signs of culture. I mean, if you flew over the planet, how do you recognise it? Because there are lights on it or there are cities on it, and those are signs of a culture. That was the starting point in the reference to that work.

You didn't see those man-made elements as in any way despoiling the beautiful landscape?

Well – yes and no. I mean, the landscape has been changed there anyway, with the skiing and everything. That is a difficult question. That is almost the crux of the whole thing. We have changed the landscape, why not change it constructively? I mean, we are going to have to change it, so it's just a question of the amount of responsibility one takes for the changes one makes.

It is the crux of the whole thing, and that's why I wanted to ask you about it. When I look at your work, I am very aware of the society we live in, the kind of materials we produce, of waste and consumerism and things being cast away. And, in a sense, of your work as seeming to be reclaimed. You do have this dual attitude: half wanting to criticise what we are doing in our present society, and half wanting to try and redeem it – or at least to initiate some kind of debate about what is happening to us.

Yes, because I really don't want to make a work which has a didactic kind of feeling about it. It is not the sense of what I want to do, being self-righteous about it. As a sculptor, you take a very specific kind of responsibility for changing the world. It's not at all bound to any utilitarian system. Making sculpture is an eminently useless thing. You can't do anything with it, it doesn't belong to a functional kind of world. It's a tool for thinking about things, or maybe seeing things differently for analysing and making up a new proposition, different from the way sculpture has been made in the past. It's changing radically. I mean, one can't just talk about formal concerns without being involved in how the thing works in terms of the meaning.

But you are concerned with the idea of vulnerability. Even if you analyse things and strive for an attitude which is removed from polemics, at the same time I think you do stress – at least, as far my response to your work goes – the frailty of things. There is some kind of feeling of a threatened culture. Take two examples. One, from the Hayward show, is a work called Minster, *built up into a series of spire forms, as its title might suggest. But at the same time there is a feeling, perhaps, of armaments pointing towards the sky. Another example is a whole series of works to do with spillage – this feeling that containers have been tipped over, and their contents spread across the ground. Isn't there an element, in your work, of a warning?*

Yes, maybe there is. It's very difficult, working from the inside of that, to say it's a warning. I am just going by my feelings and nerves in that situation, which is half the time trying to be constructive, and wondering why I am being forced to be constructive or even think about it. But it's obviously based on some kind of anxiety about the situation as well.

It also seems to me that a fundamental sense of wonder, a fascination with the world, underlies everything that you do.

Yes, I am, I am completely. I think most human beings have the idea of being very big for our egos, because we see and touch and appreciate everything through our own senses and appetites. But at the same time we are also aware of what a tiny little meaningless speck of organic stuff we are in all this mass,

in the sea of time. So one is being constantly torn between the picture of
oneself as something very, very important, and infinitesimally unimportant.
It is something that terrifies, and it is just wonder.

*Do you find that making sculpture, as opposed to painting or any other form
of art, offers you a consolation in the face of that kind of unknowable and
sometimes terrifying feeling? I mean, the presence of very large objects is very
satisfying, isn't it? Do you think that somehow helps?*

Maybe it does. Human beings are in the process of making themselves very
lonely anyway. We've cut ourselves off from nature, because we don't really
think about this borderline between the natural world and the artificial world.
It's a borderline one has to continually cross over to know where it is. One has
to go backwards and forwards all the time, in a mental sense. We do lose that
borderline or any sense of where it may be. We are just drifting away, as if we
were a separate entity to nature – which we are not, of course. And I think we
have become very, very lonely. When it gets to the point where we have killed
off all the other animals on this planet, we are just looking into the firmament
thinking: 'Is there an ET to come down and be nice to me?' [Laughs.]
So making sculpture must be a comfort. We are populating the world anyway
with something else, with beings.

*The largest object in your current show at the Lisson Gallery seems to me
particularly fascinating, because it contains at least two layers of reference.
One is to do with the idea of the container, which is one of your key forms,
I suppose. The other is a much more organic reference: it seems to invoke
the forms of the human body, in an almost erotic way.*

The two ends of the sculpture are two retorts that you call containers, but I feel
things like that are very much more like basic structures – the cell, the body.
I mean, your body next to my body is the same as the two bottles in the work,
two bottles standing in a very pragmatic way, made for their function, their
form relative to their function – a very clear relationship there. And the
merging between them, so that anything in between these two pragmatic
forms is an automatically unknown emotional blend, both formally and also
in terms of appreciation of that form. The result is that a lot of erotic forms
come out of it, whether one sees each testicle hanging from it, or a backside,
or whatever you are interested in. Yes, it is there and understandably so. I mean,
it is two bodies mingling in the same way. That is what two bodies do, you know.
That is the sense that interested me and, automatically, that is the sense that
comes off it, rather than saying, 'I would like to make an erotic form here', which
really wasn't the intention, partly giving a shock to myself – being a bit of
a prude [laughs].

*Certainly your work of the last two or three years has included a kind
of object based on the floor, rising up from the floor, often to very large
dimensions that you never used to do. It sometimes employs more
traditional materials as well. Is that part of a need to produce a more
incontrovertible presence in sculpture?*

No, not really. That is a way of looking at it, but in fact it's the other way round.
I believe in what I am doing – trying to look at some very basic structures, and
trying to identify them, trying to feel them, trying to make objects which reflect
on those structures, you know. I understood so much more about this than
I ever thought I would do, and I am just aghast at the amount of work which
is left to do. The fact that things are different kinds of technology, describing
the material being used, is just something I have had to learn. I didn't learn

all this in one moment, just progressively in time, just keeping on finding,
'Ah! I have to know how to do that, otherwise I can't get through to the next
stage of doing this,' just having to learn how to make the stuff. I didn't know
how to make, for example, bronze sculpture or carved stone. They are things
I have to learn in order to express something about certain areas. I don't
have an option.

Do you feel almost as if you had just begun?

Ah, I don't think I've even scratched the surface. In terms of making the
sculpture, sometimes I think it's not going too badly, but in terms of what ideas
I have, in terms of a culture I can't achieve on my own, we are a long, long way
from any kind of understanding.

*You seem very happy and confident with a large scale, and you have on several
occasions worked outside the gallery in public locations. Is that something you
would like to develop in future?*

I found it very difficult to work outside. I mean, the idea of 'public sculpture'
– I am not at all sure how to deal with it. I am still learning a lot. I haven't really
made that many works – maybe a dozen – which exist outside.

You did one for the new Tate in Liverpool. How was that experience?

The experience was good. It was also the first time I cast something, which was
really a valuable experience for me. And the work has its value, I still very much
appreciate having made it. It also has a very unresolved quality.

How do you mean?

Unresolved? OK: specifically in that work I thought the influences were
rather more interesting – the idea of the bollard and some sort of shells
and organic shapes.

*So you did take your cue partly from the site up there, the fact that
it was dockland?*

Oh yes, the influences are nice, but I don't really know how the work functions,
I must say. You know, sculpture is for me a way of doing things, it's not like
a definitive statement, it's not like 'here is', 'this is it'. I have never in my life
got to that point. I am probably the first person who kicks it out – the next
day or after I have my coffee break I come back and look at it in dismay.
For me, they are propositions. That is not in any sense to make a negative
or a devaluing of the work. I don't destroy work because it has become invalid
or whatever. It's just one side or the other of a conversation. They are proposals
which stand in order to help me understand a little bit of my life and my
existence. And as part of that, they have their validity. But it's not the case
that anything should stand there and say: 'This is it, this is the way sculpture
should be in the 1990s.' I think that's ridiculous. For me, it should be a much
healthier, open kind of flowering activity.

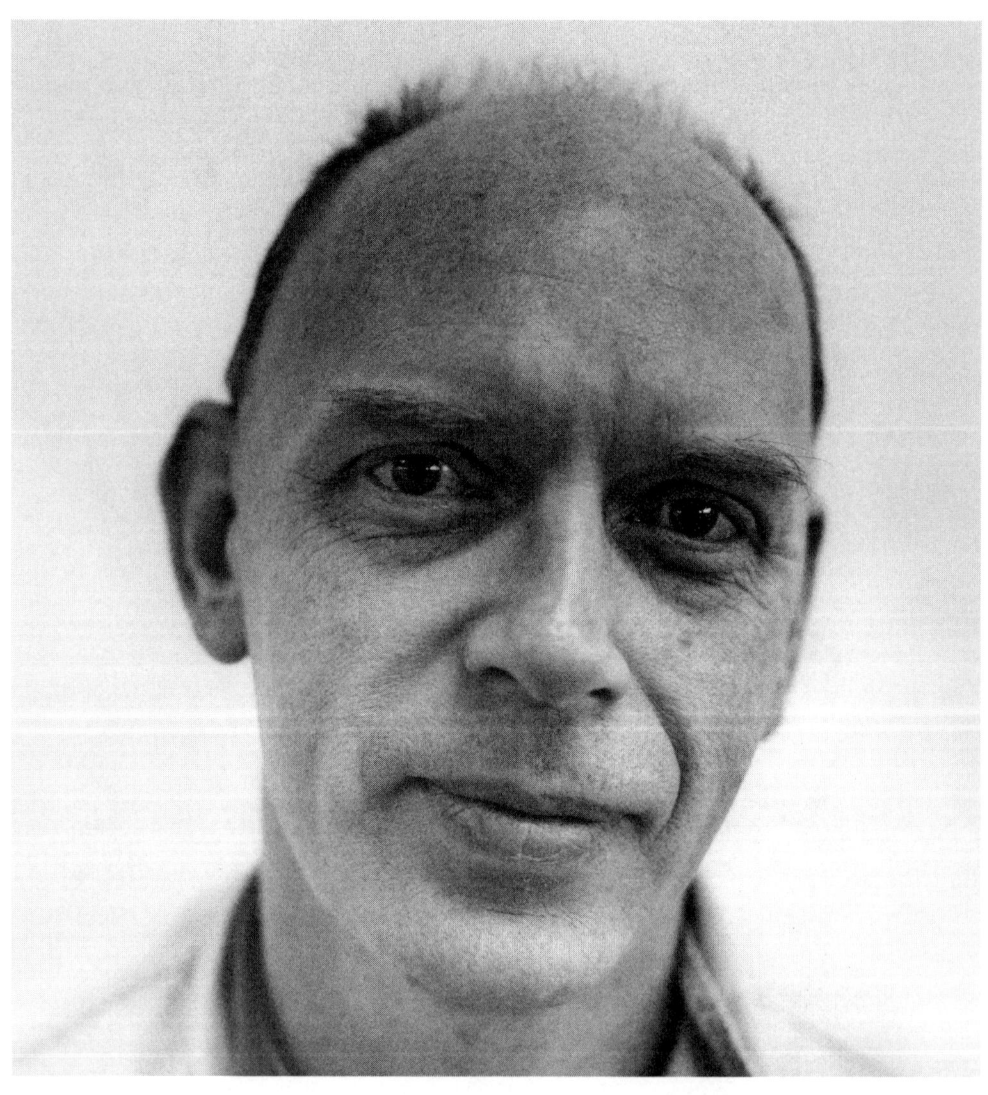

1989

Richard Deacon

'This almost double concern with the body on the one hand and, on the other, materials that you use when you're very aware of the machine age, the industrial age, the world that we live in'

I was at primary school in Hooe, when my father was in the air force
at Mountbatten. He had two sessions there, so I was at the school when
I was five and six and again when I was eight, nine and ten. Then I was
at Plymouth College from the age of eleven to eighteen. But that's not
the reason why I agreed to do the exhibition. It was an opportunity to
work ambitiously in a situation slightly off the mainstream. I mean, just
looking at my exhibition history, those are situations that I value, because
you get the opportunity to make something specific without feeling
necessarily in competition with the history of the space. And from
a personal point of view, there is an element of being intrigued about
what it would be like to do an exhibition in Plymouth.

Yes, and actually it was quite a good thing to do, because the difference between
hanging art on the wall and looking at it in galleries is a major one. I have
a memory of handling a Jackson Pollock, which is very different from seeing
the same painting purely as a spectator. Since I was already interested in
making things anyway, to handle art as physical objects seemed to be a good
thing to do. The gallery is still in the same building, although it's extended.
And as a teenager, there were not just cultural reasons for working in a situation
where you got treated like an adult rather than a junior. To find that drinking
and smoking were acceptable forms of behaviour was very refreshing. It was
a good place to spend time because of that.

No, I wasn't. What intrigued me about going to art school was partly that
I really enjoyed making things, but I also thought that there was a possibility
to find out about all sorts of different things that didn't seem determined

– in the way that, say, English or history or maths seemed determined.
And I'm not sure that, when I first went to art school, I'd decided I was
going to be an artist. It probably wasn't until I left the Royal College, some
substantial time later, that I really decided I was going to be an artist, in
the sense of engaging in the practice on a professional level. But neither had
I ever imagined that I would stop pissing about in the way that I do in the
studio. I mean, that seems to me to be vital to my ability to function in the
world. But finally deciding that it was going to be the means not only of
maintaining my equilibrium but also of attempting to earn my living, it took
a long time before I could finally resolve that.

Why do you think it took such a long time?
Well, it may have been a question of feeling comfortable with the description
of 'artist' or 'sculptor' in relation to a practice which seemed to be almost
personal. Most 'sculpture' seemed like something objective. But working in
the studio, although it was fuelled by an acquaintance with art practice, gets
its motivation from an internal dynamic and not from an external one.

So you didn't really want to fit in with any of the existing categories?
I never really wanted to be any one kind of thing. I think one of the reasons that
I always wanted to come to London was because I liked the privacy that London
offers, by the sense of its size. So it had something to do with getting on quietly
by myself, or having a kind of mental space. A physical space seemed to be what
I was looking for in its public face, but I felt very awkward about the business
of declaring 'I'm an artist'. That seemed to imply that what you made was 'art',
and I really wasn't sure that was what I did – in the sense that things that
I deeply love and move me very much belong to that category, and therefore
to think of myself as the producer in that category just felt uncomfortable.
It seemed different from being an accountant or a historian or a taxi-driver
or whatever. Most of the other ways of making money didn't seem to be
twenty-four-hour things. Some of them obviously are, and a lot of people
are very passionate about the things they do. But in different ways, I think
most of the time about what happens in this space.

Do you still have problems about being thought of as a 'sculptor'?
I have no problem with it now. You know, I make sculpture. But I think that
it took a long time to decide, because it seemed to be making claims for what
I did that I didn't know, at that age, I could really support.

*I'm interested in the fact that, at art school, you were preoccupied with the idea
of performance – the body in action. It has remained with you, in different ways.
For instance, you had a period in Chicago with a theatre company in the early
1970s. And you've done sculpture for dancers at the Ballet Rambert.*
And I like dancing.

Do you like to dance yourself?
Yes, I enjoy dancing very much. I always have done.

*How do you think this feeds into your art? Do you see it as a thread running
through your work?*
I have been continually interested in the relationship of body to material, and
the relationship of repetitive action to perception of time. Also, the relationship
of self to a material world, as mediated through a body and labour. So I think
of the sculpture as being in between me and the material world – a world made

of stuff and substance which is in some sense puzzling. I don't know how
far one wants to get into the psychology or the history of those things, but
I am preoccupied with the nature of the relationship between self, stuff and
other. So that material substance seems to be a means of dealing with the
animate and the inanimate, as well as modelling relationships to other people.
Though there is always that difficulty of locating what you see at a distance
with what you feel. The problematics of distance do seem to be quite close
to the problematics of recognising the subjectivity of other people.

*What's so fascinating about this sculpture, here in the studio, is that you see
it first of all as a large, even a grand object, sitting there in its own right. And
it seems quite abstract – it's very formal and in some ways quite geometrical.
But then I find a whole other response, which is surprisingly intimate. It seems
to bear on my knowledge of my own body and the interior as well, not just the
surface of it. You like that idea of something which has its own existence apart
from you, and yet draws you in to relate to things which are very intimate.*

Yes, if I can do that. I mean, if a physical object can transcend the boundary
of subjectivity, then that seems to be what making art is about. In a nutshell,
I think that my experience of looking at art is of physical substance
transgressing subjective boundaries. It's not a uniquely art experience: it does
happen in other situations. But those subjective/objective dialogues do seem
to me a fundamental part of what I think of as important in looking at art,
or in looking at dance. But it does rely on finding something in the way I feel
about my body, and the way I use my body, that is hard to describe.

*There's a whole series of works, stretching from the beginning of the 1980s
right up to the present, that goes under the title of* Art for Other People.
Why did you call it that?

Having made a group of larger works, I did actually want to make some smaller
works which were rather like writing letters. I anticipated that they would
end up in spaces other than art institutions – in homes or flats, a whole variety
of domestic spaces.

*Not many people could fit one of your big pieces into their living
room, could they?*

No, and so originally the title was fairly straightforward: these were a group
of smaller works which I wanted to send out into the world for other people.
But there is an ambiguity. Looking at the title in conjunction with the work,
the question arises: if the thing is art for other people, then what is it for me?
That becomes a question, and I think it's quite a positive ambiguity. I'm quite
happy to retain it.

*Looking at this sculpture, Richard, can you tell me what your starting point
for it was? How did it begin?*

I'd been doing some drawings for a proposal from Warwick University, and
in the middle here, this was one the shapes that I'd drawn. At the time that
I drew it, I was interested in having a look at it on its own, so I decided to do
that. In principle, I'd wanted to try and make something that was a solid shape
rather than a structured shape. Also, I'd done some work earlier this year
with fibreglass, which is the first time I'd used it for something like ten years.
I wanted to pursue working with it, but as a closed, sealed volume rather than
a sheet which is the way I often use material. So the first thing was making
the mould, though before we used the mould and cast it, at the same time
I was making some of the aluminium sections at the back.

The actual object goes back quite a long way, doesn't it?

Yes, and sometimes there are opportunities to make quite radical changes when you're working. That particular shape was actually very strong, and something that I wanted to act as a guide. The kind of options I manipulated were to do with the place of this section in relationship to the other element that I was adding to it. Originally, I thought about this being bracketed by aluminium on both sides.

Oh, that would have been very different.

Yes, I never did that because this was such a lovely thing, a seductive and sensitive object. I wanted this one side to be clear. Originally it was hollow and, as often happens with things that I make, I had always anticipated that this would be a vertical rather than a horizontal thing, forgetting that actually it doesn't stand up on that point. Somehow, in my mind's eye and all the time I was working on it, I managed not to notice the fact that it wouldn't stand up. It was only fairly late on that I realised, so some of the later changes are to do with addressing myself to that, rather than to things in the imagination.

Do you like to have a working method which allows you to change your mind, and to make drastic alterations as you proceed?

Well, inherent in most of what I do is that possibility. What I don't like is to have a prescription. Except that I quite like rules, so I have a generative rule that then follows through and has quite major implications, in some cases, for the way it can look. So it's not absolutely arbitrary. But I like to have some sense, when I'm making something, that I'm not building according to a plan. So there is a sense of decision-making during the course of the thing. With this one, there was a prior decision about materials: there were two materials involved, and the fibreglass had an enclosed volume and I wouldn't like to squeeze it too much.

It just flows around, doesn't it?

It didn't split up into bits, and opposed to that was the way in which the volume was constructed in the metal, by negation rather than affirmation. At least, certainly as it turns out here, on the internal shadowing of this form, so that there was a hollow space on either side which was the shadow of something of substance in the middle. If you stand over there, you get to a point fifteen feet away where all this internal construction disappears. And then that breaks up into the reflective surface at the back, a shadow of the hollow, and then on the other side you have something that's very much more prosaic, more matter of fact. And though one is just the inverse of the other – there's nothing that happens on the outside which you can't see on the inside – the difference between the character of the open body and the character of the closed body was perceptually very, very divergent. So that what you have, paradoxically, is something quite sensuous and rich – a solid shape which is clearly defined and without any bits that fly off – and on the outside you have something much more constructive and therefore, in a sense, unnatural, artificial, more prosaic, with very little ambiguity.

Yes, it's a fairly plain statement from this side. And also, of course, what you've got here, very clearly exposed, is how it's made. That's one of the great characteristics of so much of your work. I'm very aware, when I look at it, of how it's been put together – the nuts and bolts, as it were, are declared on the surface of the piece. Why is that so important to you? Why do you like to do that?

There are a number of reasons why, I think. A lot of the time, when I'm using sheet material for joining one edge to another, the way in which you make

your join is like a kind of drawing, and a certain amount of detailing becomes
a means of defining. There's also the possibility of making inside and outside
– the logic here, for example, is that the screws are always on the outside
of the bend, so that the heads appear. Whereas here, the points appear,
so there is a very rational reason: it's much easier to make than it is to make
an internal angle that's a bit tight. And I think also that things I've made in
the past have tended to slightly strip apart where the tab is independent of
the two bits they join. And at one point I started to throw the edges together,
and then I began sewing the edge, wanting to make it have a degree of precision
and exactitude. In other work, where two get opposed and you get something
that opens up, the question is why. There isn't really an answer. In the early
work I did in the late 1970s, I often found myself with a problem where 'a'
and 'b' met. The meeting of the two parts became a focus of attention, but
it wasn't particularly the focus of intention. I began to look for ways of making
work which would allow the attention to be dispersed across the surface,
so that the quality of attention to any one part wasn't either more or less
than in other parts. So the use of this kind of detail was a means of plastering
your attention over the whole extent of the work, while at the same time
maintaining a matter-of-fact character to that line. Also, it does have
something to do with drawing, and the relationship between how you
construct an edge and how you construct a line. But in laminating and
the way I work with sheet metal, the kinds of repetitive techniques that
I employ are a result of a fairly desperate search, at the beginning, for a means
of making work which disperses over its whole surface – without detracting
from the constructive nature of the thing.

*And the reason why you address our attention to the whole surface is because
you want to invite us to look at the sculpture as a totality, rather than getting
hung up on particular details?*
Well, the sculptures are intended to be whole objects.

*Does this sculpture here, Richard, does it represent a development of what
has gone before or represent some kind of change?*
I don't think I'm an artist who changes very fast. I'm an artist who works with
a developing language, if you like. So that a year ago, just after my Whitechapel
show in 1988, I was beginning to feel that I didn't know whether I needed
to change the work. But I also didn't want to get into a panic and say: 'This
has to be different.' Most of the decisions that I've made in making the work
are actually quite formal decisions. The question of departures doesn't
necessarily come up, but neither do I feel that one starts work thinking:
'Oh, let's make that one again.' Somehow, a kind of originality has become
a given in art education, in terms of the way that people discuss art as being
almost a sort of marketing. And I'm not sure that's really the issue, whether
this is radically new or whether it's pushing within recognised territory.
I've become more interested in the nature of the body clothed by the outside
of the work. But I've also wanted to have some sense of substantial, fleshy
structure, or being, present as a component within the work.

So when you talk about a body, you don't necessarily mean a human body?
Although my work does not represent the human body, some elements do
have a sense of substantial flesh. The large work upstairs in my Whitechapel
show had that sort of presence. It may well have to do with starting to make
larger projects, like the work at Munster or the commission in Toronto, picking
and handling material which has a massive weight. Whereas by only working

in the studio, which doesn't have heavy lifting gear, there is a limit to the mass
of material that I can use.

*Yes, your early work was much more open, wasn't it? Much more
skeletal sometimes.*
Extremely, intentionally light. But I think the concern seems to flow all the
way through, in particular this almost double concern with the body on the
one hand and, on the other, materials that you use when you're very aware
of the machine age, the industrial age, the world that we live in.

Do you feel that they are in any way in conflict?
I don't think the work does imply that. But when you carve there's a consistency
of structure, and when you model there's a sense of the armatures generating
the surface form. Working with a sheet material – bending, folding, laminating,
sewing – whatever I do to it, there is a sense in which the exterior isn't
predicated on the interior. So the interior remains open to interpretation.
I tend to describe the work as an envelope rather than anything else, and
that relationship is quite a critical one. The kind of material that I've used
has been arrived at by looking for a material that I could use as the structural
skin at the same time.

How you obtain these materials?
Well, I used to find materials, and now I tend to buy them. There is no sense
of the material as being unique. It doesn't have the value of particularity.
Equally, the material itself is the product of manufacture, as the work is.
So there is some relationship between the source of the material and the kind
of material that I choose.

*When I look at your work, I usually find that it suggests a whole variety of possible
meanings. It seems to spawn interpretations: that's one of the excitements I find
in your sculpture. I mean, this piece that we're looking at now: we've already
talked about it in terms of a foot, perhaps. But it reminds me of other things
like ramparts – I get a feeling of a defensive wall. I also get a strange feeling of
a billowing garment. Do you like the fact that people speculate about meaning
or would you like to control it more in the sculpture?*
I tend to think of the work as being materially and formally specific – being
a particular kind of thing and having some clarity to it. Clarity seems to me
a crucial issue, so that when you look at something it seems to be distinct rather
than a blur. The kinds of ambiguities that you mention are part of the way in
which one handles one's perceptions. You bracket them according to different
things. I don't actually think that there is an unlimited set of things that one
can think of in relationship to any work. The foot/garment relationship in this
work is the area it deals with, so it can be down to the ground and up in the air.
On the other side, there is the sense of an empty passage through it.

*Yes, it changes very much when you go round to the other side – you realise that it has
this hollowness, this sense of a flow through. It's not quite finished, of course, is it?*
No, there's another piece to go on the end, to bring it round to what I want to
do with it. I don't particularly like talking about things before they're finished.
But the intention somehow is, by bringing it round, to suggest that in these
two ends the opening functions as both an active and a passive aperture.
At the moment, I think the truncation doesn't seem to be as active as I would
like it to be.

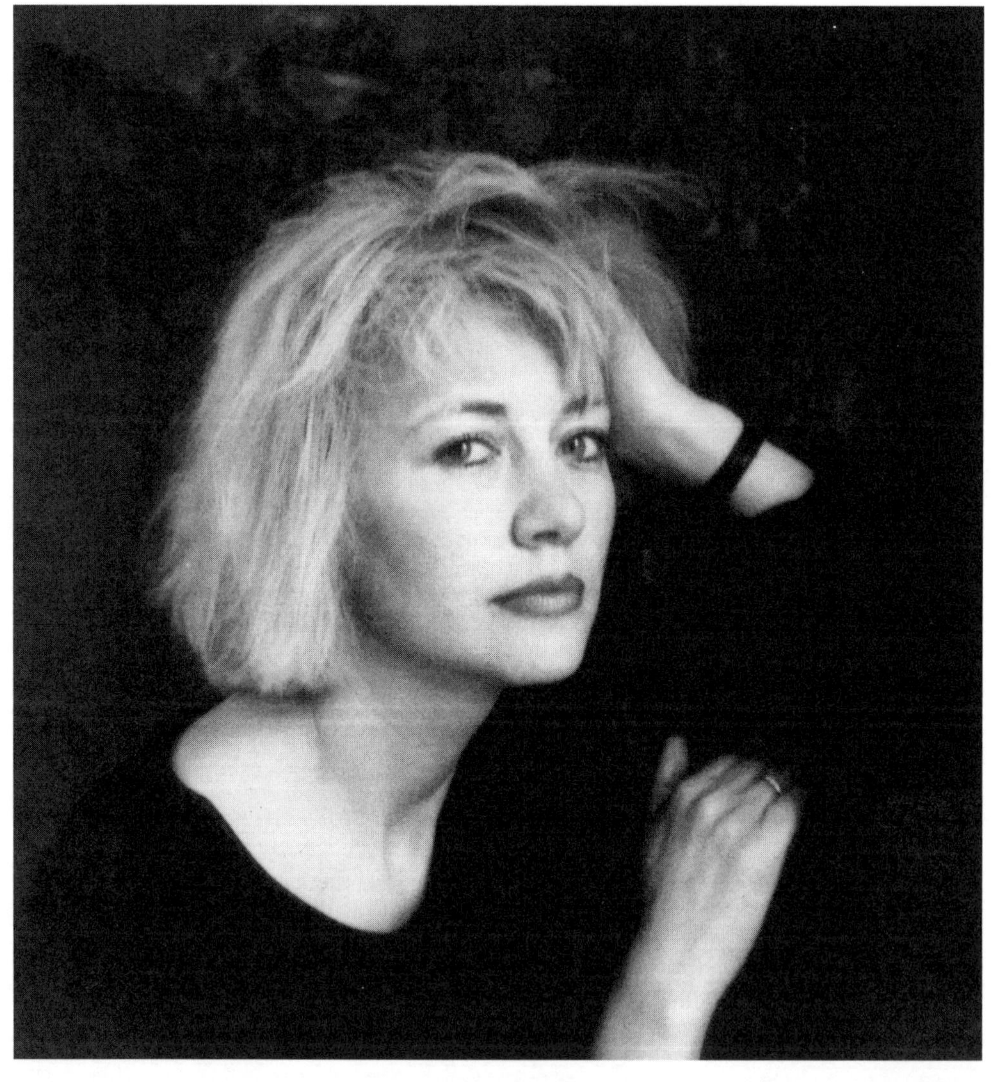

1990

Thérèse Oulton

'I imbue it with as much light as I can, and that's the true subject-matter of my paintings. I take oil paint and make it as transparent as possible, so that it can absorb, refract, sparkle, split up light, be elusive'

*The enthusiasm which greeted your first solo exhibition in 1984 immediately
made you one of the most prominent young painters in Britain. You were only
thirty-one, and some critics claimed that your expansive, richly handled
paintings heralded a revival of the Romantic landscape tradition. Words like
'sublime' were attached to your name. But the title of your exhibition,* Fools'
Gold, *suggested that you had a far less exalted, even disenchanted vision.*

*Your subsequent work has moved away from this sweeping, almost
apocalyptic turbulence, towards tighter, harder and flatter surfaces. You seem
to be searching for a way of placing emotion within a more controlled
framework, and in* Second Subject *it takes a surprisingly sumptuous form.
Burnished by colours which evoke the flaring splendour of autumn, the blocks
of furrowed paint ascend from a reflective passage resembling water at the base
of the picture. They fan outwards, with a sonorous expansiveness that calls
to mind a sequence of grand symphonic chords. 'I am switching to the realm
of music,' wrote Klee in a quotation which you included in the catalogue of your
1988 show. He discusses the idea of 'a structural net, on which musical ideas are
quantitatively and qualitatively played out'. Just as Walter Pater would have
wished, your pictures aspire towards the condition of music, and you often seem
to regard your work as a series of variations on a theme. References to landscape
are still detectable in these rock-like structures, but you undermine any attempt
to pin these paintings down. Why have you been at pains to counter the
Romantic landscape label which was so eagerly fixed to your work in 1984?*

Well, it was an odd experience, the response to my first show, because my
paintings previous to that show had been thoroughly abstract, and it might
just be that the first public showing of your work tends to classify you for a long
period of time. So for me, it's been a process of getting closer to my original
interests, or my true interests, and my brush with figuration just happened
to coincide with my first major exhibition.

*You say 'brush with figuration', but there must have been something in that
show to do with the landscape, and people seized on it. Do you acknowledge that
or do you think that they were on the wrong track?*

Oh, of course I acknowledge it, and personally I suppose landscape is the genre
I feel closest to. I also feel it's the genre that, historically, already tended towards
abstraction, and is capable of taking on the kind of philosophical issues that
I am interested in. But having said that, it was somewhat of a shock that my
work was so easily appropriated into the English or Northern Romantic
sublime, rather than being contradictions within that and criticisms of that
tradition. I certainly am critical of Romanticism. The title of my 1984 show,
Fools' Gold, was supposed to give a clue into how to read the paintings. It was
meant to set the pictures in a critical relationship to that tradition: hence the
title. But the non-critical side of the title was the elements, the type of spaces,
the vertiginous drops, the smouldering colours at the base of the pictures –
the dissolving molten colours that refer to a kind of inner world, metaphorically
and physically, to metal ores, gem stones and the colours of those elements.
This was meant to be counteracted by the way it was painted, which was so
blatantly constructed that gold wasn't discovered. It was an illusion of that,
and the romantic devices of liquid colour and wet-into-wet painting, the
exploitation of a huge scale with the consequent diminishment of the human,
were all used as very conscious devices with no attempt to make the illusion
uppermost. But that's not the way they were received. I was rather alarmed
at the ease with which the exhibition was appropriated into a nineteenth-
century sublime tradition without any of the problems or the questions that
modernism and the twentieth century had raised.

So you saw yourself, in the early 1980s, as a painter who was taking the
Romantic landscape tradition as something that needed to be questioned,
needed to be criticised.

In the following five or six years of painting, the work has addressed other periods of history. It was coincidental that those first paintings were specifically about a Romantic tradition. I think consequently I have looked at the Baroque tradition, or revived certain issues that Baroque painting throws up.

What kind of issues are you talking about in Baroque painting?

I think it was a realisation that oil painting was the perfect medium for textural description, for spatial description, and very sensuous. I could explore the sensations that one gets from counteracting textures – like, for example, in Rubens the juxtaposition of the flesh next to hard metal which makes one very uneasy, or makes a very powerful tension or anxiety. And I thought that oil painting could still conjure up those kind of sensibilities, but not necessarily attached to that same kind of subject matter, which tended to be – particularly in Rubens – violence and sensuality as an unsolvable contradiction. It might still be possible to take on those issues, but not directly illustrative of those subjects, which are not very acceptable to me as a modern painter.

Nevertheless I'd like to pursue the issue of landscape for a moment, because
it does seem to me even today to be important in your work. And I wondered
if there was a landscape, perhaps in Shropshire where you were born, which
might have affected you at some formative stage?

I think that's a continuous process. It sounds as if I am denying my northern heritage – which I am not, I feel it very strongly – but I try to underplay it as an influence on the work, because the things that go into making a work of art are so complex and probably can't be unravelled back to some cause. I object to the kind of fiction that you put something into a painting and a personality or self-expression comes out. But to answer your question: I am very close to English landscape, but it's an English landscape that I don't think exists any more – if it ever did.

So are you talking about the English landscape in English art?

Oh, exactly. My influences from landscape come from a painted landscape, and it often gets muddled for some reason: people think that it's directly from Wordsworthian walks in the landscape. Most of the ideas come from the already represented landscape.

So you are not a walker in the countryside.

But I am, you see. This is it.

Oh, you are. I can see you are difficult to pin down.

In fact, I have just been to the most romantic of English landscapes, which is the Lakes. And I was deeply affected by them, so I can't deny it. But it influences me as a person, not as a painter.

How has it affected you? Tell me about your response to the Lakes.

If there is any connection with the paintings, it's in the kind of closeness to the elements. And I have never been to such a watery place. The only sounds were of water, from bricks to waterfalls, and the constant rain. There was one walk which actually was above cloud levels: it was raining beneath me, and the peaks were jutting out above the clouds into a clear sky, which was quite startling. So I think a landscape which stressed a watery element would be somehow

quite close to my sensibilities, and in fact a lot of the paintings have referred
to the effect of something liquid destroying form. Many of the titles refer,
even if obliquely, to that phenomenon – both of light and dark destroying and
making form, and of the elements of any particular water. I am just thinking
of one example, like *Cataract*, which was two streams of very liquid paint
that physically dissolved. So it wasn't a depiction of a waterfall: it was part
of the whole question in the painting of the tenuousness, the coming into
being of form and the disintegrating back into formlessness. That, I think,
is closer perhaps to the real subject matter of the paintings. And if that
refers to phenomena outside the paintings, it's in a metaphoric relationship.
That makes sense.

*Yes, it does. Of course, in the work of many nineteenth-century painters,
the presence of God is central to their vision of the landscape. Having been
brought up in the Catholic faith, as I know you have, and indeed named
after a French saint, are you now subverting the whole idea of landscape
as a vehicle for religion?*

I think probably within the Romantic tradition itself, doubt is a very important
element. It's beginning to be the breakdown of a comfortable belief in God,
and it's a very uneasy relationship. I mean, the acting sublime is the terror
of the void, and that is also a very contemporary thing to be dealing with,
although perhaps not attached so directly to landscape idiom. I am thinking
of the American abstract expressionists, who might be seen as an extension
of that landscape tradition of the void. And I think that the void is the
beginning of lack of faith or the absence of God becoming a subject matter –
as opposed to searching for God in the sublime sunset. Landscape is vehicle,
that's what I was trying to say earlier on. Its capacity to rid itself of that imagery
and take on that subject matter, which might be to do with doubt and absence
and searching for a God through the means that are available to us. And that's
very pertinent to the way that all the reasons why I paint are given in the actual
substance. I imbue it with as much light as I can, and that's the true subject
matter of my paintings. I take oil paint and make it as transparent as possible,
so that it can absorb, refract, sparkle, split up light, be elusive so that the light
flickers across the surface. There is a literal search for that, but there is also
a kind of metaphoric quest, in that the paintings over the last two or three years
have referred to the densest kind of substances – to rock, to minerals, to gem
stones and, in the recent body of work, to the skeletal, the bones, the substance
that is most durable. To bring light into what is most dense may sound like
a kind of religious quest, but it could also be seen as an interest in the material.

*Has this interest in light, which is so important to you, become a substitute
for the Catholic certainties which must have buttressed your childhood?*

Yes, that's probably very true. That's my inheritance, those are the materials
with which I have to work as a person. And if conflicts and contradictions come
out in those terms, it's probably because of a strict Catholic upbringing. But the
same contradictions could be found clothed in a different language from a very
different kind of upbringing. I don't think that they are special to Catholicism.

*But Catholicism is of course a very strong religion, full of certainties.
Do you see yourself now as a kind of heretical figure?*

Well, heresy is a most fascinating kind of strategy, which can be useful for
an artist in a context where meaning is so over-laden, so over-burdened, that
it appears as if there were no room to move. In order to strategise out of that
situation, I have been interested in the parallels to Christianity, expressed

in all kinds of heresies. They were a strategy for survival, and for creating
meanings outside orthodoxy. In a general sense, I think that might be the
artist's task, anyway. So my references to all kinds of heretical thoughts –
including alchemy, gnosticism, Rosicrucianism – are not specifically to do with
the doctrines that they came up with, but just a clue to the viewer and myself
as to how to read the paintings. They obviously bear the mark of a great deal
of gnostic thought, absorbed into Christianity probably to make it safe. It acted
as a kind of double-speak or a secret language that, simply in its opposition, was
valuable. But it also brought along with it a great deal of fascinating imagery,
often completely inverted from the orthodox – like the elevation of the serpent
into a principle of the feminine or the good. They had various tactics like that,
and what I am trying to do is parallel this strategy of the heretics in painting.
It's bound to bear the marks of orthodoxy, but at the same time I hope that,
in my work, those things that look comfortable at first and remind one of a past
tradition will, at a closer look, start to unravel or bring doubt into certainty.

*How interested were you in all these issues when you first went to art school? You
started off at St Martin's and then you went later to the Royal College of Art.*

I think they were put into cold storage for a long while, because I came to art
school a few years later than most people, and I always felt an imposter. I learnt
very valuable things in art school, by pushing into the background certain
things that had previously interested me – including just listening to music,
reading books. It was important, for that period, to believe in the idea that
a painter just paints, which was the kind of hidden dogma in my art school.

*But when you first entered art school, in 1975, it wasn't a good time for painting.
Were you aware of this? Did you deliberately resist experimenting with all those
alternative media which so many artists were interested in at that time?*

Well, at St Martin's I didn't notice any reduction in fervour about the role of
painting, because the people who taught me certainly believed in painting. And
to be honest, I don't think I was very aware until the end of the decade that such
fundamental problems beset painting. But over the last ten years it seems there
is no problem at all, so maybe it was as well that I missed all those issues. At the
same time, though, I think I missed something at St Martin's: the theoretical
side, which belonged in other departments like the film department. It was OK
to be an intellectual and a theorist in those departments, but not in painting.
There was almost an unsaid belief that, if you thought too much, it would
damage your painting. Obviously, I don't believe in that at all now, but I would
like there to have been not such a split between the theoretical and the practice.

*Feminism was also a very live issue among many young artists in the 1970s.
Were you involved in that kind of debate?*

At St Martin's not at all, no. I reduced myself to being purely a painter. I am
pleased it happened like that, because that side was most embryonic. And
feminism was not a very polite issue at St Martin's in the 1970s: in fact, it
was subjected to ridicule, which is the best form of attack. I think I am just
a very slow developer. It only came from facing the inevitability of certain issues
within my own work, from internal questions. And then I read all the right
books, but it's very difficult in relation to a woman painter because those
alternative media that you were talking about have become acceptable arenas
for feminism. Although that's extremely valuable, I sometimes suspect that
we are still being relegated to areas that are not of prime historic importance,
just because history has decided that they are the highest form of art. So oil
painting, sculpture, composing music, writing poetry still seem to be the most

heavily guarded. Any thinking woman would call herself a feminist, so as
a person I am certainly a feminist. But its relationship to my painting is very
intricate, and to claim that it is a kind of illustration of feminism is wrong,
it's limiting. But at the same time it is actually central to the very questions
that all painters should be asking, not merely women who happen to be
feminists. And I think that, regarding the problems of representation, feminists
have asked some of the most interesting intellectual questions of our period,
in terms of how and why one produces an image, or in fact refuses to do so.
My work is about a criticism of the way objects sit in space, and how those
relationships are depicted.

*Let's look at some of your most recent work, in particular two very large
canvases called* Confessions I *and* Confessions II. *I am very struck by
how far you seem to have banished altogether now that sense of plunging,
swirling space which used to animate your early work. In* Confessions
I *you confront us for the most part with a very cliff-like structure of pale
grey paint, which stretches right across the width of the canvas. Only at
the very bottom do you allow a hint of a more nebulous world to appear
in a passage of deep brown, rather misty pigment, as if the cliff were being
revealed as an artifice, almost like a curtain lifted at its base. Can you say
what you are trying to do there?*

They are the most extreme statements yet of a slow withdrawal from the
recognisable, while keeping their feet in figuration. They feel as though they
belong to a figurative oil-painting tradition, but there is nothing that one
can actually name – even though people do struggle. It could either be this
or it could be that. I think that kind of doubt is interesting, and when they
are being described to me, the scale is often hugely varied. Some people see
it as a microscopic world, and some a kind of cosmological space. And one
of the great benefits of becoming more abstract is abstraction's ability to
simultaneously take on a range of ideas, sensibilities, textures and scale, to
present those as contradictions to the viewer. So in those two paintings you
have mentioned, *Confessions I and II*, which could be seen as a pair, for me
they have brought back into the argument the body. One is representative
of a micro-crystallised world of bleached bones – it's something that has a
bodily feel to it. And the other one is a kind of deep, dark red, with patches
on it that pulsate. It has a love-like sense of a ribbon of blood passing through
a body. So they were painted in opposition, but they are also built on the
repetition of a motif which has become the way that the paintings are
structured. Rather than the classical way of composition from a grand idea,
these are built up from the highlight on the eyeball into huge surfaces.

*Is that the way you work, starting with a tiny section of the canvas
and then gradually building up from there?*

It's built up in one surface only, there is no underpainting and no overpainting.
It spreads out across the canvas, and the works in recent years have been
structured by repeating a motif. That has become very interesting, in that
it can produce a kind of sublime. There's an analogy with a mountain range
that builds from the microcosmic unit after unit into something huge, but
it also has a terrifying side, in that lack of differentiation comes from repetition
and all the modern horrors of mass population, mass production.

Standardisation.

Standardisation, exactly. Also the idea of disease is another of the metaphoric
references in the painting. But where disruptions in that surface occur – as in

disease or scars, the idea of wearing away, of ageing, buckling, wrinkling and all
those words – they actually differentiate one individual from another, because
it's a record of the kind of experiences that it, or he or she, has been through.
And the paintings are supposed to refer to many levels of ideas and sensualities
that the very textured surface gives. The major metaphor of those two paintings
that you mentioned is the idea of painting as a second skin, which is in fact
the title of one of my paintings. The idea is that it's a reiteration of a perfection
already there, which is the nice clean white canvas. It's also only surface but, like
a human, the surface is all there is to see, and it's a record of its own making, of
its own history, of its own distress. And it does have a quality in the way that the
surface absorbs light like the skin absorbs, and the kind of scars on the surface.

By calling them Confessions, *of course, you are implying that in some
way they are autobiographical and revealing of yourself. I wondered how
far you were prepared to say that these paintings are, in the end, to do with
your own state of mind?*
I am wary of that notion. I have got a feeling that it's another of those fictions
that you put your heart and soul into your work, and they can be somehow
extricated from it again. The states of mind that could perhaps be gauged from
those two pictures do have some relationship to me the person. But I think that
those are common to all, and I am critical of a notion that says art is self-
expression. I don't even think that it is very interesting. I don't even think that
my particular history is interesting enough to go into.

Well, why therefore did you call these paintings Confessions?
The most difficult thing is to talk about the work you have just done, and
I can talk about most of my other titles. I don't think I am quite prepared
to talk about why those two are called *Confessions*, except that – like you said
in your introduction that *Fools' Gold* had a kind of tongue in cheek –
Confessions too has a slightly mocking element to it, although a serious element
as well. You would be struggling to find a confession of what, but at the same
time it is a depiction of a surface that is lived and distressed and diseased
and scarred. So the confessions are kind of self-evident.

*Let me ask you finally about a painting which was the centrepiece of your 1988
exhibition. Called* 'Lachrimae', *it presented an encrusted and almost petrified
surface of very sombre pigment – except that it was irrigated by two streams
of white, which dropped down from one ridge to the next. They were like tears,
and I did wonder at the time how closely you identified with the world you've
created in your work. It is, as you have said during this interview, a very
separate world in one sense, and very important to you. But did you identify
it as ultimately a metaphor for yourself?*
Or a metaphor for something else. I am very glad you picked that particular
painting out, because it was one of those key paintings. The subsequent two
years have been exploring the possibilities of that one painting. The tears were
certainly not my tears, and the title *'Lachrimae'* was in quotation marks: it
referred to a John Dowland piece of music that I thought was the most startling
and most magnificent piece of music I had heard at that particular period.
It was very monotonous, repetitive. It explored a kind of limited expressive
range. But because of that, a sense of claustrophobia with a narrowed range
of expression was deeply moving. It seems to be without possibility or capability
or even necessity to resolve itself. It's an endless variation, and that interested
me greatly as an expressive possibility – one that I think was possibly
pre-Romantic and has been lost under a kind of Romantic extremism.

Its melancholy belonged very definitely to the world of art, not to personal melancholy. Even though it's that as well, it was also put into art, and the tears were meant in the same spirit as that seventeenth-century melancholy attitude. But it's for real as well, and the tears doubled up because the painting still did refer to some kind of geological landscape allusion. That was also a reference to the tears of the earth, if that doesn't sound too sentimental – a kind of earth that was dying. If there was a landscape painting tradition still possible, it would have to acknowledge the death of this planet, or the death of nature as we've conceived to fit it in our art and music.

And, by extension, human mortality.
Of course, and the surface of the canvas was both a countenance in a portrait – hence the tears or the two rivulets – and referring to the larger world as well. But the tears were not illustrated. It was the actual way of structuring the painting: the streams of the tears dissolved the form in their path. The larger areas were physically dissolved by the play of substances. Some were more liquid than others. Some were destructive and some were form-making, so it was supposed to imply a whole world in flux or form in a constant state of disintegration.

THÉRÈSE OULTON

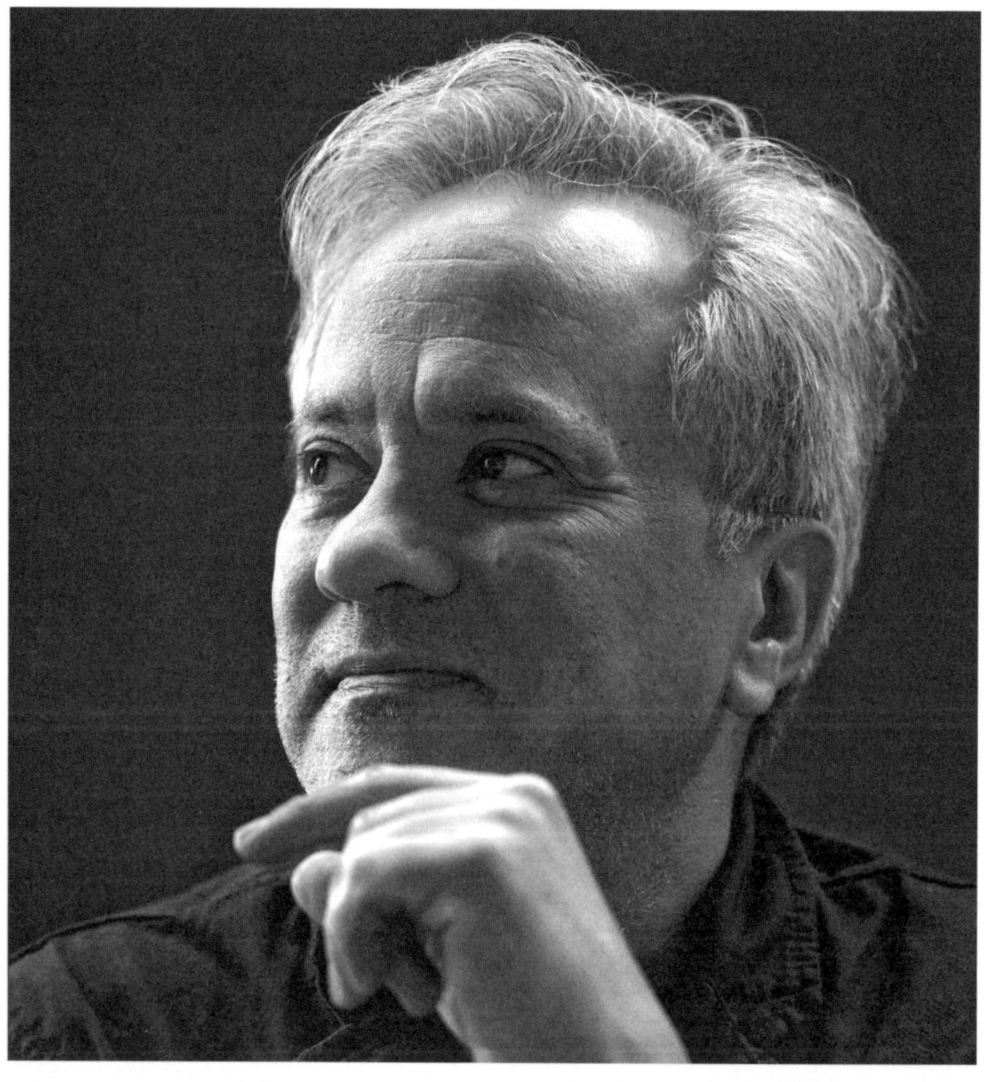

Anish Kapoor

'I do see it as an internal journey, which carries me where it carries me, and in a sense it's only of any use to me if, through it, I can act out my own internal drama'

*At the age of thirty-six, you've been chosen to represent Britain at this
year's Venice Biennale, an honour which recognises your ability to fuse
the diverse strands of your complex cultural inheritance. You grew up
in India, the son of a Hindu father and a Jewish mother whose family had
emigrated from Baghdad. Then you came to England and, after studying
at art schools here, you've lived in London ever since. You soon established
a reputation for brilliantly coloured sculpture, shimmering in red,
blue and yellow pigment-coated forms reminiscent of gourds, mountains
and breasts.*

*More recently, your work has become reliant on rough-hewn blocks
of stone and slate, most spectacularly in the main room of the British Pavilion
at Venice, where the space is filled with twenty boulder-like lumps of red
sandstone, each pierced by a small circular aperture. How much of a change
does this new work represent, do you think, away from those brighter colours
and the smaller, more openly sensual forms of your earlier work?*

I don't feel the shift has been very large. In fact, I think what's happened is
that I've moved from making objects which seem to define a place, an area of
activity. The early works of pigmented objects were in a space, and the objects
seem to be defining the edge of this place. What's happened over the last few
years is that this place has slowly moved inside the objects. Consequently
they've become bigger, and darker, and that seems to be important.

*Your concerns have remained consistent throughout this development you're
talking about, because in the earlier sculpture you favoured these very ripe,
organic and graspable forms. Often, I thought, very fruit-like and erotic, in fact.
But even then, the sheer luminosity of those powdered colours removed the work
into a more dream-like sphere. How far did you intend them to be both tactile
and ethereal, at one and the same time?*

The choice I made early on to use pigment was, I think, very pertinent, because
pigment is the stuff, in a way, of earth. It has a kind of material presence, and yet
it's made of nothing. It's ephemeral, and this kind of dichotomy – this is a central
part of my whole being, I suppose, and has always been part of the work. So
conjunction, opposition, things to do with material and immaterial are crucial.

*You also decided early in your career to place almost all your work under this
generic title of* 1000 Names. *Now, that emphasised the sequential nature of
the objects you placed either on the wall or the floor, and it implied that they
were fragmentary contributions to your search for a larger whole. Why did
you want to stress that particular aspect of the work?*

As I was saying, with pigment powder being there and not there, this issue has
been a part of what I do since I can remember making art, which is about what
is present and what is not present. *1000 Names* implies partially revealed.
The early powder pieces sat on the floor with powder sprinkled around the
objects in such a way as to define the area of the floor – and the wall, if they're
projected out from the wall – and it seemed to imply that most of the object
was either beneath the floor or on the other side of the wall. So they were partial
revelations of a bigger whole. I think, on a metaphoric level, this is evidently
a notion about passage. It's a language which I'm trying to form.

*Were you also aware of the fact that you were a young artist, embarking on what
you hoped – and what everyone hopes, I'm sure – will be a long voyage? I'm
talking about the moment when you made those works, and realised that they
would perhaps be fragmented, they would be markers.*

Yes, of course. I do believe that I have fifty years to work here, and that's

important to me. There is always this feeling that I have that I'm at the
beginning, things are just starting, so ...

So you take the long view?
Yes, it's important. I think it has a lot to do with the kind of art I want to make.
I'm not after the sensational. We live in a time where the sensational has
enormous currency in the art world. But that which lasts, that which is there for
the duration, is relatively hard to see. It's what I'm after, let's hope I get there.

*There's another issue with those earlier sculptures, too, because you often like
to group them in clusters or arrange them in lines. As if they'd almost been
set out for use in some kind of ritualistic event. Now, I know that performance
art has never been one of your interests, but are you stimulated by the idea
that an artist can almost take on a shaman-like role?*
Well, when I was a student I did do some work which was performance related.
I didn't make performances. But one could hardly be a student in the early
1970s and not be in touch with that whole way of thinking, and it seemed to
me that in the groups of objects I was putting together with the powder pieces,
I was trying to define a ritualised space – this thing that I call 'place.' There
is a very succinct Hebrew word for this, which is *macom*. It seems to be a word
that implies that this is a place set apart. Now, of course, there's all kinds
of ideas there, about passage, about ritual, about things in a state of becoming.
Powder pigment by its very nature is laid out. One of the things I like about
it, too, is that it seems to do the very opposite, that there is a way of laying
out pigment which seems to remove the hand from the making of the object.
It gives an impeccably pristine, clear surface, and this has always been
important. So on the one hand, a very tactile, physical kind of contact.
And then, on the other hand, a distance. A distance that seems to say:
'This is fragile, keep away, don't touch.'

*You mentioned a Hebrew word when you were talking about ritual just then, but
I was wondering if this interest also stems from your knowledge of Indian art?*
Of course it does, I'm Indian and therefore it's very important to me. I found
over the years that it's very difficult for me to deal with my Indian-ness on
a public level. I find I become more and more private about that, because it
seems to me that in the last ten years this has become so hugely misunderstood,
and so terribly written about, that I've become more and more secretive about
it. Although, of course, I'm Indian and what comes out of my hands is Indian
on some level, and that's important.

*Yes, I would like to discuss the fact that you made a return journey to India
in 1979, didn't you? After leaving art college in London.*
After leaving art college and being out in the wide world for over a year
or so. That's one of the events that in my early career has become
misunderstood, I think. The work that I was making before '79, before
I went to India, was dealing with the same issues I dealt with after '79,
in terms of the thematics of the work. What changed were my materials.
I feel that was a discovery, but only a discovery of a kind. The content
had always been there, so it was the same. What I found in India, however,
in fact reaffirmed for me all those things I was dealing with, and they were
to do with binary opposition and conjunction.

*But by 'materials', you mean that in India you saw the powder colours laid out,
next to the temples?*

Yes, it's used for cosmetics and temple ritual. Seeing it again, I think I saw it with art eyes. It was a different experience, it became available as a material.

*But I think that trip to India also reawoke, or made you perhaps think
again about, your interest in the whole business of Indian religion and
what the gods stood for.*

I'd spent five years or so in Britain by then, as a student, and felt alien from my culture. I didn't quite understand whether I was British or Indian, or what that amounted to. I do think I suffered quite a serious identity crisis, going back to India. I was there only for three weeks at that time, and it did make it very clear to me. I came back from that trip feeling clearer about the kind of person I am. So it was important in that sense, yes.

*I was thinking in particular of Shiva, who does actually embody within himself
this duality which I can see very strongly within your work. On the one hand
this very strong sensuality, involvement with the things of the world, and on
the other this removal.*

I have a very strong interest in that, of course, but as a student I found parallels for it in the work of Marcel Duchamp. For example, *The Large Glass* was always a very important work for me.

Why was that particular work important for you?

Because it's all about the bride and the bachelors. Because it's about binary opposition, and when I went back to India that seemed very clear. In the kind of places that I was going to, shrines and temples and so on, it seemed to be a very integral part of an Indian view of the world. But perhaps more important than all of this is the idea of origin. Opposition and conjunction are about the forming of a beginning. It's a difficult thing to articulate. Barnett Newman's *Day One* is making a statement about origin, and there are works by Jackson Pollock that seem to be endeavouring to do the same thing. It seems to be something they also dealt with.

*Maybe, because of your preoccupation with intense colour, you feel closer to
painters. I mean, you've already talked about Pollock and Barnett Newman.*

Yes, I think I'm a sculptor who's a painter, really. It seems to me that painting deals with this space, with an illusory space of the mind, and that sculpture deals with the world – it's here, it's present. I seem to have a curious combination of the two. I'm working in stone now: it's to do with the here, the present, implying some kind of illusory not-here. Something over there.

Do you think it's paradoxical that you're a sculptor at all?

No.

I mean, you can't imagine yourself being a painter?

I can. As I say, I do the two. I do both of them. But painting seems to me, after a flurry in the 1980s, again in crisis. And as a culture we have so little confidence in the truly intellectual, sculpture seems easier to deal with. Because in a sense our whole culture is a culture of the body.

*And drawing is very important to you. I mean, you've always drawn,
you've always made watercolours, collages and more recently prints.
I recall visiting your studio and seeing drawings all over the walls.*

Yes, I draw all over the walls as a way of recording my thoughts about the work. It's a good way of keeping a diary. The drawings I make on paper are work in themselves. They're very rarely, if ever, studies for sculpture.

*But are they useful for you in terms of testing colour possibilities that you might
use in sculpture later on?*
Rarely. In spite of the fact that I make a lot of work using colour, I have a small
range of colour. I use red and blue and black – and yellow, which I haven't used
in a long time. But I've never used green, and I've never used any mixture
of colours. It seems to me that they don't have the same potential.

It's also about the specific meanings that you attach to these colours.
Exactly.

Can you tell me something about that?
The early powder pieces define this kind of ritual area, space, but they were
bright and about the giving out of light. What's happened now, with this kind of
move towards the interior, the colours are becoming darker and about the
absorption of light. That's a dramatic change. I think most adventures in terms
of growth are from darkness to light. Mine seems to be the other way. Red has
always been the central colour. It's always been the most important colour, and
of course it's a colour of the earth, and blood, and it's a colour of passion, and all
of these things that we associate with it. I saw yellow as, in a sense, the passionate
part of red, and blue – if you like – as the godly part of red. But red clearly
anchoring things to the centre, or at the centre. Over the last two years I've really
only made work with black and blue. I must be dealing with something there. I
see making art not just as a process in which one deposits in the world more or
less interesting objects. I do see it as an internal journey, which carries me where
it carries me, and in a sense it's only of any use to me if, through it, I can act out
my own internal drama. In the conjunction of my works at Venice there's a play
between mass, as in *Void Field,* this mass of stones, and then their emptiness.
And the other room with *Madonna,* which is a void work.

*Yes, at first glance this massive field of boulders, in the main room of the Venice
Pavilion, might seem akin to the work of a minimalist sculptor. But these great
blocks of stone all turn out to contain a void, and the entire work could therefore
be described as subversive. Do you see it in that light at all?*
Yes, I think it's a work about mass and no mass. About what's here and what's
not here. There's another work in the show, in the back room, which is called
A Wing at the Heart of Things, the two blue pieces of slate. It's in a sense
the opposite of *Void Field,* or perhaps it's the same as *Void Field* but does
the opposite. It's two very heavy pieces of stone that are made weightless
by a coat of blue paint. Well, a very particular kind of blue paint, but the blue
gives it a kind of lightness and to my mind they float. But in a way they are
the opposite of *Void Field,* in that *Void Field* is this kind of night within stone,
earth outside and night or sky within. And *A Wing at the Heart of Things*
is earth within and sky without.

*Can you say a bit more about your interest in the fathomless object with
the mystery, where it comes from?*
There's evidently a modernist tradition for that kind of work, the abstract
sublime.

And does your own religious faith have any direct bearing on the work that you make?
Of course it does, yes, it is the medium through which I investigate that faith,
but I don't hold to any religion.

But it wouldn't really be possible, by looking at your work, to realise what
religious faith you possessed, would it?

No, and I think on a certain level, yes the work is rather distant. It's not very
much about hand, it's not very much about manufacture, and it's normally
impeccably painted surfaces. This, apparently, reveals very little. But I feel
that one of the things I'm interested in is a metaphoric language, which is
to do simply with colour, simply with mass, simply with sufficient no mass,
if you like. And that by leaving myself out, by leaving my idiosyncratic ways
out, by leaving my hand out, perhaps I might find a way to leave enough
room for you. Therefore, I don't speak about my faith. I feel really that
I have nothing to say, but maybe I can give you room for your faith. I think
that is what it's about.

I don't understand why you say that you have nothing to say. That seems
an extraordinary thing for an artist to …

Yes, I am against the cult of personality. It seems that many of our twentieth-
century art heroes cultivated huge cults of personality. We've also come through
a time in the 1980s when self-expression was the big thing, especially the
stream-of-consciousness type of self-expression. I feel that the reality of art
is somewhere else. I have a great love for art of the earlier times. Medieval
and earlier, I should say, Eastern and Western. And in it there is very little
artist. There's great art but very little artist. It seems to me that is the condition
worth aspiring to: a lot is said, a lot is touched. Great feelings are conveyed,
but with very little artist. I think that's a good way of going about it.

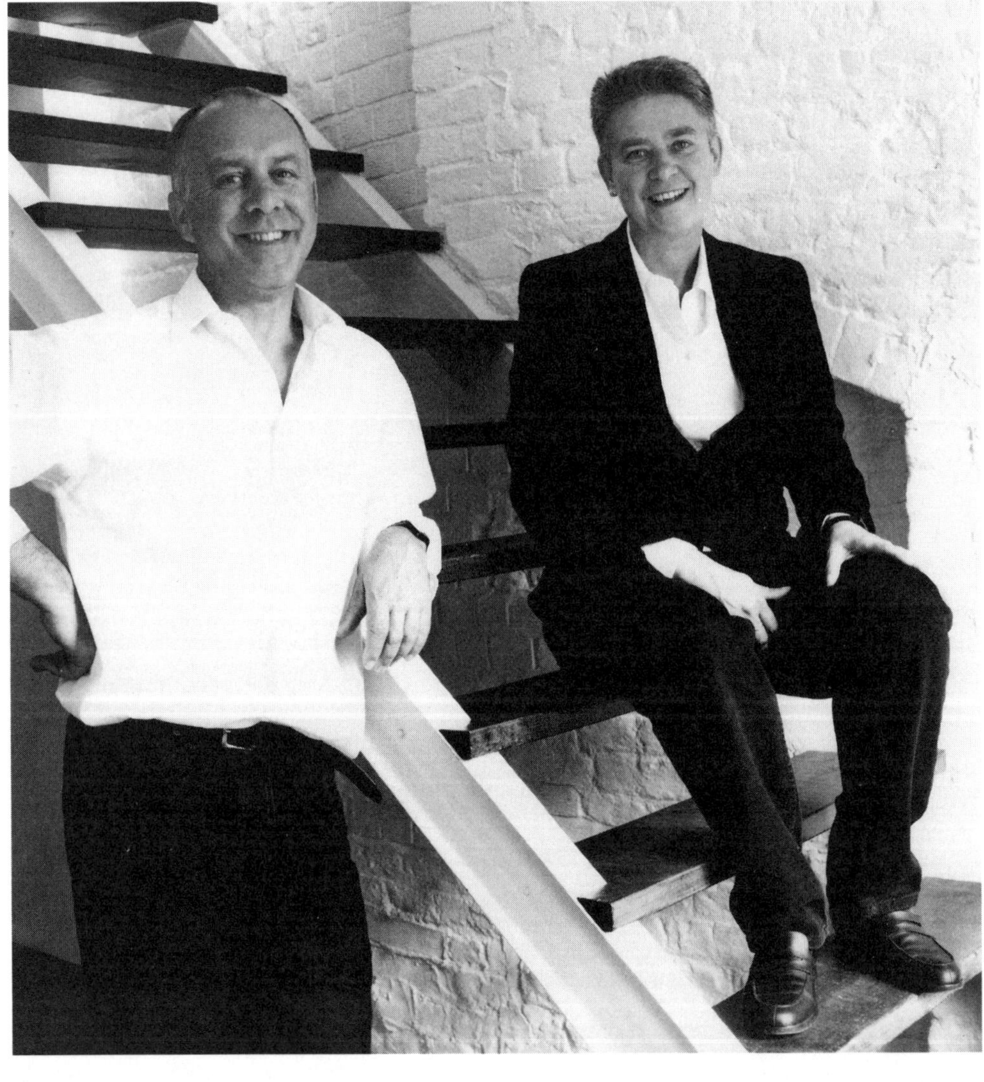

Langlands & Bell

'People are thinking that artists do have something to contribute, and can combine with engineers and developers and the whole process that you go about together. I think it's opening up, I do feel that'

Unlike most artists, who do not work with their partners, you've been collaborating ever since meeting at college in 1978. It's clear that your art doesn't really fit into any single category, but rather crosses the boundaries normally separating sculpture, painting, architecture and furniture. You refer in your work to the world of structures and places we inhabit. These constructs are often made in monochrome. The colour of the models and their precision resist traditional forms of representation by allowing a space to exist between these objects and the conditions that they question. This notion of questioning seems to be a very important part of the way in which you work. And in attempting to find a path into your art, I'm struck by the singularity of it. Although you're very well known, and many people are familiar with what you've done, at the same time it's actually quite difficult to place you.

I want to emphasise the almost determined way in which you've tried to evade any categorisation. You're called artists, and I see you as part of the context of contemporary art, but in a way you're out on your own. I can't think of any other artist who comes very near you in terms of the issues and subject matter you deal with. And although you've been included in exhibitions like Sensation *at the Royal Academy – a show based on the collection formed by Charles Saatchi, who has been a fairly assiduous purchaser of your work over the years – I wouldn't say that you were centrally located even within that exhibition. When one says the word 'sensation', one doesn't immediately think of your work. So there is this feeling that you're operating always at a kind of tangent, and maybe I could start by asking you both whether it's a deliberate policy or whether it just happens because of what you're interested in doing.*

Langlands: It's not a deliberate policy, although we do feel that at times, yes. Really we just follow our own interests and the things that excite us – and the things that we love. That's what has led us along this path. We haven't consciously sought to separate the course we're following from other art, or anything like that. But you're right: often it seems as though the contemporary art world is made up of various gangs or groups, and we don't feel as though we're in a gang or group.

You both graduated from Middlesex Polytechnic in 1980, and I think that's where you met, wasn't it?

Bell: That's right, yes.

You not only met there but decided that, both on a personal and a professional level, your interests coincided. What was it, do you think, that made you realise as students that you shared some kind of common thread, some sort of central fascination with a particular thing?

Bell: I think the first work that we did together made us realise that we would actually work together. We built two kitchens, side by side.

When you were students?

Bell: As students. As an installation, if you like. Originally, I was going to build the old half of it and Ben was going to build the new kitchen. But as it happened, we ended up collaborating and making both kitchens together. So you entered into this space, which was full of rusty objects. There was a table, there was a chair, there was rusty cutlery, there was the smell of old fat, rotten floorboards and an old window that you looked through – and there was a brand new kitchen. It was a mirror image of the old, and everything was brand new and sparkling and shiny. But you couldn't actually enter this space at all.

Langlands: Yes, at that time these kinds of installations were not called installations: they were called environments. We'd been students on the same course for about a year by the time we made this piece, and we got to know each other a bit. We didn't actually know each other that well, but we were just talking about making work – we were both fascinated by abandoned buildings and that kind of thing, just because it was interesting to explore them and to go through piles of rubbish, really [laughs].

Yes, 'rubbish' was a key concern round about 1980, wasn't it?
Bell: Well, there were a lot more derelict houses than there are now.

Quite a few young British sculptors were scavenging around then.
Langlands: We used to explore these abandoned houses full of abandoned artefacts, and we were fascinated by them. So we decided to make this piece, these two kitchens. As Nikki said, the two kitchens were mirrors of each other in terms of positioning. They were furnished properly, with tables and chairs and shelves and cookers and everything, and objects and products that you'd find in a kitchen. The objects of the new kitchen were intrinsically no better than the objects in the old kitchen, but you couldn't enter the new kitchen – you could only stand in the old kitchen and look through the window into it.

And why was the new kitchen unattainable?
Langlands: Well, partly for practical reasons, because we decided to light it from a projector that was projecting through prisms, and we didn't want people to go into it because that would begin to disturb the aura of wonder that we'd created with this light. The shelves in the new kitchen were made out of glass and mirror, and so the light ran through them and bounced off them. And we wanted it to have an element of mystery.

In this respect, and what you describe as the aura of wonder and the use of light, it sounds like a fairly prophetic work in terms of what you went on to do afterwards. The unattainability is interesting to me, too, because whatever sociological comment it might have carried, there's also something about your subsequent work which is strangely removed from the immediate experience of seeing a building. Somehow it's a different order of experience: you take away the visceral impact of going up to a building that's rearing in front of you, and you present us instead with a quite different kind of phenomenon. Can you talk a little about how your approach to that experience of a building evolved?
Langlands: It's difficult to say objectively for us. But I think when we were making works like the kitchen, and other works around that time which followed it, we were very keen to make works which brought with them their own kind of context, so that they weren't over-reliant in immediate terms on the context in which they were being exhibited or encountered. We were trying to set up a whole situation in which they could be viewed, and in time I think maybe we explored various aspects of it and started to move on. In order to survive as students, and soon after leaving college, we actually used to restore buildings for people. And as we got more competent at this, we were given plans by people and we had to work to plans, so that was the first time when we actually started to read architectural drawings and to look at buildings in that way. Then we also started to make models, and sketch models for architects, purely as a way of making money. As soon as we made the first model, we realised that it had a very kind of exciting potential – both formally and aesthetically but also in terms of telling a story somehow. I think this all happened at the same time, and we began to find ways to include this in our work. So that was how it came about.
Bell: I think also that not everyone can read a plan, but everyone can

understand a model. So by turning it into three dimensions you're almost
revealing structures which normally aren't seen from that viewpoint. So in
a way we were almost discovering, as we were making them, entire buildings
and viewpoints that you don't normally have when you enter a building.
Langlands: That's very true, and it's always been very important to us that
our work has been accessible, really, to anyone who can come across it and
take some interest in it and get something out of it without some specialist
knowledge or preparation. But going back to your question, the other thing
I suppose is that we started to work with models because we were working on
a different scale, and we could refer to specific buildings that we were all familiar
with, famous structures. We could, by combining, ask questions about how
they were connected to us. So in a sense it's just a question of scale, and we were
just widening the context in which we were finding what, in a sense, were still
'found objects'. We would find the plans to the Villa La Rotonda or Highpoint,
and we were fascinated by them. So we started to combine the plans and different
buildings in that way, and find out what happened when you put them together.

*You roam very widely, don't you? It's difficult to say where your preference lies
in terms of the kinds of architecture that you choose to concentrate on. But there
does seem to be a consistent fascination, running through the output that you've
produced, with notions of power and control. I don't want to overstate it, but
I think that quite a few of the structures that you present for our inspection turn
out to be highly manipulative in terms of what they do to the people who occupy
them. Is that one of your central concerns?*
Langlands: I think it's a coincidence more than a concern.
Bell: These things become more apparent once you've actually made the work.
We are interested in strategic buildings, but we're interested in architecture
as a whole, we're interested in buildings because they're the biggest 'found
objects' you find in a city. We're surrounded by architecture, and we're both
from London and grew up with buildings around us, so it became our subject
quite naturally. As a hobby, we loved exploring buildings, and you find
out so much about people and how they live through buildings and through
the furniture that you encounter within them.
Langlands: The other thing is that we realise that all architecture is strategic.
Maybe some architecture is more strategic than other architecture, but
basically it's all strategic in a personal sense and in the impact it has on our
lives. So I think we feel that very strongly, and that's inevitable. The way we've
worked, over time, we have tended to concentrate in phases on different types
of buildings, and we've worked in series. So at different times we've been
fascinated by or we've concentrated on, say, political architecture – or rather
the architecture of international political bodies – or prison architecture
or religious architecture or architecture associated with aviation and airports
and that kind of thing. So at different times we've honed in on that and made
numerous works in a group or in a series. A lot of the works are consciously
connected, not in a didactic way but they're linked by the route which
we've taken by choosing different buildings or different other elements
to combine with them.

*Sometimes they seem almost subversive, your choice of subjects. I'm thinking
in particular of a wonderful piece you did on the building that formerly
occupied the site of Tate Britain at Millbank. It was a penitentiary in the
nineteenth century, and a rather extraordinary building too, I think.*
Bell: Mmm – shaped like a giant flower with amazing radiant petals, where
people were segregated according to whether you were a debtor or a female

or a male. It was all categorised and very rational. We were struck immediately
by just the shape of the plan. It seemed so beautiful, and yet it was a prison.
Langlands: And the irony is that both buildings – the art gallery and the prison
– they had quite a lot of links in some ways. Particularly the prison because
it was a panopticon combined with a radial prison, and at the time people were
thinking in a very serious way about how prisons should be designed and
organised and how they would work. So it was then formulated in a very specific
way that prisons should be about observation, surveillance. And, of course,
galleries were also predicated upon observation. So both buildings were in many
ways about looking, containing and observing – that's quite a crude analogy, but
it still works. And also both buildings are in many ways about integrating people
socially in larger social norms and values, and enshrining what society's values
are, and defining them, and ensuring that people conform to them. So there
are quite a lot of links. And also Millbank was the main prison in London for
transporting people to penal colonies, for periods of enforced labour. And,
of course, the Tate fortune was built up with a lot of plantation labour. I don't
know that much about it, but certainly the sugar fortunes were built up with
plantation labour in the West Indies. So there are quite a lot of links, actually.

*Yes, and I do think that you're one of those artists who, the more we dig into
the work, the more fascinating it becomes. I mean, how satisfied would you
be if people simply glanced at your work and saw it from a purely aesthetic
point of view, rather than finding out what it did actually represent? How
important is it to you that people understand that it really was the Tate
penitentiary, rather than some wonderful leaf-like, petal-like Victorian plan?*
Langlands: I don't think we mind at all. In a way, that's how we started making
our work initially: we were fascinated by buildings, we love the subject, we love
the material we work with. It's a kind of journey of exploration in many ways.
And a lot of our works start off when our attention is just caught by a formal
element, or a typology or some other attribute of a plan or a building. Really,
it's a journey of investigation or discovery. So we don't mind at all if people
just view it in that way. It's entirely up to them. Hopefully, nothing stays the
same: people's interests can change.

*Another way in which you differ from a lot of contemporary art is the well-made
aspect of your work. It's extremely well constructed, it's beautifully finished
and it must take a long time to produce. There's something immaculate about
it, combined with the way it's displayed, on which you also place a great deal
of quite fastidious emphasis. How do you actually go about the process of
working? I'm quite intrigued by the fact that there are two of you at work here.
This is pretty rare. I know – thinking off the top of my head – we have Gilbert
& George, we have Jake & Dinos Chapman working together, but it's not that
common. And most artists would, I think, find it intensely difficult to work with
anybody else. So how do you go about the process of collaboration – if, indeed,
you think of it as collaboration?*
Bell: Yes, we do think of it as a collaboration, but I think initially it comes from
sharing the love of the same subject. We talk a lot about what we're going to do
before we actually make it. We often research a lot as well, so we both have to
feel right and happy before we make a work, you know, because it's going to live
on beyond that time. So we care a lot about making that decision and leading
up to that decision.
Langlands: Yes, as Nikki says, we're continually discussing different things.
If we decide to try and make a work, we look at the material we have and we
gather other material. Although the making of it can be very hard work and

can take quite a long time, that's in a sense only a relatively small part of the whole thing that we're doing. Once we make the decision to do it, then basically we draw it up and we do what's necessary to make it. We just divide the labour between us, and if we need to modify it as we're working on it, we do, and we discuss it and eventually the piece is finished.
Bell: The exciting thing is the transformation, when it's nearing the end, when you can feel it coming together, and then you feel very excited.

I'm sure that's right. And talking of transformation, one of the things that fascinates me about your work is its richness of meanings. It is to do with buildings, out there in the real world occupying a social and political context very often, and it's to do with people usage and all the rest of it. So you root it very much, in one sense. But in another sense, when I look at some of the images that you're exhibiting and presenting to us, it's quite the opposite – it's almost as if you're throwing them up into space and letting them float. Some of the images look like planets oscillating, free-flowing. So that's a very strange kind of double thing going on.
Bell: I think buildings have the power to reverberate over time. Once a building is set in motion, once that plan is there, once that building exists, even if it's demolished those reverberations continue to affect people if it's a significant building or has had an effect. That's why buildings are so important over centuries.
Langlands: Yeah, I think that's very true. There are lots of buildings which have been demolished but which we're aware of, and they are still having an influence on architecture being built today. I think also it goes back to being fascinated by things, and in some ways trying to ask if there is a kind of essence – or asking how they connect to other things. And in a way, part of our strategy is to isolate them and look at things with quite a strong stare. That's true, and it's ironic because, as I was saying earlier, we were intent on creating a context or looking at things within the context, but sometimes, yes, we're removing them from the context. But also that's quite a strong strategy in all art, I think: to relocate elements and to reconnect them.

Mind you, it's actually true to say that this whole notion of things suspended, things being isolated in a void, things travelling through space, does link up with your interest in air travel. Quite a few of your more recent works are looking at the whole imagery of what one is presented with in airports. Maybe it's a change in your art, to do with emphasising more the notion of words, for example, lit up on big screens – circular forms containing codes for airport destinations, and this kind of imagery.
Bell: In a way it links up to buildings as well, the poetry of places.

Sure, but it also invites us to, as it were, travel with you through space.
Bell: We hope so, yeah.

It's quite a releasing thing to look at, I think. Can you talk about those airport destination works which you've been doing?
Langlands: I think one thing is that we're conscious there's a kind of trajectory with architecture, and certainly one of the things we're envisaging with our work is a network, which starts with the individual or a group and moves out to the building and the street and the city and beyond that to the whole world. So it's a kind of route of expansion and connection which is moving ever outwards, if you like.
Bell: I think more and more people are moving between places, and time

has collapsed between places. It's much easier to travel, and so people's notions of time are getting compressed all the time, getting shorter between places in our lifetime, and it is an important subject.

Langlands: It's also again a question of scale and magnification, moving out along that route so that one can indicate cities with three letters. In a way, it's again another kind of template of circulation or movement or connection, so we're very curious about that.

I have a feeling that you might be tempted, particularly in recent years, to move in to the process of designing architectural forms yourself. I know that you're involved at the moment with this extraordinary new development at Paddington Basin, and the notion of designing a bridge. How did that come about?

Langlands: There was an opportunity to design a footbridge over the canal by Paddington Basin as part of this new development, and we were invited to look at it and see if we were interested. We thought it was a great opportunity and something we'd be very interested in doing, so we made a proposal. We're working on it at the moment: we're working with a group of engineers called Atelier 1, and it's just about to go to planning. What we've done is design a very simple structure: it's basically a spine wall which crosses the canal, and suspended off the spine wall is the bridge deck, and cantilevered off it are access ramps and staircases. It's a very minimal blade, if you like, which crosses the water vertically. And it's steel-framed and glass and quite monumental, but in a transparent kind of way.

What do you think that you, as artists, can do with a commission for a footbridge which an architect maybe wouldn't think of doing? Or do you expect that the result will be more or less indistinguishable from something that an architect would have designed?

Langlands: That's a good question [laughs].

Bell: I don't know if it's for us to say, but it'll be very interesting to hear if people think there is a difference. Obviously, it's going to be lit as well, at night, and lighting is also part of our work. We do see lighting as an important element, especially because it brings up the modelling of something and we do feel it's important.

So once lit, it'll be more like the kind of thing that you exhibit in a gallery, anyway, won't it? Or a kind of extension of that.

Bell: In a sense, yeah, it'll be like a light box.

But I wouldn't imagine there'd be much danger of you wanting to encroach permanently on architects' territory. Because you recently applied for, and won, this exciting new commission to do an enormous sculpture – it's so vast that it almost becomes architecture. It's kind of poised between the two states, and it's actually sitting on a piece of architecture, a bridge-like form which is there already, in Sunderland. What was it about this commission that attracted you to trying to propose something? What was it that fired your imaginations, because it's a very dramatic site, isn't it?

Bell: Mmm, initially the site we thought was very interesting. But also the visibility: it has an incredible range of views as you approach it from different angles. But also the bridge itself, being this ancient truncated structure in the middle of this vast urban wasteland.

Very strange.

Bell: Yeah.

*Not that you've tried in any way to replicate either the form or the material
of the bridge. Certainly not the material, because your proposal is to construct
a glass structure.*

Langlands: Yeah, our proposal is a structure in glass and steel. But it does
refer to the site. The site is a sandstone Victorian railway viaduct, which
has been sort of abandoned – it's just a section of it, which is about 60 metres
long on a sloping site by the River Wear. And it fell out of use about thirty
years ago. It's just been left there, and it got listed about ten years ago.
It's a beautiful, monumental relic, and the viaduct, of course, is made
up of a series of arches which support a deck on which these trains used
to run. We proposed a screen or row of four arches, but they're flat arches
made of glass with a steel frame, and – I don't quite know how to describe
it – the columns of the arches, the posts, are set at 45-degree angles off the
horizontal plane, also alternating. So are the beams, and so that makes
a kind of prismatic arrangement of planes. The idea is actually to make
it out of a semi-transparent mirror, so it will be alternately reflective
and transparent. Because it's a screen of arches, it does refer to the site.
But at the same time it's very different.

*One thing that fascinates me about it is that although when constructed it'll be
quite a dominant object, it's not at all oppressive. For one thing it's luminous,
but also it's not conventionally solid like a lot of monumental sculpture. Is this
part of your thinking, to get away from heavy monumentality?*

Bell: Yeah. Glass is a material which we've used a lot in our work and like a lot,
and we discovered that glass in Britain originated first in Sunderland – the first
glass was actually found there. So this was a material to use, as opposed to the
brick below.

*Absolutely. We ought also, I think, to talk about furniture, because that's
another key element in a lot of your installations, whether it's chairs, tables
or curious amalgams of the two. The chairs seem to extend into space, so that
they almost become – well, not tables so much as structures in their own right,
occupying quite a lot of space sometimes. Chairs that fuse together or become
kind of bipolar images. There's a concern running through quite a lot of your
work, over a long period, to do with furniture. How did that originate?*

Langlands: It originated in the found environment that we would reconstruct,
where we'd find abandoned furniture.
Bell: Furniture mediated between the body and the building. It was such a
fundamental aspect that it was something we wanted to develop. When we
first moved to the East End, we were living in the basement of a tenement flat.
And the only work surface we had was this table, so we started making books
on the table, and that was sort of the beginning. But it is essential: a table and
a chair is what you start off from, in your space.
Langlands: Yeah, and when you discover furniture in a building, it records a lot
about the way a building is used. So when you go into a room, it might be empty
of people, but the way the furniture is arranged will say a lot about how the
room is normally used. And, of course, that carries on into public buildings
– it's very explicit there. So we've done quite a lot of work where we've looked
at that, and been fascinated by it.

*Sometimes they're quite disconcerting. I'm thinking in particular of the IMF
table, the table where the IMF hold their doubtless deeply alarming conferences
about the state of the world economy.*

Bell: It's a negotiating table.

Exactly: like something out of Dr Strangelove.
Bell: We love the shape of the table as well.

Yes, I can well imagine.
Bell: It's such an extraordinary shape! We were fascinated by the fact that
it was open at one end and why this was, and was it significant? But then we
found out it was just to let the lady in with the tea trolley to give the delegates
their tea [laughs].

*Another way in which you're developing is to do with installations.
You've always been interested in them, but in recent times you've actually
been penetrating space in a more dramatic way – leading elements through,
round corners, inside tunnels. So you're presenting the viewer with something
much more difficult to pin down, even, than before.*
Bell: I think we're getting more physically involved in the space.

You are, yes.
Bell: We're quite excited about making transformations of spaces at the
moment which you physically enter. That's another aspect, really, which
we're developing right now.

*And you're getting more interested in a tactile experience, shoving people
up against the physical actuality of the work that you're producing.*
Bell: In a way we are, yeah.

So does that mean you're getting less removed, maybe?
Bell: What, more involved? [Laughs.]

Well, I don't know – what do you think?
Langlands: When we started working together and making this work in
the early/mid-1980s – which crystallised in this way we were working with
models and this furniture which we were making ourselves – we were very
determined that it should be non-utilitarian, so that the chairs shouldn't
be sat on or the tables shouldn't be eaten off, or used in that way. Everything
was for contemplation only: we were very determined about that. And
I think we needed to somehow create a certain amount of space around what
we're trying to do, a space in which we could operate, so that we could think
about the structures we were using and not just automatically use them.
Bell: I think by placing a glass top on a chair, and putting a model
underneath it, you are subverting the chair. It looks like a normal chair,
but you realise that there's a model underneath and you're looking down
at this other world.

*And sometimes it's the basement of the National Gallery or something
else really rather surprising that you're inviting people – at least by
implication – to sit on.*
Bell: I think often in basements of galleries or national institutions they're
the works which you don't normally see. So again we're trying to reveal
the structures to people that you don't normally see, if you like.
Langlands: Anyway, maybe we're more relaxed about it now, and more
interested to make things which we can all use.

You certainly like Japan, don't you?
Bell: We love Japan, yeah.

*I think, when I am looking through your work, that there is something distinctly
Japanese about it. A certain kind of economy, a certain love of conciseness, and
even this sense of something purged and clean-cut. The Japanese influence has
spread through so much western art, especially during the course of the twentieth
century, that you're not alone. Do you find yourselves drawn to the kind of art
that may well have been turned on by someone like Hokusai?*

> Langlands: Not especially. Although we don't know that much about
> it, formally speaking, we're conscious of the enormous influence and the
> very big recognition in modernism of Japanese art and architecture.
> Bell: I think they have a different timescale as well. The history of Japanese
> building is so different to ours, which is rooted in history and heritage.
> In Tokyo a building has a maximum life of twenty years, which is almost
> unheard-of here. The land prices are so high that they will destroy the building
> and put another one in its place. They also have earthquakes there, which
> affect the whole way of looking at buildings. It's so different, and interesting
> to us to look at them.

So you have been influenced by the whole Japanese way of handling things?

> Bell: Subliminally, yes. Definitely.
> Langlands: I think we feel quite a strong personal connection to geometric
> abstraction and design in the twentieth century. And, of course, that's been
> influenced by an awareness of Japanese art and architecture, so we're aware
> of it in that way.
> Bell: Also, the Japanese respond to and aren't afraid of beauty, for instance,
> and that's interesting as well. Over here, probably, there is more fear of that:
> an artist is a messy, dirty thing, you know [laughs].

You think we shy away from beauty here?

> Bell: I think so.

Yes, that's probably true.

> Langlands: This is something we're often criticised for.

What do they say?

> Langlands: People remark – it's how you described it earlier – that our work
> often appears purged or detached or precise, and some people think that art
> shouldn't be like that.
> Bell: But actually, you know, we put a lot of love into it as well, and a lot
> of emotion, so when you enter it, it's quite humane.
> Langlands: Basically there are no rules – art can be what you want it to be.

*Absolutely, yes. How did you feel about being included in the context
of the* Sensation *exhibition? What sort of experience was that for you,
in terms of the show?*

> Bell: Our work isn't sensationalist, but we hope that it's quietly sensational
> [laughs].

You had some noisy neighbours in that show – not literally noisy, but visually noisy.

> Langland: Yeah, I think that was interesting.
> Bell: The emphasis was more on the sensationalist aspect of work, so it was
> on the louder works, generally speaking, in the show. We were happy to take
> part and to be there.

Finally, to widen this conversation out, I think myself that there's still too much

*of a division between architecture on the one hand and art on the other.
I often find it very surprising to think about how many architects attempt
to rid themselves of art and artists in their buildings, especially when the
Bauhaus tried so hard to bring things together. So maybe my last question
to you would be whether you feel that lack nowadays – a lack of a greater degree
of dialogue between the two sides, and whether you would like to see much more
active collaboration between architects and artists?*

    Bell: Yeah, I think it's exciting.

    Langlands: And they can be the same people. I mean, there are times when certain energies in culture and society are very particular. The early period of the twentieth century was obviously very important in that respect, especially the period in Russia soon after the Revolution with the developments that happened there in architecture and other visual arts leading to constructivism. I think we're very conscious of that.

    Bell: Architects are becoming less wary of artists, which I think is a good thing. Because up until about ten years ago, there was a real suspicion: people looked down on artists, they didn't want to include them, they were tokens to be added.

Yes, they were too much trouble, weren't they?

    Bell: Absolutely! Whereas now, people are thinking that artists do have something to contribute, and can combine with engineers and developers and the whole process that you go about together. I think it's opening up, I do feel that.

    Langlands: The culture generally at the moment is more open, and the interests of corporate culture have converged in theory much more closely with the interests of art recently. Whether in art and architecture or other spheres, people are not so frightened of artists. So at the moment, corporate culture believes that they've got something to get out of contemporary art, but that could change.

    Bell: At the moment art is fashionable, galleries are full, people want to look at art a lot. So there has been a swing in that respect.

*But corporate culture is not necessarily at all interested in the whole notion of
a genuine collaboration between architects and artists. As it happens, I was very
intrigued yesterday when I went along to a little ceremony at St Mary's Hospital
in Paddington, to celebrate the restoration of some murals that Bridget Riley
executed there around twelve years ago. Because they're on the walls from floor
to ceiling, they've been bashed by hospital traffic one way and another. So the
process of restoration was quite extensive, but it's been done with great love and
care. The people gathered there yesterday were all very committed to the whole
thing – including the hospital staff – and both Bridget Riley and the architect
John Weeks gave little addresses stressing the fact that they had worked together
very closely. John Weeks even went so far as to use the verb 'subsume', not once
but twice, to describe what went on between him as architect and Bridget as
artist. Which quite astonished me, because I didn't think either architects or
artists were particularly interested in going so far as 'subsuming' nowadays.
But there it is: one example, probably a very unusual one, of such a thing
actually having taken place. So maybe it could happen again.*

    Langlands: Yeah, it does happen from time to time, and it's very important to support it when it's possible to do it. I think those initiatives and that support should come from wherever they can, whether they come from architects or artists or developers or whoever has some influence and leverage in the situation.

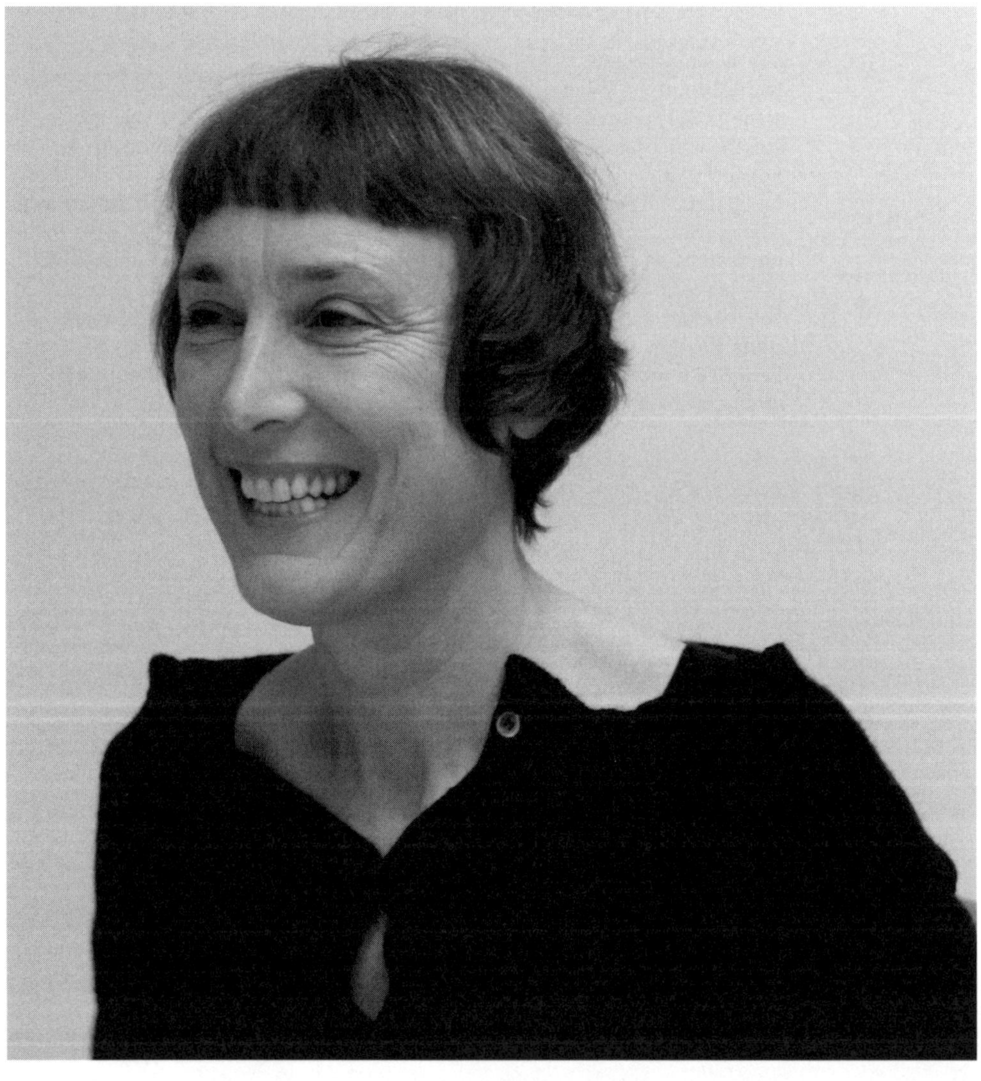

2012

Cornelia Parker

'I've been fighting these dark thoughts, which have been with me since I was a child, but I'm making sense of them through the work, trying to overcome it and project my optimistic side'

Visitors to the 1997 Turner Prize exhibition were confronted by your arresting installation. Deftly and poetically, you suspended in a vertical downpour the scorched fragments of a Texas Baptist church struck by lightning. But many of your major works are the outcome of destruction initiated by the artist. In 1988 you asked a steamroller driver to flatten 1,000 pieces of silverware carefully laid out in a curving line. Then you picked them up and set about making a spectacular installation from the squashed remains.

Your most celebrated work, Cold Dark Matter: An Exploded View, *is even more dramatic. With expert help from the British army, you blew up a shed whose shattered contents were then transformed into a suspended masterpiece, which threw shadows on the surrounding walls. But aggression is always countered by dry humour in your work. And the fragments in* Cold Dark Matter: An Exploded View *achieve an alternative beauty of their own as they float and spin, like something resurrected, in the air. The outcome could hardly be more removed in impact from another controversial work you made in 2003, for an exhibition at Tate Britain. It was called, very intriguingly,* The Distance (A Kiss with String Attached). *And you had the audacity to wrap Rodin's monumental carving* The Kiss *in no less than a mile of string, to 'capture the moment of erotic poignancy'. But destruction lies at the centre of your work, and the idea surfaced quite early in your career. I remember you telling me once about a piece you made way back in the Orwellian year of 1984. It was an eerily prophetic image of major world monuments drowned in a gutter.*

Including the Empire State Building.

Yes. Where does your sense of apocalypse come from, do you think?

I think I've always had a very vivid, dark imagination. As a child, I was a loner, fearful, shy and introverted.

Oh, were you? I would never guess, knowing you now. You don't seem fearful or shy at all.

No, perhaps it's because I've been making art for a long time, and it's helped me bring out my more extrovert side. My outlook on life has always been a bit doom-laden. I've been fighting these dark thoughts, which have been with me since I was a child, but I'm making sense of them through the work, trying to overcome it and project my optimistic side.

Where do you think the dark thoughts come from, or is that too personal a question?

I think perhaps, as children, you have dark thoughts naturally.

Well, we all do to a certain extent, yes, but it sounds as if you had darker thoughts than most?

I'm sure we've all been there. I grew up in the countryside, in quite an isolated spot, with a mother who was German and an English father. When I was about five, before she became mentally ill, my mother used to read to my sisters and I, *Grimms' Fairy Tales* from a very old German copy, vividly illustrated with scary images. I don't know if you know Straw Peter's cruel cautionary tales, another book she would read, they could induce fear in any child's heart. My mother said he would come along and chop off our thumbs with a pair of scissors if we didn't stop sucking them. So I grew up with all that.

Those stories obviously ignited your imagination. Did she read them to you in German?

She did, which I understood when I was an infant, and now I don't understand a single thing. It's very bizarre! I think I became prejudiced against Germans when I was around five and started primary school. It was in the early 1960s, when the Second World War was still a recent memory, and other children poked fun at me and called me a Nazi.

Did they really? Because your mum was German?
Yes, obviously that wouldn't happen now – well, but who knows? But it did at that time. I was not happy with the fact that I was half-German: I was kind of keeping quiet about it, but that was hard being called Cornelia, rather than Alison or Jennifer, which were my sisters' names – I got the more German-sounding name. It's not very popular in this country, in fact I have only just met someone with the same name as me. So when I was a child I was really wishing I was called Anne or Janet [laughs]. So I might have cultivated this vivid imagination because of the guilt of being half-German or perhaps because my father was a very larger-than-life, dramatic character. I might have inherited my drama from him rather than my mother.

And he wasn't anything to do with art, your dad?
No, he was a peasant, in the proper sense of the world. I'm not joking: he worked on the land, and his father had worked on the land. He worked on land that belonged to the Queen. We lived in a tithed Tudor cottage, where his father had been born, and his grandfather before him.

Was this in Cheshire?
In rural south Cheshire. He worked on the land for the Duchy of Lancaster, planting trees and laying hedges. So he was always working with his hands, and not really that educated.

So you must have roamed about quite a lot when you were little.
That's an understatement!

And I can see you, feeding your gothic imagination as you're walking through those woods.
Yes. I spent a lot of time walking, a lot of time climbing trees. But I also spent my childhood working very hard, because we had a smallholding to maintain and we were pretty poor. I was the middle one of three daughters, and the surrogate son [laughs]. As far as my father was concerned, I was a boy that he never had. The Christmas presents I received were things like a wheelbarrow, wellies, tools, not too many dolls. He ignored the fact that I was a girl, and trained me up to help on the smallholding. Playing wasn't on the cards. I wasn't really allowed time to play. There were too many chores like mucking out the pigs, brushing the yards, tying up the tomato plants, all that kind of stuff. Part of me really liked that, but also I badly wanted to play. So I would escape, go off down the fields and go AWOL! I'd steal time and disappear into my own imaginative world. So I think the practice of sculpture might be me going AWOL [laughs].

Did you draw a lot when you were little?
I did, children draw all the time – my daughter, who is eleven, she's constantly drawing. So I drew a lot.

And your drawings tended to be quite grim, with a double 'm'?
Fairy-tale images?
Very Arthur Rackham-ish [laughs]. Arthur Rackham was somebody I loved when I was twelve, but now I can't bear him!

*You mentioned the early 1960s and being at school. There was a moment then
– which I remember so vividly and I'm sure you do – when we were confronted
by the Cuba crisis, and what we thought was the end of the world.*
> I was six then.

Of course, so you were a little bit too young.
> But at six you're thinking about the end of the world, and I'm still thinking
> about the end of the world. It's still a possibility: I haven't ruled it out
> as subject matter.

The first piece of yours that really knocked me out was Thirty Pieces
of Silver, *which I saw in the 1990 British Art Show. All those pummelled
silverware pieces, flattened by the steamroller, were suspended from
the gallery ceiling.*
> The pools of silver were shown quite close together in the British Art Show,
> in the grand downstairs room of the Hayward Gallery.

*And I thought it was very poignant, surprising and dramatic, because
what you had done, it seemed to me, was rob them of their original identity
and give them an unlikely new life.*
> I'd robbed them of having any kind of worth in terms of value to someone.

Certainly!
> They were trashed, basically, and then resurrected again. I suspended them
> to hover just above the ground, to replace the volume they once had. The
> steamroller was only ten tons, and I really wanted them to be flatter. But
> it was still pretty brutal, so it broke them into bits. I'd shown it at the Ikon
> Gallery in Birmingham in 1989, and it didn't get a single review. There was
> an enthusiastic audience but it didn't get any media coverage. And I thought:
> 'Oh, that's it! It's never going to be shown again – I might as well throw it
> away.' I remember writing to a few galleries in London to see if they would
> exhibit it, and getting polite letters back saying: 'I'm sorry.' I remember
> writing to Andrea Schlieker, then a curator at the Serpentine, saying:
> 'I've got quite a big piece here, I'd like to show it in London.' It was very
> naive of me [laughs]. And she wrote: 'Oh, we would prefer to commission
> an artist from scratch.' Anyway, I did show it at the Serpentine a few years later
> in my solo show there. It's funny that I've ended up showing it in all the places
> that turned it down originally.

That's right. And the biblical title, Thirty Pieces of Silver, *does of course
suggest that you associated all those gleaming goblets and teapots,
or whatever they once were, with greed and betrayal?*
> They were only cheap silver-plated objects with vague ambitions of being
> grand. There was all kinds of stuff – I remember a lot of friends giving me
> their wedding presents, including Antonia Payne who was Director of the
> Ikon at the time. She was the one who commissioned the piece.

*So you persuaded other people to give you their wedding presents, which
you then destroyed? How come they were willing to do that?*
> Well, I'm not sure, perhaps they were unwanted presents, but they all seemed
> very keen.

This strikes me as quite bizarre, actually.
> Obviously they got some perverse pleasure out of seeing their things smashed.

Whoa!

But what I liked about the squashing was that it united all these objects in one tragi-comic event and gave them a common history, as well as having their disparate histories. They all met their demise on a lonely road getting smashed by a steamroller. And the steamroller driver enjoyed it.

Where did you find him?

I got him through the Steamroller Association. It was November, I remember, and almost everybody had stripped down their steamrollers for the winter. So I was trying to find someone within the radius of London whose steamroller was still working. And this guy had his own scrapyard, and luckily he also had a concrete road: you can't just squash silver onto tarmac because it is too soft and it would become embedded – which would be very nice, but wouldn't have helped me with the show [laughs]. So he said: 'Yeah, we've got a concrete road, and we haven't stripped down our steamroller yet. Yes, please come along – I'm very keen, very keen!' And when I arrived with a few friends, he'd invited a few of his friends and their families, so about thirty people turned up, with sandwiches and cameras. So it became a kind of performance by default.

But did they think you were mad?

Somehow, no.

Because Brits often think that artists are mad, don't they?

Yes, but steamroller drivers, all they want to do really is squash stuff. So then it was like a dream come true, that some person would come up with all this stuff and he would squash it. They were very keen and happy, and believe it or not, the guy who drove the steamroller had been an extra in a *Carry On* film dressed in drag as Barbara Windsor.

Cornelia, you're making all this up! [Laughter.]

No, it's true. He said that he'd had a little glimpse of fame because he'd been in a Barbara Windsor film, dressed up as her, and driven over a bike or something. He was really up for it, so it was just finding the right person. Part of the saga of making new work for me is finding the right person to help, because very often I'm asking somebody else to help.

But they must have asked: 'What are you going to do with the squashed and flattened victims?' And what did they say, when you explained that you were going to exhibit the remains in an art gallery?

I told them I was going to resurrect the pieces, and I don't think they really minded what happened. They just enjoyed the process. And I think the process, for me, is what a lot of the work is about. You know, the work is obviously the next stage along the line, but the process for me is pretty important. But not only the destructive part of the process, but also the restoration: I suspended every single broken piece on wires, and actually when I first did that, I thought: 'I'll just drop the wires down and tie the stuff on.' But I realised that if I got a squashed plate, it's got to have four points, and therefore you have to have a plan for it. So I made these very rough plans. I cut thirty pieces of paper out and put all these objects on them, and spent about five minutes in each pool, drawing round them. Now the Tate owns the piece, they've still got the same plans that I made, and they've made beautiful drawers for every piece with its own negative shape cut out of foam.

So they are very carefully looking after all the things
that you, wilfully …
> … destroyed! But in terms of sculpture, you can see all the work embedded
> in it. All the endeavour is visibly recorded, because of the wires, you can see
> all the time it's taken to build. Whereas, with a carved wooden sculpture, you
> can't see all the strokes that have gone into it, because the surface that remains
> at the end is the last surface. But I quite like the idea of somehow being able
> to log all those hours, just to say: 'Look, I've worked really hard!'

But would you go so far as to say that you were, on one level at least, mocking
the whole notion of prized, middle-class wedding presents?
> Er, yes.

So you were being satirical?
> A little satirical. But that wasn't the only thing, really.

No, no.
> When I made this piece I had a tiny budget, so I bought the cheapest silver
> plate I could find – they were simulacra, signifiers for something wealthy.
> It wasn't really that these things cost lots of money, but it's what they aspired
> to, what they symbolised that I was more interested in.

So what proportion of them were gifts from friends?
> Not that many – about 5 per cent.

Oh, I see.
> And the rest I bought from car boot sales: they were all used, they weren't
> new. They'd all been prized objects at some point, but then people let them
> go, we just litter our lives with stuff. I was just helping get rid of it all – not
> realising that it'd end up in a museum and be added to the other end of the
> food chain. At the time I made this, I had just met a tree surgeon in the Forest
> of Dean when I was doing a residency, and he said he'd got a steamroller.
> And that's what started the idea off – I thought: 'Oh, wow, somebody who
> owns a steamroller! Perhaps I can find something to squash!'

Now I also want to pursue this title, because it does interest
me a lot. Thirty Pieces of Silver *is a very, very pointed title*
indeed. And you wanted people to recognise the biblical
reference, did you?
> Yes, definitely, it was a found title. I was brought up as a Catholic, now lapsed,
> but it was very much part of my childhood – all these biblical stories that embed
> themselves into, became part of the vocabulary, and still is. I've just been
> in Jerusalem, and the last couple of days I spent visiting the Garden of
> Gethsemane, which is where Judas betrayed Christ for thirty pieces of silver.
> So I've finally returned to the scene of the crime, literally.

You have, yes. For the first time?
> No, I've been three times to Jerusalem this year, because I'm working on a show
> there. But curator Jonathan Watkins and I went to another garden, very close
> to the Garden of Gethsemane, and it was on a Palm Sunday and I picked up this
> rock. But in the real Garden of Gethsemane you can't steal any rocks because
> it's all penned off, and it's got all these warning signs telling you what not to
> do in the Garden of Gethsemane. Don't betray Christ! But there was no sign
> for that – so that's obviously why it happened! [Laughs.]

*What is your attitude towards organised religion in general? I ask that
question not only because of the thirty pieces but also because your Turner
Prize installation in 1997 was dominated by the remnants of this hapless
Texan church devastated by lightning.*

I was in Texas at the time, and I was working on this series of works which were
about killing things off – things falling off cliffs, things being steamrollered,
being blown up, being stretched or drowned. And finding things that had been
struck by lightning was something I wanted to do. They have hugely dramatic
storms in Texas. So the likelihood of things being struck by lightning there
seemed to be greater. So I thought: 'I'm going to Texas, I shall look out for
things being struck by lightning.' I alerted lots of people, like the fire brigade
and lightning protection people and just generally people who might keep their
antennae … I was only there for a few days, and I got this phone call from a guy
who was a fireman. He told me that a church had been struck by lightning
in a town 13 miles south. So I was like an ambulance chaser. I went and got
my pick-up truck, drove down there, went to see the minister and asked him
if I could have some of the remains of the church for a piece of work.

How badly had it been damaged?

It had been razed to the ground, and they'd taken away the crucifix that had
fallen from the spire, which was a shame. But looking at the rubble, the thing
I was drawn to most was the charcoal. So I asked them if I could have that.
Then I resurrected the church.

So was the charcoal still hot?

Warmish. The idea of the piece I wanted to create being called *Mass* came
to mind when I was actually picking up the charcoal. I made several trips
with someone else to help, a Texan artist from San Antonio, who had offered
to come and help me pick up the church pieces. I thought it was quite sweet,
us gathering this church together, especially as we got married a year or so after.

*You're very hands-on as an artist. You like to get involved and
actually do things.*

It's about being hands on, physically touching stuff.

Some artists don't – they're quite removed, aren't they?

I can rely a lot on the expertise and experience of whoever's helping me, like
the army, for example. I like to be out and about, doing stuff on the hoof. I'm
not at all interested in spending years in the studio perfecting a technique.
I want to try lots of different things. And the idea of using natural disasters,
as well as disasters I have orchestrated myself, seems quite compelling to me.

Absolutely.

They call it 'an act of God' when things get struck by lightning. I talked to the
minister at the church and I said: 'What about this fire being an "act of God"?'
And he replied: 'Oh, I think God wanted me to have a better church!'

So it wasn't God damning them for doing something wrong?

He could have construed it that way, because that was what I was wondering,
but because of his unshakeable belief he interpreted it as being positive.
The church had a white congregation, and when I was there picking up the
remains of the church, about four or five guys came with another pick-up truck
and began measuring up the site. They told me they were church builders,
a group of retired guys, a plumber, a carpenter, an architect and an engineer.

They went round Texas building churches. And I said: 'Wow! Does that mean you get struck by lightning all the time?' And they said: 'No, they're usually black congregation churches that get burned down, as racist hate crimes.' I was rather horrified by this and thinking: 'If I'd had enough time, it would have been great to make a diptych to this called *Anti-Mass*, using the remains of an arsoned church.' Which is what I did.

Yes, that was eight years later, in 2005.
Using the charcoal from an arsoned church, in Kentucky.

Which had a black congregation?
Yes, bikers would drive up on the porch of the church and rev up their engines to disrupt the services. It was an elderly congregation, quite small, and they would intimidate them, they would drown them out. Then gradually, they started to decamp to people's houses to have their masses, and the church got torched by these hell's-angels guys.

So it was an arson attack?
A deliberate arson, sadly one of many. I've had a Google Alert for arsoned churches for years, and they come in regularly, perhaps two or three a month. They're usually in the southern states of America, not anywhere else in the world. And it's still going on now, it's not a thing that gets talked about.

But it hasn't stopped?
It hasn't stopped – it just carries on.

I don't think that, over here, we do realise it.
It's quite extraordinary. So I had a show in San Francisco in 2005 where I borrowed back the original church, *Mass*, which was in a museum in Arizona, and I showed it alongside this new church, *Anti-Mass*. The white congregation church was destroyed by an act of God, and the black congregation one was destroyed by an act of man. I thought of them as two giant three-dimensional charcoal drawings, silhouetted against a white wall.

Yes, absolutely.
The formality of the way I show suspended work is usually determined by what the thing was before. So the churches took on the form of an architectural cube. If it is flattened, it's usually hovering near the floor, or over a surface. I often think about my work in terms of drawing.

I tend to think of you first and foremost as a sculptor. But looking at these images now, the first thing I thought of was paint thrown into space.
Well, I've always been drawn to the abstract expressionists.

You must have liked Jackson Pollock when you were quite young.
I'm not sure – I don't like him very much, I don't mind the work looking painterly, though. It is exploring the idea of things hovering between abstraction and representation. I take very representational things like a church or a house or a silver spoon or a famous monument like Niagara Falls or a souvenir of the Empire State Building. Taking something that's very clichéd, ubiquitous, a part of society, and then I try and reduce it to an abstraction. Unlike minimalist art, where they use the most simple units of raw material, trying to get away from the idea of representation or content. So with my churches you get this black cube that can be read as expressionist,

or minimalist, but then you read the titles and realise it has this specific
content. It's not a drawing of a church that's been arsoned: it is the church that's
been arsoned, so I'm using the church itself as itself. So everything's dead literal.
It is what it is, hopefully liberating the viewer to create their own metaphors.
I was brought up at art school with this ethos about 'truth to materials', which
is using a material for what it does best. When you're carving in wood you've
got to go with the wood-grain, rather than trying to make it do something
it won't naturally do. So in some ways I'm behaving like a traditional sculptor,
using things for their own qualities. I often use a found object which already
has its own history, and by adding another layer, I'm transforming it into
something else.

So you wouldn't deny, in one sense, being a sculptor?
Oh, no.

*And when you were at art school, did you think of yourself primarily
as a sculptor?*
I wanted to be a painter but wasn't very good at it. I reluctantly moved into
the sculpture department and realised it was my true home. I think I'm edging
nearer to painting now through my sculpture. It's so funny – the *Mass* piece,
the church struck by lightning, was in a show called *Post Mark: An Abstract
Effect*, which was all about taking painting to the edges of what painting can
be. There was this big symposium about 'Abstraction', and somebody put their
hand up and said: 'But your work's not abstract!' I said: 'It's the curator that
has put me in this show about abstraction, so it's up to you. Without the
caption, my work appears abstract, but with the caption ...'

If viewers wandered into Anti-Mass *without the caption, they wouldn't
know that it was the result of a deplorable, malicious attack.*
No, but they'd know something bad had happened. What's interesting about
the Texan church struck by lightning, because its frame was made of lots of
2 x 2 wood, the charcoal was all very delicate and ethereal-looking, made up
of hundreds of small pieces. But the other church from Kentucky was Victorian
and built entirely out of wooden clapboard, so the debris was made up of these
big heavy timbers. There were no little pieces, so although I was trying to use
the wood in an identical way to *Mass*, it turned out to be very different. So
Anti-Mass is much more strident and angry than the other, just because of the
size and shape of the available wood. It was just by chance that was the case,
that's what I mean by 'truth to materials'.

But in the piece that really made your name, Cold Dark Matter: An Exploded
View *– a great title – you were the one, effectively, who blew up the garden shed,
although you very sensibly got professional assistance from the British army.*
It was the first show Jonathan Watkins and I worked on together. He's a curator
extraordinaire: if anyone's aspiring to be a curator, this is the man to watch!
He was the Director of the Chisenhale Gallery in 1991, and asked me if I'd like
to do a show there – it was a big black box, no windows. I wanted to use
something with a light as part of the piece, and he'd just laid a lovely new
concrete floor, and he said: 'What would you like to do?' And I said: 'I'd like
to blow up something in your space.' He said: 'Oh, my new floor!' [Laughs.]

So it was simple, really!
Well, why not? But then we realised we couldn't obviously, because there
were studios above and artists would be complaining. Then I thought:

'What do I want to blow up?' And I thought: 'Well, I'd love to blow up a house, but that would be impossible.' So I thought the garden shed could become a surrogate for the house – in that it's full of all the overspill of stuff you normally have in a home. So we assembled the garden shed and contents in the gallery with a light on inside it, and photographed it prior to the explosion. Then Jonathan showed his diplomatic skills by talking to the army with the idea of getting sponsorship. We were invited along to visit them at the Army School of Ammunition in Banbury to discuss the idea, not knowing if they would say yes. Then before we knew it, they were blowing up a car for us. One of the majors, an Arnie Schwarzenegger type, said: 'Well, if you put a pig in the car, that would be a real simulation of what would happen in a terrorist attack.' So they were very gung-ho about showing us their skills. But one of the other officers, Major Hewitt, was much more sensitive and really got into the idea. So on a later trip we took the shed and all the contents out to the ammunition grounds, where they blow things up. We modelled the Semtex, plastic explosives which hung inside the shed, and then I got to press the button. There were all these Kenyan soldiers who were there doing exercises and watching us, and the sergeant said: 'Yeah, this is a British sort of ritual – we blow up one of these sheds every so often, it's like a tea ceremony or something.' I think they had a lot of fun with it, the army! But what I do love about working with people who are not from the art world, you get a real creative friction that goes on, which I think is interesting. A testing of prejudices. They're probably thinking: 'Art – what a waste of money!' And perhaps I bring to the table my own preconceptions about the armed forces. Somehow, that's a very fertile locking of horns, and both sides usually enjoy the process.

I'm wondering about your childhood in this respect as well, because when you said 'garden shed', my mind went right back to the young Cornelia in the countryside.
Plotting to blow up her father! [Laughs.]

Well, with the Grimms' Fairy Tales, *possibly spending a lot of time on your own, in your own garden shed?*
We didn't really have a garden shed – we just had outbuildings, barns and stuff. But Yinka Shonibare said to me, a few weeks ago at the Tate, he said: 'Your shed was all about blowing up the male domain, wasn't it? Was it anti-men?' And I said: 'Oh god, I need some therapy, I haven't sorted that one out!'

Can I ask you what the shed actually did contain?
It contained all kinds of things you normally have in a garden shed – it had a bike, old tins of paint, tools, it had a pram ...

A pram?
Yeah, from my next-door neighbour's garden shed in Leytonstone, where I lived. I got all my friends to donate stuff from their sheds: a bit like wedding presents. Some of my next-door neighbours had moved away and left the pram. I blew it up, and then they had twins a few months later and said: 'Where's that pram?' [Laughs.] But in the end they were very pleased that I'd used it as part of a now famous artwork. There were parts of a scooter, tools, lots of books and there was a big box of curlers I'd got from Walthamstow car-boot sale – because every stall-holder in car-boot sales sells the contents of their sheds.

When I actually look at Cold Dark Matter, *my eyes are always caught not only by the fragments themselves but also by these extraordinary shadows which the fragments cast on the walls all round the installation. There is this dialogue*

between solid things, even though they're very fragmented, and things that
you can't actually touch – things that are, again, almost painterly images
cast on the walls. And the shadows seem to have as much vitality as the solid
objects when I'm encountering this piece.

I like the fact that the viewer is standing in between the shadow and the shed.

Fair enough.

You're caught in between, and then you become part of the piece. I was so
pleased about the shadows, because I didn't expect them, somehow. I thought
of the light bulb having all this stuff formalised around it – small, medium,
large objects and then the wooden walls of shed, and that it would blot out all
the light. It would be very dark. I was trying to describe this thing called 'Cold
Dark Matter', which is a scientific name for all the stuff out there in the universe
that they know is there, but can't quantify. So when the shadows proved to
be so dramatic, that was a wonderful bonus. It appeared as if the fragments had
reanimated themselves, like the shed was unexploding and reconstituting itself.
That's the way things can often work out. I quite like working under pressure,
building things in an exhibition space to a deadline. You haven't too much time
to waste prevaricating about how things should look. You just do it swiftly,
intuitively and instinctively. And I think that's when my best work comes
out – when I'm under pressure.

So can you remember the moment when you thought, 'I must put a very
strong light right in the middle of this'?

Well, very early on. Because that was the very first thing I thought of, the
light bulb.

That was the first idea?

Yes. Because the gallery was a big black box, I knew that I wanted light to be
in it. So it was almost the centre of the universe, or the centre of the explosion,
the big bang or whatever. I quite liked the idea of *Cold Dark Matter* sounding
like a personal matter, something like a dark deed or a dark thought.

You're actually very interested in words: you're quite literary. Do you read
a lot, in the wake of Grimms' Fairy Tales?

I do read a lot and love literature. In fact, if I hadn't done art I would have
done literature.

That doesn't surprise me.

It's my second love. Failed writer, failed painter [laughs]. I've got this book
coming out next year with Thames & Hudson, a monograph, and I've written
short extended captions about each work in the book, 22,000 words in all!
It made me appreciate how hard it is to write.

Very few artists would do that.

In their right mind!

Richard Hamilton did it.

Oh, he was much more academically inclined than me. But I found it was
a very good way of processing stuff.

Can we just pursue, for a moment anyway, this notion of death? Because
I remember, when I visited your Serpentine Gallery show in 1998, I was
very aware that you had a preoccupation with death. One of the installations,

called Another Matter, was dominated by a coffin lid leaning against the
far wall, which you'd obtained from an undertaker in Brazil soon after suffering
a serious car accident.

I had the idea before the car accident. I shattered my pelvis, so I ended up
in hospital for six weeks, and then spent three months in bed getting over
it. Then I went out to be part of the São Paulo Biennale: I was going to make
a new work out there, and I knew I wanted to make a piece with a coffin.
Talking about these cliché things – the house, the pearl necklace, the silver
spoon – the coffin seemed to be the ultimate clichéd object. It's got more
or less the same shape wherever you are in the world, and we all have to
negotiate it at some point in our lives.

And, of course, a coffin is incredibly sculptural.

It is, and I wanted to somehow break it apart, to see what it was made of,
metaphorically as well as physically. So I used a hammer and chisel to break
down the coffin into lots of splinters. I decided to make the splinters into
matches by going to a Brazilian match factory and dipping them in match
material. What I do not like about this piece is my decision to leave the frame
of the coffin lid intact. At this point in my work it was still important for
me that the viewer recognised what the object was that I was destroying.
It was enough of a marker having the metal handles of the coffin intact.
So after that, I felt liberated and got rid of the object altogether, letting
go completely, and allowing things to be completely abstract. Months before,
when I was in hospital delirious with the effects of morphine, I decided
that I didn't want to make a piece with a coffin any more after having such
a near-death experience. The British Council phoned me up and said:
'We've got a couple of undertakers for you to see in Brazil, where you can
go and buy a coffin.' I said: 'The last thing I want to do is to see undertakers,
I've gone off the idea.' And they said: 'You can't go off the idea! You can't be
ruled by fear! You're British!'

Is that what they said?

They were right. I should rule the work rather than it ruling me. I don't think
anything could have cured my post-traumatic stress better than me picking
apart a coffin. I worked in a studio in São Paulo for a few weeks with all these
Brazilian artists. When they saw me with this coffin, chiselling away in a
corner, they were all completely blown away by it. They were mostly painters,
and they came over and they were all very excited. It felt really good – a real
ice-breaker.

But what about the fact that the whole work seems about to ignite?

Well, it's actually safety-match material – otherwise the whole thing would
have gone up within the first thirty seconds. I wanted to communicate the idea
that all these thousands of different-sized matches had the potential for a life
and death of their own. Instead of being about darkness, the piece was going
to be about light. It's a curious work, normally you would only buy a coffin when
some loved one has died, and then you're not really thinking about it. The idea
of doing a pre-emptive strike, by dismantling it, somehow defuses fear.

So it was quite therapeutic.

Sometimes I think quite a lot of the work is about me trying to keep a grip
on things.

Yes, yes. And in the same show at the Serpentine in 1998 you also

exhibited Room for Margins, *a series of canvases taken from the back
of paintings by Turner.*
> Yes, all his works were double-stretched, as it was common practice then.
> Artists would stretch up two layers of canvas and then only paint on the
> top surface. So the canvases that I displayed had lain as a support underneath
> his paintings for about 150 years, having acquired this wonderful patina from
> having their backs to the wall. I gave them the titles of the paintings they were
> backs of – like *Rough Sea with Wreckage* or *Venice at Sunset*.

Or Richmond Hill at Dawn.
> Yes, that kind of thing. So you've got these dramatic or evocative titles, and
> you're looking at these faded pieces of canvas. They had accrued Rothko-like
> stains, the shadows left by the stretcher bars, and tidemarks made by a flood
> in 1927 at the Tate.

A very disastrous flood.
> The Tate had kept blotting paper, which they used to salvage Turner pastel
> drawings which had got soaked. The paper bore beautiful offset prints from
> the Turners, and looked like washy abstracts. So I exhibited a set of those, too.
> I'd just borrowed them from the Conservation Department at the Tate for the
> Serpentine show, and they would just go back there after. I thought: 'Oh, I
> would really love for the piece to remain intact so it could be exhibited again in
> the future.' The only way I could do that was for it to become a piece of my work.
> So I wrote this very cheeky letter to Nick Serota, saying: 'Could I possibly
> acquisition this piece for the Modern Collection at the Tate as a piece of my
> work, and not as Turner's, please?' And so, after plenty of wrangling between
> the various departments at the Tate, that's what happened – now they're my
> works in the Tate rather than in the drawers of the Conservation Department.
> My husband Jeff jokingly said: 'You can call this piece Turner-Over!'

*You mentioned Rothko, and quite understandably, because they're like
melancholy Rothko-esque images. So he might be important to you, Rothko?*
> Turner's more important to me than Rothko.

Why is that?
> Because Turner is one of my favourite artists.

I don't think that he would leap to the minds of people who knew your work.
> Yes, I know, but I love the way his work gradually became more impressionistic,
> more abstract. His were some of the first works I knew as a child, we had prints
> on the wall of *The Fighting Temeraire* and the *Snow Storm*. They have an
> intensity which I really liked.

And, of course, destruction?
> And destruction. There's a great one of a big rock falling on a tiny shepherd's
> hut, right up my street!

Oh yes, that must have been a major influence!
> Huge! I don't dislike Rothko, but Turner really does it for me every time.
> The later works, the more abstract works.

*But what we're also looking at here, apart from Turner and Rothko, is to do with
dirt and damage.*
> And neglect – not being looked at, hence the title *Room for Margins*.

Yes, but I want to pursue dirt. I think dirt is very important to you, Cornelia.
Oh, dirt is, actually.

*You're absolutely fascinated by the kind of detritus which most of us would
shy away from in everyday life. You very much admire Man Ray's photograph,
taken in 1920, called* Dust Breeding. *It's a photograph of Marcel Duchamp's
iconic* Large Glass, *which is shown covered with dust in Duchamp's own studio.*
It lay under his bed for a long time.

Why do you like this so much?
Well, I love the idea of not working, and neglect, allowing dust to settle on an
idea. I love the gestation period in Duchamp's work. That he might work on
something over a long period of time. I think I do that myself – not in the same
way as Duchamp, but things can mull away for a long time and then finally
insist itself when it absolutely has to be made. I love this idea that Duchamp
and Man Ray could celebrate neglect and dust. The first time I saw this
photograph, I just could not work out what it was. I thought perhaps it was an
aerial photograph of the Nazca Lines in Peru. It's totally fascinating and elusive
as an image. It's extraordinary, it's one of my top ten favourite artworks.

*I'm not surprised, and you also made a homage to that photograph with the
Chinati Foundation, down at the Don Judd Museum in Marfa, Texas – yes,
Texas coming back again in your work.*
Well, I married a Texan. When I met my husband, we went on a trip to
the Chinati Foundation. It's an old air-force base, where Donald Judd used
the huge aircraft hangars to make works in. Every year the Foundation invites
an artist to make a print to give to their main benefactors, and they asked
me. The major sculpture of Judd's there is 100 untitled works, large square
constructions made in aluminium, which are really sublime. So I asked if
they'd clean them for me.

Because they were covered in dust?
Inevitably they collect dust, so they're cleaned regularly. I asked them to keep
the dust and send it to me. I scanned it on a scanner – a whole bag of stuff,
insects, wasps, sand blown in from the desert, feathers and goodness knows
what. So I liked the idea that all this wild life was settling on minimalism.
I'm sure the patrons, who obviously love Judd and his aesthetic, were not
expecting this! I can't help being cheeky sometimes.

But didn't the Chinati Foundation suspect you of subversive motives?
I hope they happily embraced it. The piece I made was called *Dust Breeding
(on Judd)*. I made another one called *The Fly that Died on Judd*. Just a scan
of a bluebottle fly with no legs, I liked the fact that it looked like a face. But it
was just too minimalist, so I thought I'd give them the other one.

So is this your critique of the minimalist aesthetic?
I love minimalism.

So you're not saying: 'Come off it, minimalism!'
Oh no, I'm just jealous, because I can't do it. So I might as well embrace
my gothic senses, but heavily hint that I like minimalism.

But it really is gothic, because it's teeming – it's just extraordinary.
It's just a humble fly, but it happened to die on Judd. At the time I was collecting

spiders which had died in famous spaces, like in the Tower of London or in
the Alamo. I told Rob Weiner, who was the Director of the Chinati Foundation,
about my collection. And he showed me this huge tarantula that died in an
Ilya Kabakov piece in there at the Foundation. But I was horrified and said:
'Aargh, no, that's far too big!' Because I tend to put my spiders in glass slides
and project them. But he sent it to me anyway in the post, so I got this huge
tarantula, which I had in the fridge forever, and then my flatmate threw it out.
He objected to having to look at this tarantula every day. I was very relieved,
because I didn't know what to do with it. The burden was too great!

So your flatmate said: 'Cornelia, enough!'
Enough!

*Maybe your most disturbing and controversial intervention in another artist's
work isn't Don Judd, but what happened in 2003, when you had the audacity
to wrap Rodin's sculpture* The Kiss *in a whole mile of string for an exhibition
at Tate Britain.*
It was for the Tate Triennale 2003. When there used to be only one Tate, before
it became a franchise, Rodin's *The Kiss* used to sit in the prime spot, which was
the rotunda. It was always there when I visited. And then it was moved to Tate
Modern when it opened, but this is not really a modern work of art.

Yes, it's not Rodin at his most adventurous.
No, it's just a separated-out part of something much more complex, and on
its own it somehow became too idealised, too romantic. But then it's the most
well-loved sculpture in Britain, perhaps because it seems to celebrate romantic
love. I love Rodin, but I also love Duchamp – such opposites, one retinal and
the other non-retinal. So somehow I thought it would be great to put the two
together. Instead of calling it *The Kiss*, I called it *The Distance*. It was an echo
of what Duchamp did with his mile of string – he draped it all over a surrealist
exhibition in 1942 and he messed everybody else's work up. It was a very
mischievous act. So I wrapped *The Kiss* with string, working closely with the
Tate Conservation Department. Hence the way it's draped around the body.
I wasn't allowed to tie it really tight, except around the heads where protective
tissue could be concealed by the string. So the process was a kind of 'truth
to materials' – I was going with the flow.

Did you have to persuade the Tate staff a lot before they agreed to do it?
Well, after my working with the Painting Conservation Department, on the
backs of Turner paintings, they were a bit worried that I was going to ask for
The Kiss to be re-accessioned in the same way. I was thinking of writing a letter
to Nick Serota, just as a joke. But just as well I didn't, as there was a big
brouhaha in the press when this piece was shown.

You bet.
It was only wrapped for the duration of the exhibition. When they first unveiled
this sculpture in 1904, in Lewes, the public couldn't take it: they thought it was
too lewd, and so it was covered with tarpaulins for two years.

So you were referring back to that, in a way, as well.
I was withholding it again. That which is withheld can be much more
erotic than something that's not. Its full title was *The Distance (A Kiss with
String Attached)*. It alluded to the human condition, intimate relationships
— it was more to do with the things that bind you together, which can also

suffocate you. It became much more about the human condition rather than
about Rodin and Duchamp. So it wasn't really art about art. The general public
got quite outraged that I withheld *The Kiss* from them for a couple of months,
so it got reinstated at Tate Modern, upgraded from its former spot languishing
on a landing outside the toilets to pride of place in the main gallery display.
So it had a kind of resurrection.

*But it wasn't just the general public, it was the stuckists. They actually invaded
the exhibition and cut the string to 'liberate Rodin'.*
They did a fake seminar around the sculpture with about twenty people.
One of the guys had a big pair of scissors, and he snipped all the string off,
except the stuff around the heads, which he didn't manage to cut because
it was too tightly wound. They said they were liberating Rodin, and then
the guy who did it added to my Wikipedia page with lots of links and
photographs of himself. Then the Tate said: 'Right, we're going to prosecute
him for vandalism of Cornelia Parker's artwork.' And I was: 'Ooh, I'm not
sure about that.' And then the police said: 'Oh, I'm not sure we could defend
a piece of string in a court of law.' And I thought: 'Oh no, this is giving far too
much oxygen to the whole thing, I don't want to prosecute him.' And then:
'What would Duchamp do in the situation?' And I thought: 'Well, I'll knot
it all together and put it back on.' Which I did, which made it even more
perverse, less lyrical, more strident and punk!

*We're running out of time, but maybe I could ask one last question about
Jerusalem. You just got back from there last night?*
Yes.

How was that as an experience?
I've just been in a show called the Jerusalem Show, which happens every year,
but this year it was under the bigger umbrella of an international Palestinian
Biennale called *Gestures in Time*. I've visited Jerusalem a few times now,
and I made a video of these two guys making crowns of thorns in Bethlehem.
When I was visiting Jerusalem for the first time with Jonathan Watkins, it was
around Easter and everywhere you went there were these crowns of thorns
outside every shop, so pilgrims could buy them.

Really?
As a lapsed Catholic, this was just too much for me to bear. All round
Jerusalem and the West Bank there is razor wire everywhere you go, because
of the constant building of settlements and the conflict and resentment
it causes. This process of making crowns of thorns has been going on for
2,000 years. So I was curious about who made them and if it was a painful
process. I went to Bethlehem and tracked these two guys down, who were
a Muslim family.

So was it really just one firm?
Well, I'm sure other people make them, too, but these are the family who supply
the biggest distributors. They produced hundreds of thousands of crowns
of thorns. So when I was filming I asked them, through an interpreter, what
they thought about when they were making the crowns of thorns. And the
older man, Mohammed, talked about what it was like living in an occupied
state, how he wished for peace and dignity for the Palestinian people.
He made a very impassioned speech. And then I asked his son the same
question, and he said: 'Oh, I only think about how to make as many as

I can.' He just talked about the practice of making crowns of thorns, how to produce more, and that was it. The sheer numbers of crowns in piles seemed like something from a Grimms' fairy tale.

That's extraordinary.

I asked Mohammed how long he had been doing it, and he said 'thirty-three years', which was the same age as Jesus when he was crucified. It somehow seemed to sum up the whole situation.

And what do people do with them, once they've bought the crowns of thorns?

Well, I don't know – wear them to bed! I've just bought some, I think they're beautiful objects. The thorns on them are pretty big, and I thought: 'God, it must really hurt them to make these – it must be quite a painful process.' They are obviously very adept at doing this, and they've been doing it for a long time. But somehow, it just seemed almost sadomasochistic, making this very spiky thing that you're mass-producing. It was very short, an eight-minute video encapsulating the history of an object that's become a cliché, but it still signifies so much.

It's funny, because although you're a lapsed Catholic, religion is one of the things that goes through your work like a leitmotif – from Thirty Pieces of Silver *to the crowns of thorns.*

Another piece I showed in Jerusalem is a *Bullet Drawing*. It's a minimal line drawing, made out of lead from a bullet which has been made into a wire. The bullet wire gets wound round nails, to map out a square 1.2 x 1.2 metres. The wall in Jerusalem was tough concrete, so I had to put these masonry nails in, which were big and dark. So twelve nails, with this bullet wound round, mapped out a territory. It was kind of curious – it somehow became less and less abstract the more I thought about it.

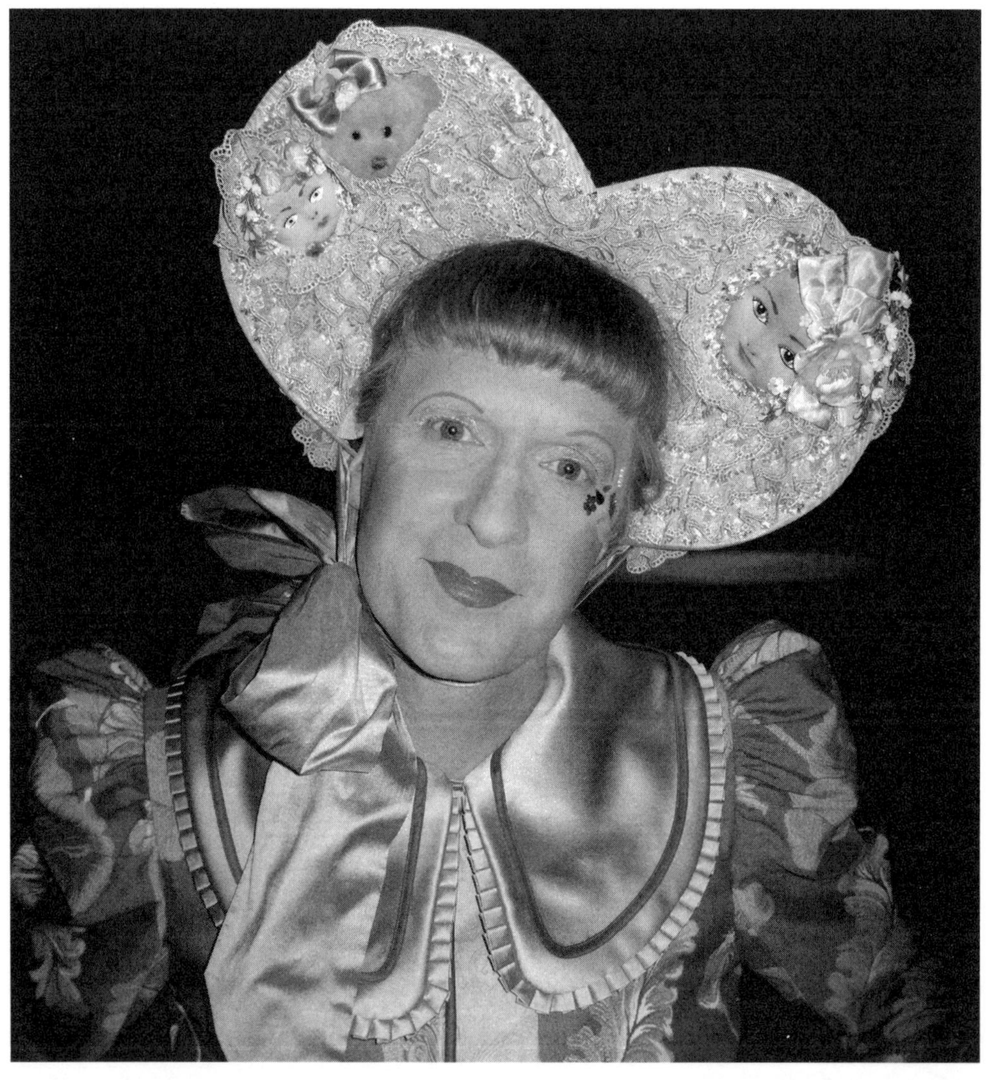

2009

Grayson Perry

'In the middle of the
night I wake up, tossing
and turning over what
I'm going to wear the
next day. It's so exciting!
Of course, I have fantasies
of being humiliated in
my outfit, but they never
really happen'

Dressed as your notorious alter ego Claire, you have now become even more recognisable than the work you produce. Growing up in a rural part of Essex, you escaped as a child into a fantasy world dominated by aeroplanes and your teddy bear Alan Measles. But the most decisive moment in your life as an artist occurred in 1983, when you discovered the Victoria and Albert Museum's ceramic collection. It prompted you to make your first plate, Kinky Sex. *And your subsequent prowess as a subversive, controversial potter earned you the Turner Prize in 2003. I happened to witness at close quarters the extraordinary moment when, at the Tate's Turner dinner, you walked up from your table to collect the prize. A crowd of newspaper photographers rushed forwards to snap the event, but a disturbing number dived down beneath your voluminous transvestite dress and took pictures of your underwear as well.*

Some of your work undoubtedly reveals a seasoned sense of satirical humour. A large ceramic pot called Queen's Bitter *is enlivened by oval photographs of the artist wearing a headscarf. Posed defiantly against derelict urban buildings, you look like a resolute working-class forerunner of your* bête noir: *none other than Margaret Thatcher. The effect is hilarious. Even so, you don't allow us to laugh for long. Take your* Head of a Fallen Giant – *a large, recent bronze skull pierced by bolts and nails. The violence seems alarming at first. But the more we look at it, the more elegiac this skull becomes.*

Nor are you afraid of vigorous protest against inhumanity. Womanly courage and honesty are celebrated in The Mother of All Battles. *Saddam Hussein's infamous war cry is subverted here, by a headless mannequin wearing a full-length, folk-style dress. You used computer-controlled embroidery techniques to festoon the cotton fabric with heinous scenes of torture, the underbelly of tyrannical regimes like Saddam's. Helpless figures are pierced, muzzled, butchered and crucified as we walk round the garment, and the decapitated mannequin only adds to the sense of universal suffering. Would you agree that* The Mother of All Battles *is a wild, angrily impassioned work?*

I'm not wild. That cliché of the artist as a passionate beast, I'm a cliché-allergic person, because my mother ran off with a milkman. So I can't do it – I'm not wild. Sorry, sorry, Richard, but carry on [laughs].

Feel free, Grayson. I thought you would feel free, actually! It's difficult to know where to start with you. But maybe, since you're looking so splendid tonight, we ought to start …

My outfit is getting applause …

Yes, we should start with the attire – that's a good word! How do you decide – take today as an example – what to wear? And where do you get it from?

The first thing I do is look out the window at the weather, because heat is the enemy of drag, right? So you don't want to get too hot, and you don't want to freeze, either. So I look at the weather and I look through my range of outfits. I do prefer winter because I like something quite complicated. But today it's quite sunny in London, so I wanted something not too hot. And yesterday I wore an outfit I quite enjoyed wearing – it was really poncey. So I wanted to carry on with the really, really poncey. I have grades of ponciness, really. When I work with students – this has been designed by a student at St Martin's, this romper suit with the teddy-bear-shaped breasts – I ask them to make the outfits where I need to take a deep breath before I leave the house. So I put this on today, because it's Frieze Week in London and as a transvestite I love it, because I can just dress up all the time. I have the week off and I go to parties and openings and book launches and signings and …

*I'm somebody who can't bear to think about what to wear – I find it all very
boring and irritating having to even think about it. So isn't it tremendously
hard work having to think about all this stuff?*

It's my passion, though. I'm driven lustfully – literally – to think about it. In the
middle of the night I wake up, tossing and turning over what I'm going to wear
the next day. It's so exciting! Of course, I have fantasies of being humiliated in
my outfit, but they never really happen. Even builders have given up shouting
at me now. They do it half-heartedly – they go: 'OI! HELLO DEAR – dearie ...'
It's like that. Oh, anyway.

When you think about it, do you make drawings or is it all in your head?

Oh no, when I design things – like my lovely clogs here – I'm meticulous.
I really work it out, and it's my hobby. It's what I do when I'm doing leisure
art, if you know what I mean. Because when you become an artist, you're
basically taking on something you used to do solely for pleasure and enjoyment,
and then suddenly it's your job! So that takes on a little bit of a different
character then. I still love it and enjoy it, but also I'm obliged to finish things
and I have deadlines – blah-blah. But fashion designing – clothes, hats, dresses
– is my hobby art. It's when I'm off the hook. And I think it's really important
for all artists to have that, because it reminds you of what it feels like to do art
for pleasure.

So it's good for the soul and good for the mind. It's deeply therapeutic, is it?

Yes, it is, in all departments. And it's also good for PR, of course, which is
an afterthought. I mean, I didn't really predict how useful it would be in that
department, and how PR would become so important in the modern cultural
landscape, though I don't call myself an artist now – I call myself 'an engine
for social change'.

*OK, to take that literally, what kind of 'social change' are you supposed
to be engineering?*

That's a cynical joke about the government. I once did a pot called *This Pot
Will Cut Crime by 29%*, because the government at one point were getting
up on their high horses and building art centres and hoping that house prices
would go up in the areas and crime would go down, and the 'carbon footprint'
of everything would go ... you know, it's just ... Artists are as good at politics
as politicians are good at art. You make art because you really love it and are
interested in it. And if it happens to beat global warming, then great. But if not,
don't worry about it.

*I made the question about social change pretty much in jest. But I remember you
saying once that the whole transvestite thing is a part of the male psyche, which
has repressed a lot of urges and impulses that come out in your transvestism.
Me included, I suppose. I mean, look at me: I deliberately dressed very, very
opposite to you today. I thought: 'I'm going to come all in black.'*

I think it's very personal. For me, it's about the idea that when we bring up boys,
we perhaps don't necessarily give them affirmation over just how they look.

How do you mean?

Well, we always talk to boys about what they do – they kick a good football or
they do a good bit of homework, or something like that. It's very much a man
of action. And girls are praised just for how they look, and that's quite an
attractive thing. So it's a mixture. There's no one cause for why people become
transvestites. When we go through childhood, we collect up counters on the

way, and then we cash them in at puberty. It's like when you pupate, at puberty, you come to the gatekeeper and he says: 'OK, give us your chips.' And then he'll say, 'Yep, tranny', and you're off. Or 'You're gay'. Or 'You're straight', or whatever. And everybody's a little bit of a mixture, because every tranny has a slightly different permutation of the things that make it up – there's a bit of S&M, a bit of gay, a bit of that. You fall into a slot, you've got the right counters, and once you've gone through puberty I think it's pretty much hard-wired. I don't think you can be cured from any particular branch of sexuality. The idea that you can be cured of being gay is just – well, it's just wrong.

But what do you think when you look back to the Elizabethan portraits at Tate Britain? There they all are, in their peacock finery, especially the full-length painted portraits: the Duke of This, the Lord of That, the King of Whatever, and they are extraordinarily ornate.
If you look at women now, they wear not far from what you're wearing! More women look like you than me [laughs].

What are you suggesting? [Laughs.]
What I'm saying is that – we're going to get on to my art in a minute [laughs] – in those days the codes of gender dress were different. There would've been transvestites then, just as there are now. It's just that the codes would've been different. It might have been a subtler thing, but it's existed as long as there's been gender difference.

Oh yeah, sure. But do you think that, in centuries subsequent to the Elizabethan age, male attire just got more and more repressed, to a ridiculous extent?
I think the change was in the Victorian era. What happened was industry, and men had to be functional, they had to earn the bread and they had to wear functional clothes and be seen to be doers. And of course women became almost like furniture. Most trannies, if you ask them what period of history they'd like to be transported back to, it's the Victorian – bonnets, corsets, crinolines – generally swanning about with a perfumed hanky. That's good, I'm liking it! That might be my personal thing, though.

May I ask you when your transvestism first manifested itself, and what kind of effect it had on you?
It's not a family sort of thing to talk about. I mean, it's arousing, transvestism is a sexual fetish. A lot of transvestites say there isn't a sexual element to it, and I can believe it, because sexuality is all different for different people. Also, I've met trannies – quite old ones – who say, 'Oh, I don't like sex any more', but they still dress up. So there is an emotional structure as well as a sexual structure. It's a complex business, being human. Our sexuality is about emotions, really, what we access whenever we've any sort of fetish. It's about the emotions that are attached to it. So if somebody has a thing about train crashes – believe it or not, there are people who have a thing about train crashes – it's because of the emotions that come up. And that's what turns them on, that particular blend.

Roughly how old were you when you first had the desire …
Oh, I had S&M twinklings from very early on.

Twinklings?
Twinklings of S&M, oh yes. All my fantasy stories used to involve getting tied up and stuff – I would have been about six or seven. And then I tried on a dress at about twelve, thirteen.

Teenage.

Yeah.

And did you just feel it to be a huge release and a huge source of delight, or were you also at the same time puzzled by it, bewildered, even anxious?

What is interesting is that I didn't really think about it consciously, because it was just a dialogue between my unconscious and my conscious. I didn't have to talk about it at all, so I didn't even have a word for it, because I never even knew transvestites existed.

Really?

And I had a revelation when I finally saw it, maybe a couple of years later, in a paper. No, I just did it spontaneously.

So you weren't at all surprised by it?

I dunno. It's like you're surprised that your nose itches. You just do it, you're it, you're in it. It's like saying: 'Is a baboon surprised when he wants to have a poop?' I doubt it, you know.

So the culture that you grew up in – you're very much an Essex boy, born in 1960 – contained no hint of this? You never came across anyone who was a transvestite when you were a child?

No, I grew up in a background which was sort of acultural – no paintings, no books, not really any music, apart from maybe pop music with Radio 2 on.

Was it aggressively acultural, or just non?

It just wasn't very aspirational, to use the modern parlance. We weren't particularly poor, but culture really didn't figure in it at all. So I didn't have any idea about what middle-classness was: I hadn't ventured out into that particular ethnic safari that is class mobility [laughs].

But was it to do with looking around you, and the whole landscape of the culture?

I was a kid! You just absorb stuff, I was completely unconscious, and I had this very strong fantasy life. I lived in my bedroom, with my teddy bear Alan Measles. He was the king of my universe, and I played with model aeroplanes and Lego. And I built him fantasies and I just played out an imaginary world, which was very strong, until I was about thirteen or fourteen.

But that's quite usual for a lot of kids.

Yeah, and very healthy!

Totally, yes. The difference being that you have actually foregrounded the transvestite world to such an extent that here we are, on a stage in the Cheltenham Literary Festival, and you're looking gorgeous and it's part of your art, isn't it?

No. It's not part of my art.

Whether you like it or not, it is.

Well, I don't turn off my creative energies when I get dressed. Mind you, if I'd been dressed up maybe fifteen years ago, even ten years ago, I'd have been dressed in something from the high street, from Whistles. Because I had a Damascene moment when I kind of …

You mean the Road to Damascus?

> That's what I mean, not Damascene, I got the wrong word, didn't I?

No, no.

> Working-class people are always trying to show off how knowledgeable they are – I still have that terrible trait! You always know, if somebody uses a long word in the wrong context, they are struggling to escape their class background. Sorry, I digress [laughs].

Feel free, it's good stuff.

> Yeah, ten years ago I'd have been wearing something from Whistles or Monsoon, probably. And it wasn't until I bought from an Oxfam shop a bridesmaid's dress, and I tried it on when I was on one of my transvestite weekends, that it gave me new access to why I was a transvestite and these feelings of vulnerability and embarrassment. And I thought: 'Ooh, that's interesting!' I didn't really look back from there, I just abandoned the high street look and went for my fantasies. And then I had the budget – and the confidence as well – to do it, to have them made. I've had enormous fun from being a tranny. It's great!

And you gave her a name, didn't you?

> Because you had to have a name when I joined the Beaumont Society, which is named after the Chevalier de Beaumont who was a famous eighteenth-century French aristocrat. He was a spy in the Russian Court, but dressed as a woman, and an expert fencer as well. He's buried in St Pancras Churchyard, and they named this Society after him. That's the oldest Tranny Society, and you had to have a name for anonymity.

So how did you choose your name?

> My girlfriend chose it. She said: 'You're a Claire.' I took it on the chin, I didn't really know about these things. I don't particularly like Claire – I don't use it much any more.

No, you don't.

> I'm a man in a dress now. I don't have tits, I don't have bosoms – apart from these teddy-shaped ones.

So you're not really Claire tonight – you're Grayson, aren't you?

> Yup, really I am.

Yes, I don't think of you as Claire.

> I don't put on an act, or a funny voice or anything. It's quite fun to do that, but in private.

And you were always very, very visual, I'm sure – right from the word go. When we talked on the way down here, you were saying that comic books were very much part of your childhood.

> Yeah, the only piece of art from my childhood that I wish I hadn't lost was these comic books I used to do. And they were like typical boy's adventures, you know: the male hero RAF pilot got into various James Bond-type things. But as puberty struck they became quite sexualised, and so he ended up getting tied up quite a lot, and having to put on women's clothes to escape the baddies. That's why I like outsider art, because it shows that raw impulse of how our creativity works. We think, as human beings, that we are rational. But neuroscience is

showing us that a very small part of our brains is actually the rational bit. All that is doing is desperately trying to find out what most of it is doing, and trying to make up a reason. It's the Baloney Generator, desperately trying to say: 'What the fuck? Why is he doing that, why is he dressing up as a woman? We've got to think of a rational reason! Oh, I know – he's a woman trapped in a man's body.' That always sounds to me like the most male idea of what transvestism is.

Yes, and it's also rather melodramatic.
Yes, like most things it's a difficult mixture.

Was there ever any doubt in your mind, when you were a teenager, that you wanted to be an artist?
No, I never thought of being an artist. I wanted to join the army!

Oh, that's what I guessed: you can tell – army man!
When I was a child my mother always thought – my father was in the RAF, and because my father had left he'd become a kind of hovering icon – so the idea grew that I'd become a pilot. I loved jet planes. And then I joined the cadet force when I was at college, and I really loved that, running around pretending to have wars and firing guns and stuff. I was on track for Sandhurst, when I was like sixteen I was talking to the careers officer. And then it all went pear-shaped because of my home life and my sexuality, so I abandoned that. And I was in a slight limbo for a short time, till my art teacher said: 'Oh, I think you'd do really well at art college.' And I thought: 'Oh! Good idea!' It's almost like I wrote the idea 'you will be an artist' on a little imaginary bit of paper, and put it under my imaginary mattress and I left it there. And then – pdah!! [Laughs.] And that's how it happened.

That's very interesting, because I always imagine in my innocence that all artists are born artists, and they want to be nothing but artists all the way through their childhood. But it's never quite like that, is it?
No. Some do – there's a great film called *Sick* with a guy called Bob Flanagan Supermasochist, which I really recommend. It's quite stomach-churning, but a really good film. He had cystic fibrosis, and he went on the Johnny Carson Show when he was very young. He was the poster-boy for cystic fibrosis, and there's this great scene where he does some drawings of doctors and Carson says: 'So, Bob, do you want to be a doctor when you grow up?' And he goes: 'No, I wanna be an artist!' And his art was pretty strong stuff – he's not called Supermasochist for nothing!

When you went to Portsmouth Poly, which is where you studied, did you more or less straightaway want to start making pots, or was that a very gradual process?
I don't think I knew what art was much – it was a dour business in those days.

Did you really not know much about art when you went to art school?
No, not really. I don't think I'd been to many galleries or anything.

You were a bit of an innocent.
Yeah. I'd been to the National Gallery and the Tate Gallery once, I think, in my teens.

But you're not an innocent now, not at all.
No, I've had therapy! But no, in those days I didn't know what an artist was. I was very influenced by my teacher, and that is one of the things about art

colleges – your audience is your tutors and your fellow students. And I was
in Portsmouth, it was a real microcosm: small, quite rough town, and the
art college was very small. We were like a little island, and I never thought
about the wider art world that much.

So the townies were always after the art students, were they?
A bit, yeah. I was used to being shouted at a lot. I didn't have a formed idea
about what being an artist was. All I knew was that I hung out with a group
of people who had a really good sense of humour. That was very formative.

That's really important, because humour is so much part of your work.
Yeah, and it's also a very creative business. It's like intuitive playing with things
and flipping things and seeing things, and always being a bit contrary was very
important. When you're in the art world, you have to be contrary with the
art world, and that in a way is the basic mechanism of the art world. Once you
are the young artist approaching the art world, you will go: 'Grrr! I'm rebelling
against you!' And the art world will look down and go: 'Ooh! Nice rebellion!
I like it! Come in!' It's true. I always think of it like that advert for Babycham –
in the 1980s, I think – where the woman goes into the bar and she says: 'Oh,
I'd love a Babycham.' And everyone goes: 'Er!' Because it was a really naff drink
to have then. And then this real cool dude comes in and he sees the drink on the
bar and he goes: 'Hey, yeah, I'd like a Babycham.' And then everybody wants
a Babycham, and that's how the art world works [laughs]. And I'm the girl
going in asking, and you're the cool dude. Or people like you [laughs].

*And you couldn't wait to come to London? Was it the great Mecca to which you
aspired from your base in Portsmouth?*
Our teachers used to talk about this thing called networking, and we never
really understood. And I never really twigged how important it was until fairly
recently, when I started going to more and more things, and I suddenly realised
that nobody wants to work with an idiot. If you can go out there, and of course
you have to produce nice work, but also it's very important that you have
a personal contact with people in the art world. Because you can be the most
talented person and clever, but if you're – let's face it – a bit low on the
emotional intelligence, nobody really wants you. There are a list of artists
that curators will give you, of people: 'Never do a show with that person again,
because they're an arsehole.' So that's what networking taught me – it's a nice
little social club full of, on the whole, good and passionate people.

*But you must have had to change quite a bit, because I was fascinated, just
before we came up on stage here tonight, to meet an old friend of yours, and
I asked her: 'What was he like when you first met him in college at Portsmouth?'
And to my astonishment she said: 'Oh, well, he hardly said a word.' I said:
'What? Because he's not short of a word or two now, is he?' And she said:
'Yeah, he would just grunt occasionally.' So you have changed, haven't you?*
Yeah, it was a real mixture. I was probably a bit shy and unconfident,
and I had what is very common with people from my background, which
is Imposter Syndrome.

What's that?
You talk to sociologists and they'll tell you what it is: it's often working-class
people, when they're climbing the ladder and going out into the cultural world,
you feel an imposter. You constantly think that someone's going to tap you
on the shoulder and say: 'Sorry, lad, you don't belong here.'

I can understand that fear.

I had it, really strongly, the first time I got a museum show. I sat in the foyer at the Stedelijk Museum and I was waiting for the curator to come down and collect me. And I thought no, she's not going to come, someone's going to come and tap me on the shoulder and say: 'It's all been a mistake.'

Really?

Yeah, it was really strong. That is a very recognised social constraint. You see it all the time. People say: 'Those museums, they're not for the likes of us, boy. They're for posh folks, from the big house!'

But when you emerged, I suppose in the early 1990s, it was very much the generation of the so-called YBAs, the Young British Artists.

They're all a bit younger than me.

Many of whom, though by no means all, had studied in London at Goldsmith's. Did you feel very much apart from them, or were you interested in what they were up to?

I didn't really know any of them. I met Damien Hirst fairly early on because of my dealer – I don't really know him that well to this day, but I know most of them now because the art world is relatively small and we brush up against each other. But at the time, I didn't know much about what was really going on. And then, when the whole boom started to happen – the Saatchi thing and Tate Modern – I started to think: 'Oh, this is good, I like being an artist in London now.' Because when I left college it was a really dour business. There must have been – what? – a quarter of the galleries there are now?

Oh, less than that.

Yeah, less than that. I never knew anybody who had sold a painting or bought a painting, and a lucky artist was one who got a residency in a coal mine – when there were coal mines, of course.

There was also a very serious economic slump, in the late 1980s and early 1990s. It wasn't funny at all, was it?

No, but we had the dole, we had squatting, we had the enterprise allowance, we had the community programme. I availed myself of all of those – that was my kind of MA. It took me through the mid-1980s, that series of government initiatives. But I've paid it back tenfold, I can tell you. That's very Essex – my wife calls that me 'talking in Essex currency'!

Yes, Essex boy. But when you left art college, were you a potter? Were you someone who was making pots a lot, or was that yet to come?

Oh god, no. I left college, like most art students, with not much technical facility. What you learn at art college nowadays, you pick up a bohemian sensibility. That's basically what they teach you. We were trainee bohemians, really, and you pick up the kind of atmosphere of the art world.

Bohemian is rather an old-fashioned word.

Yeah, I use it slightly in inverted commas. But what would be the modern version of it?

I don't know. Artists nowadays have to be so worldly, I often think.

All students nowadays look as if they've been sitting in a cafe on the West Coast, in Seattle or something, with their Apple. Anyway, my girlfriend's

sister was a potter. She trained to be a potter, and she was squatting around
the same place as us.

Squatting and potting.
Yes! She went to evening class to keep her hand in, because she didn't have
any facilities, and she said: 'Come along.' Because it was practically free when
you were on the dole. And I just went because I didn't have a studio. I'd just
left college, and I thought I would make some little clay sculptures – some little
figuriney things. But while I was waiting for them to dry – because pottery
basically involves a lot of waiting around, any potter'll tell you that – I thought
I'll have a go at making something a bit more conventional. Because people
around me were being taught the basics.

Oh, I see.
So I thought I'll just listen in and have a go at that. I made a little plate and
a mould and tried a few of the techniques. I thought I could do one of those
plates in a week! So it was great – I got something substantial, finished out,
every week. I had them lined up on the mantelpiece in my squat, and then
someone came round – he turned out to be my first dealer – and bought one
of them. He came round to see my girlfriend's paintings at the time, and he
gave her a show and then he gave me a show as well. I was selling them for,
like, £30 or something, at the time.

Done! I'll buy one!
Yeah? [Laughs.] Part of the appeal was, all my fashionable arty, night-
clubby friends I had at the time, they all said: 'Pottery?' But they were
also smart enough to know that there was mileage in it. And that was a
bit encouraging. Cerith Wyn Evans was a squatter in there with me, and
his partner at the time was this guy called Angus Cook, who was a writer
and very funny. We'd have a real laugh, and if it was a really bad joke, he
used to say: 'Was it raining in that joke?' He was like having Paul Merton
in the house – you could not get away with anything. The slightest
pretension, he would jump on it! And so if pottery passed muster with him
and his ilk, I thought: 'There's something in this!' The art world will accept
canned shit, canned shark and whatever, you can do anything. Yet pottery
somehow still has a little bit of an edge to it.

*Well, that's what I wanted to ask you. It's not so bad nowadays, because
the whole thing has eroded to a certain extent, but there's still this huge divide
between art on the one hand and craft on the other. That used to be a big one:
art people would look down on craft people, and I guess craft people would often
despise art people on the grounds that they didn't know how to make anything
– they were just messing about. And it's still there, isn't it?*
It's like a mind/body split, almost. And it's very important, even to this day,
how one defines oneself. I always define myself as an artist who happens to
use traditional craft techniques and templates. That's been very important
to me over the years, because if you're a craftsperson and you want to expand,
you're forever shackled to that definition. Whatever you do, even if it's brilliant
art, it's by a craftsperson, so there's something holding it back. I think that's
quite important, because it's about the way you approach what you're doing,
and that's what you learn at art college. I came out not being able to tell the
difference between earthenware and stoneware, but I did have the right
sensibility, which was a certain sort of mischievous experimentation and
willingness to be surprised and delighted.

*But you must also have had the ability to be a craftsman to a certain extent,
because you couldn't have made them otherwise. And you've always insisted
on making them yourself. That's another divide between what you do and
what so many concept-based artists do nowadays. Very often they don't actually
make it themselves.*

Most artists can make things OK. I think that's because a lot of high-profile
artists use fabrication studios, and make big flashy things that are incredibly
shiny and gorgeous, and that's fine for them. I'm a great fan of Jeff Koons
and Murakami because they make things that are extraordinarily right for
our times. We get the art we deserve. And I like their work: that's their modus
operandi and that's fine. There's a quaint pair of half-timbered inverted
commas around what I do, in that 'I'm being a craftsperson'. But I do enjoy
it as well, I do genuinely enjoy it. I started maybe more ironically, because
when I first made things they were, of course, very inept. I sold my very, very
first piece from evening classes, and it was inept. I remember my pottery
teacher getting out one of my early things, and she says: 'Oh, it's cracked!'
And I said: 'Yes, but at least it's a genuine crack, not one of your pottery-style,
Japanese-style cracks!' I was an angry young man. I wore my ineptitude with
pride, and they thought it was an ironic comment on craftsmanship, but it
wasn't. It was genuine ineptness. I've since abandoned that strategy.

*But another barrier that you've had to crash through is the tastefulness barrier.
And I'm sure you've been absolutely delighted to do that. Because craft was
always associated, particularly by art people, with a kind of tastefulness.
And it's safe to say that your pots have never been tasteful, have they?*

Oh no, they are. I strive for tastefulness – I love tastefulness. It's underrated:
it's probably one of the most powerful things in our society. If you asked me
to define middle-classness, I would say it's someone who pays over the odds and
is inconvenienced by the beauty of their home. Here in Cheltenham, probably,
you know [laughs]. But that's a loose definition. No, I do feel that taste is an
OK thing, I quite like it. Someone once described British modern art as
'tight-rope walking six inches off the ground'. Because it was so tasteful, always.
If you look at the classic movements of modernism going through Europe,
there's a kind of brash confidence in them in many ways, but the British did
a kind of tasteful version – with a muted palette. And I love it!

*What I mean by 'crashing the barrier' is to do with the content of your pots –
the fact that they contain all kinds of things which just do smash straight
through what one expects ever to find on a pot.*

I did a pot fairly recently called *Good and Bad Taste*.

Ah well, there you go.

And what it's about is this. It's a classic Japanese shape, and I did it in a nice
yellow colour with some grey-blue drawing on it, because I regarded that lemon
yellow as a very Georgian-interior type of colour, somehow – it had that look
of a Nash-interior type of colour combo, slightly adventurous. You know, like
these very posh men that wear quite brightly coloured shirt/tie combos, sort
of like dandyish a bit, I associated with that. And I drew some pornographic
drawings in that shape, and I juxtaposed it with some images out of a really
tacky clothing catalogue – really horrible, cheap, nylony clothes. I was trying
to say there's a group of people who would find the clothes tasteful, and there
are people who would find the colour and the pornography tasteful, and that's
the difference. It's that acceptance of radical chic, to a certain extent. It's like:
'Oh, I'm a very cultured person, and I'm unshockable!' You know.

But deep down – well, maybe not so deep down – you are at bottom satirical, aren't you? You're a satirist.

I don't try to be self-conscious about it.

No, I didn't say you're self-conscious about it.

I am how I am.

Yes.

I don't see myself as a satirist necessarily.

Don't you?

I dunno. I suppose I am! But I don't consciously try at it, no.

No?

I just do what amuses me.

And you're hugely a social commentator, I think.

I feel very often that I'm on an ethnographic study of life. If I go to a shopping mall, for instance, I really feel I've gone to see the Bunga-Wunga Tribe. I did a recent piece about Westfield, and I had to go there to research it.

It's got about 500 restaurants, hasn't it?

It's absolutely enormous. And it's like the Death Star of consumerism landed in Shepherds Bush, all shiny and new and full of designer shops. It's horrible in many ways, and soulless, and it came on the day that Lehman Brothers went bust, practically.

More or less, yes.

So it's a great symbol for me. I made this pot with a map of Westfield on it, and I took it to my restorer's studio and I smashed it. He mended it with gold, and it looks lovely.

I also think of you as a novelist or a playwright, because you have a huge cast of characters on your pots – at one extreme a very dumpy, frumpy housewife, and at the other extreme there's the porno fantasist.

They don't sound very apart to me, no [laughs]. I'm interested in social stereotyping to a certain extent, so the thing I became aware of, very early on, was that visual language had its limits to communicate the kind of ideas that I was interested in. So often I resort to language – a lot of my pieces have words on them. Because I was kind of stuck to get the complex social ideas onto the pot with just images – I find it really tricky sometimes. That might mean I'm not a very good artist or whatever, but that's the way it is. I found myself asking how do I convey the class, the occupation of that person it concerns, because I want to make some kind of comment about it. But I quite like using words as well, because being a literary culture we feel obliged to read them. So very early on I noticed that people spent a lot longer in my exhibitions if there were a lot of words on the pots. Because they were obliged to read them.

Can you sum up what it is that appeals to you about pots? Why do you make them? What is it about the shape of the pots, the physical aspect? Do you think of them as sculpture?

No, they're pots. That's one of the disturbing things the art world finds – they're real pots.

So you don't want to enlarge our definition of sculpture to embrace pots?

No, they're pots. And I make a tapestry, it's a tapestry. And I make a print, it's a print. I make a sculpture, it's a sculpture. I make real things, I don't make sculptures of them.

OK.

D'you see what I mean? Because I think beauty is an interesting thing. I've got a pot right at the front of my book, it's called *I Love Beauty*, and there's something like: 'Ooh, that's a bit of a dangerous statement to me.' But anyway, one of the components of beauty is familiarity. I think Proust said something about when we see something in a gold frame, we're ready for it to be beautiful. So I see the pot as like a gold frame. When you see a pot across the room, all of the stuff comes into my mind: 'Oh, that's going to be a pretty, decorative thing.' And I'm very aware of that, so I like that because it's done half the work before people even see what's on it. And I can go with that, or I can go against it. And there's various stages as well. You start to see what's on it, and then you see the details, and I like to reward people right up that close to the pot. So some of the detail on my pots is very, very intense.

Sometimes, to my way of thinking, you have a very savage view of what is going on out there in the world. I mean, sometimes I reel away from a Grayson pot and think: 'We are going down the road to hell, and Grayson must be really quite pessimistic.'

I am.

Are you?

When I'm on stage like this and talking, yeah I definitely am. Because I just feel, especially with global warming and everything, I just see it all and I think: 'Oh god, we're not going to do anything about it, because we're so lazy and we're so addicted.' I'm not very hopeful about it, and a lot of it at the moment seems like middle-class window dressing. I just can't see us really getting up off our arses, unless it's legislated for. This sounds like me being a politician, I don't really like it. I think life is meaningless. That's comforting to me, it's only the meaning we can give it. If I can dress up and have fun and make art, that gives a kind of mythological story. I see my work more and more evolving into my own civilisation, my own religion, almost. With Alan Measles as God! And that gives my life meaning. When I started, I had an exhibition in Japan and I thought I was like an exhibition of a foreign culture going there. So I thought I would call my show *My Civilisation*, and I thought we've got to have a religion. So I thought of my teddy bear, of course, because he was the king when I was a child. So I did a few sculptures of him in a shrine, and made a sort of prehistoric gold version, and I made a Muslim version of him.

A Muslim teddy bear?

Yeah, I made a sort of Islamic sculpture which I copied from a piece of Islamic ceramic, with him looking wise. It's called *Wise Alan*, like a scholarly man. And anyway, I thought it wouldn't have much mileage in it. But the more I thought about it, cuddly toys are like God because they're like this inanimate object that we project all of our feelings onto. When I was a child, Alan Measles held all of my positive male qualities. He was like a kind of psychological left-luggage locker. So whatever dysfunction was going on in my family, I felt it was very sensible to put them into him, and he'll look after them until I take them back from him. Thirty years later, I took control of them. So he is the God, and I think he's just as valid as any other God. So now I'm really warming to him, and I'm trying to make him slowly into a bit of a cult. Not that I want everyone to worship Alan Measles. I want everyone to worship their own Alan Measles, in a way.

And it is true to say that you're bursting out of the confines of the pot at the moment. You're becoming quite wide-screen, almost epic, because you've started making these massive tapestries. I couldn't believe my eyes when I saw one, quite unexpectedly earlier this year, in a chateau in Switzerland. It's the Walthamstow Tapestry. *Why is it called that?*

Well, the most famous tapestry to us in Britain – which isn't even a tapestry – is, of course, the Bayeux Tapestry. And so I thought: 'That's called Bayeux because it was made in Bayeux.'

I think that's even bigger than yours.

Yes, it's very long – but very thin, though [laughs]. Anyway, my studio is in Walthamstow, and then I thought: 'William Morris, he was born and raised in Walthamstow and he was a big tapestry fan.' And also, of course, Walthamstow is a typical suburban place with all different sorts of people. So there's lots of reasons why I call it that. It's basically 15 metres long, so it's longer than this stage [at the Cheltenham Festival]. It's birth to death, and it's like our life, it's what I would call 'The Shopping Trip of Life'. The seven ages of man in brand, basically.

Do you mean like 'The Westfield of Life'?

Kind of is, yeah. What it is basically, there's seven main characters who represent the seven ages of man, and then there's also hundreds of little characters and incidents all the way across in quite a decorative, folky kind of way. And each one is labelled with a different, familiar brand.

Yes, it is full of shameless product placement.

Part of the reason was I had this book to promote, and we said: 'We'll have a book launch in the gallery, in this bloody great room with a big wall.' So I thought I'll put something on there like those logo boards, which they all stand in front of – you see them in *Hello* magazine, in their red-carpet dresses. So the initial inspiration was this idea of a logo board, but mine's a very up-market, very classy folly – nice one! And I'm very pleased with it. Because the effect I didn't predict was that when you see the words away from their logo, away from their product – they're all written in the same font, each brand – they have an emotional resonance. And it's all about what they mean to us quite deeply, positive and negative. If you say 'Rolex' to someone, they might go: 'Ooh, Rolex!' If you're a drug dealer or someone like that. But if you say 'Rolex' to someone else, they might go: 'Ooh, tacky!' So it's like that: it has two edges, it's quite interesting. Anyway, I'm very pleased with it, and it's very big.

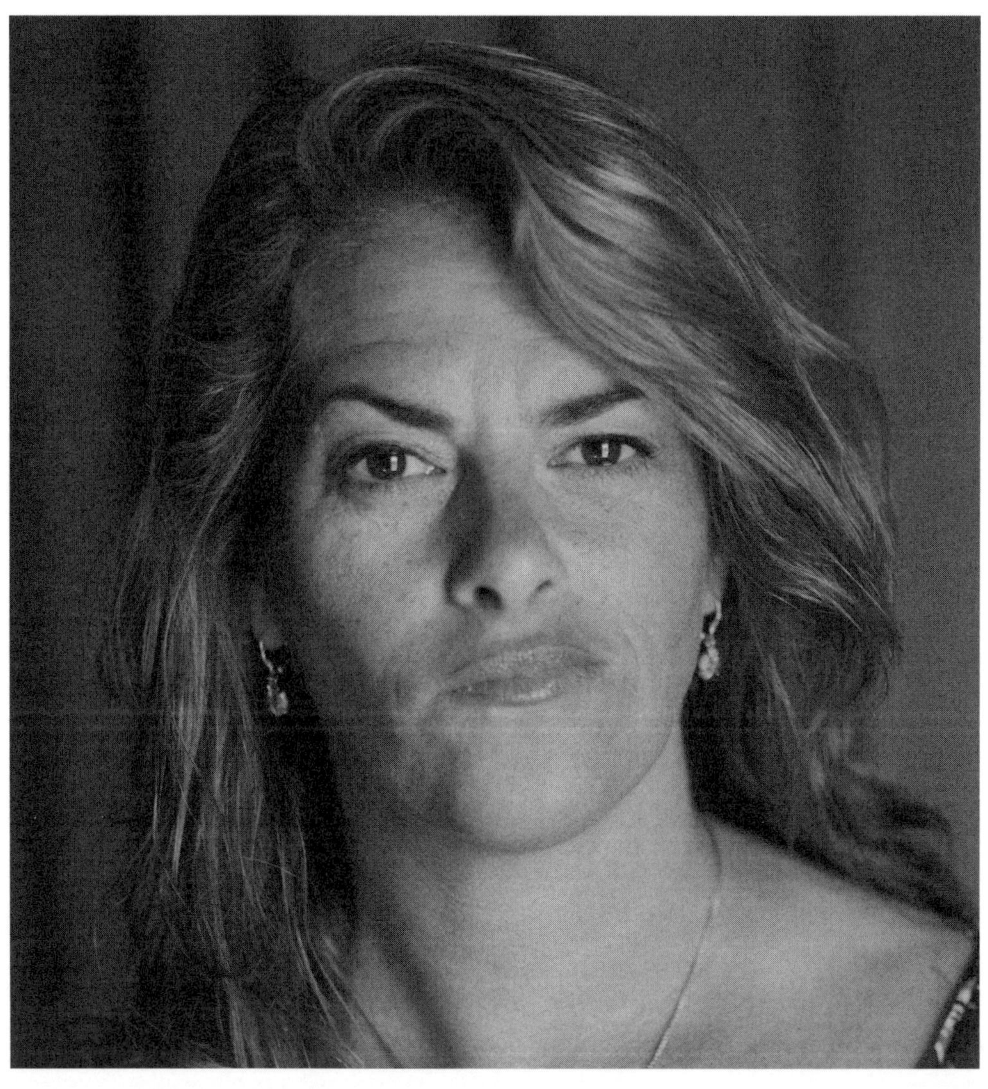

Tracey Emin

'Every time I try to run away from art, art has chased after me like some wanton lover: "Don't leave me, don't leave me!" Art is always there to pick me up. Art is my best friend, art is my salvation'

I'd like to start by saying that there is nothing discreet or cosily reassuring about your work. In the notorious Sensation *show, held at the Royal Academy in 1997, you encouraged visitors to crawl inside a tent embroidered with the names of 'everyone I have ever slept with'. And two years later, you astonished visitors entering the Turner Prize exhibition by inviting them into your bedroom. At the centre of the Turner show's opening space, your double bed was displayed in a shamelessly rumpled state. Unlike the tent, your bed could not be climbed into. But once visitors had walked round it, any urge to lie down there quickly evaporated. The sheets were discoloured, and the heap of belongings dumped nearby proved that you were able to fling away all English inhibitions.*

In your outspoken art – using neon, video, appliqué blankets, drawing, photography, words, furniture, documentation of all kinds and much else besides – you explore memories of your childhood in Margate and adult life with tough, defiant, wry and painful honesty. In fact, I think 'explore' has been a key word throughout your career. In a video called Why I Never Became a Dancer, *you made powerful use of traumatic spoken memories accompanying blurred, hand-held footage of Margate revisited. While we glimpse sand, sea and the Lido Leisure Centre, you recall in a voice-over how your attempt to win a dance contest was wrecked by 'a gang of blokes, most of whom I'd had sex with at some time or another'. When they all started shouting 'slag', you ran off the dance floor and escaped to the beach. But instead of ending on a tearful note, you then tell us that you left Margate, and the video shows you dancing alone with wicked delight on your face. Looking back now, from the vantage of 2012, can you pinpoint the moment when you decided to place your own troubled existence at the heart of the work you produce?*

Yes, easily!

Really?

Yeah, I was about fifteen, I was in the Albion Bookshop in Cliftonville, Margate, Kent, and I was pulling down off the shelf a book on German Expressionism. And I was looking up the name of Egon Schiele. So there you are!

Fascinating. And what was it about Schiele that persuaded you?

I'm a really big David Bowie fan. And David Bowie has an album called *Lodger*, where he's kind of, like, this shape, and then there's one called *Heroes* which is, like, this shape. And they're both taken from Egon Schiele paintings. I had a boyfriend at the time who was doing graphics, and I said: 'Oh, I really love the David Bowie covers!' And he said: 'Oh, they're just ripped off from Egon Schiele.' So I said: 'What's Egon Schiele?' [Laughs.] And so I went up to the local bookshop and found out about it. And I thought: 'Wow! I really like this art!' Because at that time, at school, all we was doing was, like, pop art, actually – Andy Warhol, Lichtenstein, whatever – and then I suddenly saw this other kind of art that I really liked, and I've been stuck in that groove ever since, actually, Corky [laughs].

Can I pursue the Schiele thing a bit further? Because I can see it absolutely now, there's something quite painful about Schiele, the way in which he unearths things and brings them to the surface.

Yeah. But also, because he died so young – he was twenty-eight when he died – I'd like to see what he was like when he's fifty, and see him when he's got through it all. He might have changed radically, he might have become a minimalist and moved to New York and become some kind of, like, avant-garde – god forbid – like a friend of Jackson Pollock or something. Who knows? The main thing is that a lot of people think that all artists of my generation are inspired by, say, postmodernism or contemporary ideas or whatever. But me, I'm actually coming from the school of Van Gogh and the school of Käthe Kollwitz, the school of Caspar David Friedrich. Edvard Munch is my favourite painter of all time. I really am not very close to conceptual art, apart from the fact that I use my intellect in what I do. It isn't just some kind of gut reaction: I actually think through what I'm doing.

Yes, you're very much out on your own, actually. Because you became one of the most well-known members of the so-called YBA generation, a lot of people still imagine that you somehow studied at Goldsmith's with Damien and so many others.

Mmm. It's really funny!

Yes, it is, isn't it?

Yeah. Michael Craig-Martin, who's like the Daddy of Goldsmith's, he curated a show in Berlin a couple of years ago with his favourite students from Goldsmith's, and there's all these articles saying: 'He didn't choose Tracey Emin!' [Laughs.] So me and Michael always have this joke that I was actually his favourite student, but we fell out so badly! The only connection I have with Goldsmith's is the fact that I used to teach there, and I've obviously got a lot of friends who went there. But weirdly enough, it was my friendships with those artists back in the 1990s that rubbed off on me, and also being shown by Jay Jopling at White Cube. Had I shown at Marlborough Fine Art, for example, I would probably have been perceived as a completely different kind of artist. So I was very lucky: it was one of those cases of 'it's not what you know, it's who you know' – definitely. I somehow got put into this other kind of echelon.

Yes, the truth is that you actually went to study at Maidstone College of Art, and then you finished up at the Royal College of Art in London.

I took my degree in 1986 and my MA in 1989, and a lot of my friends who went to Goldsmith's didn't start their courses until 1989.

It's true.

And I'd finished my MA by then, so there was a big leap of time. And also I was coming from a different direction.

What were you like as a student? Can you give some indication? I remember once, when I went to the Royal College of Art's Senior Common Room, where they display a lot of work by ex-students, I was fascinated to see a big early painting by you, and it was definitely in the lineage of Edvard Munch.

Yes, well, when I was at the Royal College of Art my paintings were like a cross between – wait for it – Edvard Munch and Byzantine frescoes! [Laughs.] I'd like to say they were really, really awful. But they weren't, because I was genuinely responding to something I wanted to learn about. I left school when I was thirteen. And then, by law, I had to go back when I was fifteen otherwise my mum would have been in trouble. So I went back to school for three days a week when I was fifteen. But I left when I was fifteen as well, and all I did there was art, basically, three days a week, and I didn't even get an O level in art [laughs]. But anyway, when I got in to do a degree at Maidstone College of Art, I was nearly twenty. I was so happy and grateful that I only missed three days of the college – that's when I had chicken-pox – and otherwise I went in every single day and I stayed there till 8 o'clock every single night.

Whoa!

And I loved every single moment of it. I didn't miss one lecture, I did every thesis, I read every book I was supposed to. It was like I couldn't get enough of it, and it's because I was doing the right thing. All that school crap I didn't have to go through it! My brain was: 'Ah! Ahh! Ahhh!' I loved it. I was even Social Secretary of the Student Union!

I didn't know that! [Laughs.]

I was asked to be President of the Student Union at the end of the third year! But I didn't want to, because I wanted to do an MA course and travel and see the world. At Maidstone, in the first year we had to do a corridor show, in the second year we had to do a seminar and in the third year we had to give a lecture on our own work – in the lecture theatre, to the whole school, which would be to 300 people. And so the main thing at Maidstone was that you were taught really confidently to speak up about your work. And if you were clever, like me, if you'd really fucked up on a project or it was a real mess, you'd go in and you'd go: 'I did this project wrong, I now see where my mistakes were.' And you'd start back-pedalling on yourself, and you'd start talking about what your faults are, with your work. Which means you're addressing where you're going wrong, and what you have to do next. And at Maidstone you actually got rewarded for that, and I left with a First with Distinction, and I got a First for all my theses, and my lectures and everything, and I excelled.

Is it true to say that painting really was your absolute prime medium, your goal, at that point?

No, when I was at Maidstone College of Art, I went from printmaking and then I went to the Royal College of Art to do painting. And before I applied to the Royal College of Art, you had to take a year out, so I took a year out, and then the year I applied they changed it, so you could apply straight from your degree. So the year I applied, 2,000 people applied for 20 places! And I got in, although I hadn't done painting, I'd done printmaking. And I got in because I persuaded them that I wanted to learn to paint.

Mind you, looking back now, the 1980s was in many ways dominated by the idea of painting, wasn't it? Painting was very, very big in the 1980s – it's hard to imagine or remember now.

It is. And another thing: students now can't paint, can't draw, can't even take their own photographs. Everything's digital. They can't print their own photos, they can't do a stone lithograph or whatever. When I was at art school, you had to do every single thing yourself. Before you could have the use of the Photography Department, you had to learn to print all your own photos and learn to use every single format camera. Even if you were bad at it, you had to prove you could do it. And I think it was a different kind of time and a different era.

It really was.

But even though I was terribly unhappy at the Royal College of Art – I was really unhappy, for two years – I learned so much from being there. I learned about the kind of artist I didn't want to be. I did not want to have the debutante's day out! [Laughs.] There were so many people there who just went to art school like it was a finishing school, and I knew I really didn't want to do that.

So you were surrounded at the Royal College by posh people, were you?

Well, no. But if you do art, the majority of people do actually come from …

well, by the time you get your A levels and you've done your Foundation
Course and your degree, and you've done your MA, usually for a lot of people
there's a support system supporting them. And it's not a class thing or
anything like that, it's a support system. So I didn't have that support system,
I had to support myself.

Is that why you were so unhappy?
No, I was unhappy at the Royal College of Art because it was the height
of Thatcherism: I felt quite trapped, and I wasn't enjoying London.
I preferred to be by the sea, or by nature or something like that. I was very,
very unhappy with my personal situation, mainly. But the best thing was,
at the Royal College of Art I learned about the kind of artist I really didn't
want to be. So when I left art school, it gave me a really good idea: 'Right,
I'm going to go that way, I'm definitely going that way!' I went and did
a philosophy course.

Yes, why did you do that?
Because when I was at Maidstone, I really loved all the extra-curricular,
everything that we learned, all the art history and philosophy to all the
supporting courses. When I went to the Royal College of Art, it really went
downhill. Everything at Maidstone was taught with a Marxist doctrine,
which I find interesting. I didn't agree with it, but I found it really stimulating.
The art history was really superb and major, and your brain bounced around
it and you got excited by what you were being taught. When I went to the Royal
College of Art, I thought: 'Wow! 800 students from all over the world! It's going
to be even better!' And it wasn't: it was really, really tired, and the Humanities
Department was really slow, and I just wasn't satisfied. So by the time I left
the Royal College of Art, I felt that my brain had died a bit, and then I went
and did a part-time Birkbeck philosophy course for two years. And that was
one of best things I ever did.

*Well, I can't think of many artists who would want to do that, having left art
college. I think it says something quite important about you, because reading
is important to you, isn't it? And words are incredibly important to you.
Have they always been?*
Yeah, always. Ever since I was a little girl. I don't keep a diary any more, but
I always used to keep a diary. And the reason I don't keep a diary any more
is because I know I'd have to burn them, or it's quite obvious someone's going
to read them, or they'll be published when I die. So it means I'm not generally
writing a diary, if that makes any sense. I know there's an audience for it, out
there somewhere, so I don't write a diary any more. But I write lots of letters,
and I write extensively. I was thinking about it this week, and I must write –
on average, with letters that I write to friends and different things – between
8 and 10,000 words a week.

Really? That is a lot.
Mmm. That's a lot!

Are you sure that you're not going to end up as a novelist, Tracey? [Laughs.]
I wrote a column for *The Independent* for four years, every week 1,000 words,
and the fastest one I did took me 15 minutes!

I can't believe that!
I'm not saying it was any good! [Laughs.]

I'm really jealous.

My friend Lynne Barber, who's a journalist, said: 'You never, ever tell another journalist that!' [Laughs.]

Yes, yes, because that's awful! [Laughs.] But now I want to take you back to 1993, by which time you'd learned about philosophy and you'd teamed up with a Goldsmith's graduate, Sarah Lucas, who had just staged her own solo show. It had a very interesting title: it was called Penis Nailed to a Board. *You got on very well with Sarah, and together you decided to run The Shop.*

Definitely not a boutique!

The Shop was in East London, where you created objects like a Rothko Comfort Blanket, and an ashtray where people could actually stub their cigarettes out in Damien's face. You had a good time there, didn't you, Tracey?

Yeah, we did. I actually hadn't made any work for about two years, and I'd been pregnant and had an abortion. And after I had an abortion, I decided that I couldn't make any art. I definitely couldn't paint – I couldn't paint! And it was a mixture of, like, the admission of being a failure, within my own world and with my kind of morality, and the abortion thing affected me so much that I couldn't make any work.

Well, I'm not surprised.

I was doing the philosophy course and I was teaching at Southwark Council with latchkey kids. So it was kind of like a good combination, really. And then Sarah came into my life.

How did that happen?

I went to see her show at City Racing, and I just really loved it – it was the most exciting thing I'd seen in a long time: no perspex, no frames, just bits of cardboard and glue. And I was looking at this thing, which I always call *Cock Soup*, but it wasn't called *Cock Soup*, it was called *Soup of the Day*, or something. And it was this big picture of, like, soup, like tinned vegetable soup. And she just had all what she calls nob-ends, like the ends of a penis, like photos, just stuck on it. And I remember looking at it and thinking: 'He was circumcised.' And I was looking at this penis and I could hear someone behind me say: 'Oh, poor Sarah, she doesn't even know how to use a computer.' And I was sitting there thinking: 'Wow! This Sarah's really fucking cool, she's not using a computer, she's making things, she's actually making things!' And at that time in the 1990s it was the beginning of high production, and everyone was like: 'Right!' You know, they'd show their work and they'd make a list of, like, 'three stainless steel screws, brass pack', making a list of every single bloody thing. And there's Sarah actually using paint, using glue, using pictures, photographs, cutting it all up, and it was very creative and natural. And we just hit it off so well. Sarah wanted me to share a studio with her, and she'd just sold a lot of work to Charles Saatchi, and she said: 'You don't have to worry about the money, I'll pay for it all. I just think you're creative, and I like hanging out with you, and we'll just share a studio together.' And I said: 'But I'm not sure I want to be an artist. I think I might want to be a writer.'

Oh, interesting, yes.

'And if I share a studio with you, I'll be dragged into this thing I'm just trying to get my head around at the moment.' So I said: 'Look, I'll help you look for a studio, and maybe I'll come in and have cups of tea and stuff like that'. [Laughs.] We were walking down Brick Lane together, and in those days there were so many boarded-up shops, like much more than now, and we were both walking round and we both said, at exactly the same time: 'Let's have a shop.' We both said it, and then we both said: 'No, a real shop – shop, shop!' And that was it, and so we opened a shop for six months.

Instead of a studio?
Yeah, instead of a studio.

So it was like a shop/studio?
No, it was a shop.

Oh, just a shop [laughs].
We only got this lease for six months, so this is diligence: we worked in the shop from Tuesday to Friday, from 11 to 6, and then in the evenings we made all the stuff to sell in the shop. And then on Saturdays we worked from 11 o'clock at night through to Sunday afternoon, because Brick Lane was one of the only few places where things were open at night there. You know? There was no late-night things, like there is now, anywhere in London: it was just the bagel shop, the newspapers, and the Market would open at 5. So Sarah and I just decided to have this all-night thing, and in those days there was nowhere, no clubs or anywhere for us to go at night, so all artists and different people would come to The Shop at 11 o'clock at night. And of course we'd just drink all night long and play games and just be really stupid. Sarah and I always said it was like a collaboration between ourselves and not just artists but critics like Carl Freedman – who's a gallerist now – and Gregor Muir, who's Director of the ICA now. I can't tell you the things that went on, but we had a really wild time!

Gregor has written about it quite extensively.
Yeah, Gregor has a book called *Lucky Kunst*, and if you read that you'll read a lot about The Shop, and a lot about me in those days as well.

And a lot about booze, I seem to remember.
Yes, exactly. Sarah and I did what I think now is a phenomenal performance, really, behind a shop counter for six months every single day – apart from Mondays. Monday was our day off.

So do you think it was like a performance art piece?
Yeah, I do, when I look back on it, definitely. And Sarah and I would do, like, the most maddest things. Like we said: 'We got to have a name for the shop!' So we got really drunk! The other thing was, we had like a hexagon-shaped goldfish pond in the middle of the shop, which we painted the inside like Ken Kiff's paintings. And we also liked Ken Livingstone, so all the fish were called Ken [laughs]. And then, when people came into The Shop, we'd encourage them to make a wish and throw some money in the pond. And we'd use the money in the pond to buy the fish their fish food and their weed, and stuff like that. But also there was a pub next door where you could get a pint of Guinness for 50 pence then. It was so cheap! And Sarah and I, if we didn't sell stuff in the shop we had no money, so we'd take the money from the fish, and we'd write the fish an IOU note and pin the IOU note to the fish pond, and then we'd sell the IOU note [laughs]. The other thing we used to do was, I'd show Sarah how to make, like, a really cute little cat out of a cigarette packet – we used to chain-smoke all the time, Marlboro Lights – and then we'd put all the cats along the top of the window in The Shop and we'd sign them. And then we'd sell them for £3.25, which was the same price as a packet of cigarettes [laughs]. We had

so much fun, just being really silly! And then Anthony d'Offay, who was
probably the most powerful gallerist in Europe at that time – he's retired since
– we used to joke: 'Oh, I wonder what would happen if Anthony d'Offay came
in?' We'd have these insane conversations where one of us would be Anthony
d'Offay and had to come in The Shop, and then we had, like, a stuffed octopus
with a wig on it and laid it across the radiator, and we'd have this pretend
conversation that Anthony d'Offay would come in and say: 'Hi! How much
is that octopus?' [Laughs.] And we'd say: 'It's £8'. Anyway, whatever [laughs].

That was a lot of money in The Shop, wasn't it?
And lo and behold, what happened one day, Anthony d'Offay walked in! And
what did he say? 'How much is that octopus?' [Laughs.] So everything with
The Shop was really, really funny, and really, really good. And lots of people
pretend they went to The Shop and we know they didn't. Sometimes, during
a whole week there, no one would come in. We got people to write their names
in a book, and we gave them a choice: we'd either do their star signs or
something, or we'd do an anagram of their name. So we know which people
came to The Shop, yeah. That's what art is about!

It lasted six months, The Shop, and then you must have focused quite quickly,
because soon after that you had your first solo show at White Cube. I remember
that very well. You called it My Major Retrospective *– it's a good title.*
I called it *My Major Retrospective* because, in my heart of hearts, I didn't think
I'd probably have another exhibition.

Really?
Yeah, I didn't know what was going to happen next. And Jay would actually
say: 'I think this is it. She's got no more fans after this.' Which was true!

Why did you think that, though? You must have been very focused to do the
work: you filled the show with your diaries, letters and memorabilia of all kinds.
Yeah, well, the thing with *My Major Retrospective*, a lot of it was objects which
I had. I put together families of objects and then I wrote stories that went with
the families of objects. And so I knew that once I'd done this, I'd have no more
objects left, which was true.

Oh, I see.
And I made my first blanket, out of one that I had from when I was a child,
and a blue sheet that I'd bought in Geneva, and I cut up all my old clothes
as well. So then I knew that I had no more clothes to cut up, so I was thinking:
'How am I going to make another blanket?' I mean, obviously I wasn't thinking
ahead, I wasn't thinking of all the skills that I had at the time or anything.
But it was a really, really, really successful show, in terms of criticism and
people coming to see it.

It was. Loads of people came, and not just at the private view to get pissed, either.
No, I'd be there every Saturday afternoon, from 2 to 4, and people would be
queuing round the block – not just to see the work, but to see me. It was kind
of like this weird kind of thing, because there I was showing all my real objects,
and telling all these real stories, and some people even thought it was all
constructed and not real. So, for example, one piece of work was my passport,
and the tooth that I'd taken out, with a story. And my passport had run out
on the 17th of November, the day the show opened, and people just thought
I'd got a highly produced, mocked-up passport. Because people couldn't

accept it was all really true and all real and all my life, that my life was true, because it sounded so bizarre, so over-the-top.

Well, that's very interesting. So performance was very much part of the show, wasn't it?
Me.

Yes, you. Much more you than had been the case in The Shop, much more the real you. Was it the real you, Tracey?
It's always the real me, yeah. So when you go into a gallery and read that this woman was raped at the age of thirteen, had an abortion that didn't work – the foetus ran down her leg – diddle, diddle, one story after another, people don't expect to read that when they go into a gallery. And they certainly don't expect it to be true, either. Because there's an air of cynicism.

You mean among the visitors?
Yeah, people were cynical, and they couldn't actually believe what they were seeing.

They thought you were just making it up?
Yes.

Why do you think that was?
But lots of people didn't – some people stood there and cried. It depended on how it affected people.

It definitely had a very confessional feel, that show.
Yes.

So looking back now, do you think it was actually cathartic for you to do that?
Yeah, because I thought it was going to be my one and only show, so I'd get it all off my chest now, you know, definitely! [Laughs.] But also, when I look back on it, it was seminal, it was ground-breaking. What I was doing was really, really radical as well. At that time there was this kind of like glossiness, this veneer of making everything look all right, kind of stiff upper lip and everything being cool, you know. And I'm just not a cool person: never have been, never will be. And I was making a work of art about not being cool, about being on the outside of society looking in, but using myself as a vessel to talk about it. So instead of painting neo-expressionist, angst drawings of myself – which I could do now, or at art school – I was doing it in a sort of, like, much more sophisticated way. And that is why I showed with Jay Jopling and not with, say, a gallery that would be interested in figurative drawings.

And then, soon after that, you published this book, Exploration of the Soul, *which really did explore your life from birth through to adolescence.*
Well, it was from my moment of conception to being raped. And it wasn't just a book. My grandmother gave me her armchair and she said: 'There's a lot of money in chairs.' So I decorated the chair with lots of my life story, and I took the chair round America, and I did performances with the book and sold the book on the way to take me on this journey.

Yes, there's an extraordinary photograph of you in Monument Valley, sitting in the chair with the book.
And also at that time I was with Carl Freedman, and I had the idea to write this

book and to go round England, and he went: 'Think big!' And suddenly
we were going round America, which takes it into a completely different
context and really pushes things. So it wasn't just me that was doing
things like that then – it was a lot of ambition about bigger ideas and taking
art to bigger places. Whereas previously people were quite myopic about
what was possible.

*Did you ever think that you didn't want to own up to stuff? Because on the front
cover of the book were the words 'All the Love that I Have Made', but on the back
there's this counter-dedication which conveys regret for 'All the Love I Have
Destroyed'. That's quite a thing to own up to, isn't it?*

Yeah, well, there's two things going on. I'm really, really an amazing friend.
My loyalty to friends is amazing. And I'm really, really terrible at relationships
– really awful. So I don't have one any more now I'm an adult. I'm useless at
it, terrible. So I actually have in my life destroyed a lot of the love that's been
around me, intentionally, because I couldn't have it close to me. And also
I think I was still very much upset about the abortions, and physically still
felt this thing attached to me, pulling me up, which was like the foetus of
love for me. Because I realised that, had I had a child, god knows what would
have happened. But there would be a lot more chance of having unconditional
love there, and I buried all that by having an abortion. But there we go ...

*Some of your prints around that time seem incredibly bitter and accusatory.
They're scrawled with outbursts like 'You Were not Men, You Were Less than
Human'. Do you think that was a fair accusation?*

Yeah, I think that was a fair accusation – someone who was twenty-six years
old fucking a thirteen-year-old. I think I was actually being quite nice about
them, Richard.

Really.

Definitely. In my late twenties and early thirties I was very, very angry then,
you're right. I was angry about the stuff that had happened to me.

Well, I don't blame you.

I was angry about being fucked up, I was angry about being psychologically
unhinged, I was angry about being a mess. And when I make mistakes,
I still get angry with myself now.

Do you?

Yeah, definitely, but then all that gets driven back into the work, so I have more
control over it now as I get older.

Sure.

I was more crazy when I was young.

Why do you think so many of your teenage years in Margate were so hellish?

I don't think they were hellish.

You don't think they were?

No, I don't. Hell is – hell is – how can I describe hell? Hell is growing up
in Africa and having to walk nine miles to get some water, and on your way
back you're raped by fifty militia who then bayonet you up the vagina and
stab your womb out. That is hell, Richard, not what I went through. What
I went through was kind of manageable.

But a lot of people haven't been through what you went through.

Yeah, but we all have our crosses to bear, don't we? You know, that's why we're here. One person's hell may not be another person's hell. What people can live with is, yeah, we all have our pain threshold. And when I look back on it now, I sort of think, because my life has turned out to be so positive and so brilliant, I can't really go round moaning about everything bad that happened to me. Because it's all going to be all right in the end, and it is. I'm an incredibly lucky person: all of those things that were bad that happened to me, I've been able to channel into my work and just be really positive and productive with. I feel lucky because of that, not unlucky because of the things that happened to me.

But I think you were absolutely right to get it all out of your system at the time that you did. I remember being impressed in 1997 by a show you had at the South London Gallery. You called it I Need Art like I Need God, *and the videos were especially powerful. You talked to camera so frankly about the time you were raped, about your depression, about your attempted suicide and the anger that you felt about your abortion. This is really difficult stuff to talk about, but you managed to, didn't you?*

But then, you didn't expect to walk into an art gallery and see that as art. It wasn't what was expected.

Totally not.

And also, being a woman as well and actually taking hold of all the subjects that were taboo and you're not supposed to talk about. I really did grab hold of them by the balls, and I just threw them back in the face of what hurt me. I turned it around, so it's a bit like playing tennis when you lob it back as hard as you can, and then you win. It's so much better than just letting everything crawl over you and say: 'Oh, I'm a failure, I can't do anything.' Just turn it all around. And at my South London Gallery show, when I went to the opening I got out of the taxi and I said: 'Oh, that's weird, my watch must be wrong, because everyone's queuing outside, they're not in it, my watch must be wrong or something!' And then I went and looked, and they were queuing all the way to get in, and I got down to the front and the gallery was so packed and so full. And then the garden was so packed and so full that people were waiting for people to come out before they could come in. When I walked in, I'd bought a new dress and also I used to wear big, thick glasses because I couldn't see, but I'd gone and got some tinted-lens glasses. And it was May and there was blossoms on the trees, and *Vogue* was there and people were snapping and the BBC was there, and I just thought: 'Wow! This is good! This is how it should be! I've arrived, I've arrived!' [Laughs.]

So you weren't nervous?

I was so excited!

You weren't shy. Do you do shy? [Laughs.]

Yeah, I do sometimes shy – a bit [laughs]. No, but do you know what? I was in Frankfurt, today actually, and I was installing my bed for a big exhibition there, and I had to unpack everything from the bed. And when I'd made the bed I get in the bed, and then I sort of whirled around the bed and then I, like, threw the duvet back so that it has its own natural thing. So it was quite strange when you were talking about the bed earlier, I was thinking how close I've been to it this week.

That's funny, yes.

But the South London show was my moment when I thought: 'It is possible, I can be an artist, this may work for me!'

*I'm not surprised, and in one of the videos I remember your mum says: 'You
would have gone to the dogs if you hadn't gone to art school.' Was she right?*

Yeah, absolutely, 100 per cent! My mum actually thinks I'd be dead if I hadn't
gone to art school. Which I think is true. Art saved me. Hence *I Need Art like
I Need God*. Every time I try to run away from art, art has chased after me like
some wanton lover: 'Don't leave me, don't leave me!' Art is always there to pick
me up. Art is my best friend, art is my salvation, art saves me constantly. And
whenever I feel really lonely, or I'm in the city and I feel isolated, the moment
I'm in an art museum or the moment I'm in a gallery I feel safe and I feel looked
after. Because my mind has been absorbed with what I really love, visually,
aesthetically. That is what I'm really good at. I'm definitely never going to be
the greatest artist in the world, I'm not saying that. But visually I know what's
good and what's bad. I can run round a museum show in ten minutes and tell
you what the best paintings are, definitely. Unless there's an art historian who
wants to argue with me about it: 'Why?' [Laughs.]

Yes, I bet there are a few of them here at the Courtauld tonight [laughs].

But if we're looking for the same premise, then people will agree with me.
And it's because I love the visual dilemmas, I love the testing, I love the teasing
of it all, it excites me.

In fact, 1997 was a key year for you. In the autumn Sensation *opened at the
Royal Academy, and immediately one of the most notorious exhibits in the show
was this blue tent, where you invited everyone, really, to get down on their hands
and knees and crawl into it – which was an extraordinary idea – so that we
could all read the appliquéd names of* Everyone I've ever Slept with. *You even
had the dates: 1963 to 1995. And all these names ranged from members of your
own family and sexual partners even to the foetus that you had aborted. It was
all there, wasn't it?*

Yeah, 102 names. There were some that just went, like: 'John – '. And people
said: 'Why didn't you want to put his name?' And I said: 'Because I never knew
it!' [Laughs.] So there were people I'd just slept with, and perhaps half-an-
hour's shag, somewhere on a green, shagged and just maybe got a touch of their
first name. And there was people that I really loved, and then there was, like,
my grandmother who I would go and stay with, and I'd get into bed with her
and listen to the radio and I'd hold her hand. So then I wrote about all these
different people and different situations, but I didn't put the anecdotal stories
next to the people's names. I gave people a bit of distance on that. But oh god,
did I get in trouble! Oh, my god! Because there were some names, some people,
I shouldn't have put in the tent. I'd never do it now – never, ever, ever. But when
I made the tent, no one knew who I was. It was my first group show that I'd
done, and I was nobody. Who the hell would be interested? I really didn't think
anybody would be interested in what I was doing. I was with Carl Freedman at
the time, and Carl curated the show called *Minky Manky* at South London
Gallery, and I was originally going to be in the show with Sarah Lucas. And then
Carl decided that he wanted Sarah to make individual work, and Carl just said
to me: 'You can't be in the show, because you're my girlfriend and it would look
patronising. If you put one of your little tiny things in, it would look like:
"Why did I put you in the show? Only because you're my girlfriend." It would
be more harmful to you.' Oh, I got so angry with him! And he said: 'All right
then, you come up with a really big work, with a really big idea, and I'll put
you in the show.' And that's when I came up with the tent, and there in the
tent-flap it said: 'Carl Freedman'. And people who didn't know that Carl and
I were together said: 'God, she slept with the curator!' [Laughs.]

Yes, shameless! [Laughs.]

> Yeah, do anything to get a show! [Laughs.]

Looking back to your childhood, were tents important to you when you were a kid?

> No.

No?

> No, that was my first tent! [Laughs.]

So where did it come from? You just dreamed it up?

> No, it wasn't that, because I was sewing on lots of different things, sewing on chairs, sewing on this, sewing on that, and the tent was a really good thing to sew on. But I didn't know I was going to get the igloo tent until I saw it. And it was kind of nice, because of the Mario Merz thing – it was a nice kind of connection.

The Mario Merz connection is interesting, yes.

> And the tent – I lived in a tiny flat, not far from here, Waterloo. My living room was about 10 foot long, and I had nothing in the living room. It was my studio, where I worked, and I had the tent in there. And inside the tent I had my TV, I had my dinner and I'd sit in the tent the whole time sewing. And my neighbours could see me, and they said: 'Why has she got a tent in there?' [Laughs.] And it took me six months to sew it all on!

But from the point of view of your notoriety, it was a TV programme that turned you into the most celebrated British woman artist of your much publicised generation. I know, because I was there on the programme with you, and I'll never forget! It was after the winner of the 1997 Turner Prize was announced, and it was a live TV discussion with a panel of guests on Channel 4.

> Yeah, tell 'em what it was called – brilliant title!

I can't remember.

> I can – I'll never forget: *'Is Painting Dead?'*

You're right, and I remember you arriving drunk for the debate. You were quite clearly very, very pissed, and you had your finger in a kind of …

> I'd broken my finger in half, in New York, and I had a splint. And I was on really, really strong painkillers, and I was drunk, just to make it even more interesting! [Laughs.]

And then, I remember, because I was within earshot of this, you went up to one of the Channel 4 producers, just before the programme began, and said: 'Can I say "fuck" on Channel 4?' [Laughs.]

> He said: 'No!', so I said: 'Oh, all right then, I won't say it!' Then they were setting me up for the programme and I said: 'Oh, I think I'm too drunk to do this!' And they said: 'Just put some coffee down your neck and you'll be fine.' And I wasn't, was I? [Laughs.]

During the programme you shouted abuse at several panellists – including me, I'm sure. And then you announced, to the TV cameras and all the people watching the programme, that you were walking out of the room to 'go home and see my mum!' [Laughs.] And it was extraordinary, because overnight you became the talking point of the nation!

> Four million viewers – there was a power surge! [Laughs.]

It was really quite weird, wasn't it?

It was very weird! Especially because the next day, I didn't remember anything about it [laughs], but me and my boyfriend at the time, Mat Collishaw, we went into a greasy spoon to have, like, eggs, bacon and chips or whatever during the afternoon. And I opened up the *Guardian*, like that, and I went: 'Ohhhh!' [Laughs.]

So you didn't remember anything about it at all?

No, because I left the programme early! [Laughs.]

You certainly did! [Laughs.]

I just remember being in someone's house on a red sofa smoking, but actually that was the Tate Gallery! [Laughs.] And then I rushed to go to a party to meet my friends, and talked to my mum on the way. And I got to the party and then we stayed up all night – that was what we did in the 1990s, stayed up all night partying – had a couple of hours' sleep in the morning, got up, went to the greasy spoon and then the rest is history.

So were you able to watch a video recording of the programme?

No, I didn't. I didn't watch it! But Gregor Muir made me watch it about eight months later, because I was so embarrassed about it and I was a bit upset that I'd caused a scene. I'd rung up Nick Serota and I apologised. I wrote a letter to the Tate apologising, you know, and I felt kind of embarrassed because on the programme, apart from me, it was like men who'd made all their life being art historians.

Yes, it was all men with you on that programme.

And then there was little me, telling them that they didn't know what they was talking about, because I was the only artist on the panel.

You were!

And as an artist, I knew what it was like to be an artist, and they didn't. And actually, I had quite a good point, I think! [Laughs.] But it's on YouTube, and now it's really funny and you should all watch it! [Laughs.] No, it's really tame and sweet: 'I want to go home and see my mum.' It's not exactly rock n' roll! [Laughs.]

No, it's quite safe, in a way.

Yeah, very safe. But it did get into the Top 100 Best Moments on TV – number 81 [laughs]. And I did get into the Top 20 Most Drunk Moments on TV, and I came in at number 3, I think. There was Oliver Reed, the Sex Pistols, and me! [Laughs.]

I remember coming home that night and my family – my wife and four kids – had all been watching it, and they all turned to me and said: 'Dad, who was that extraordinary woman?'

Yeah, because there was this really boring, boring discussion, with all these men going: 'Is painting dead? Yes, I think painting's dead!' [Laughs.] And little me!

I remember that Norman Rosenthal was one of my fellow panellists, and he had kiss-lips on each cheek. Someone had planted them there during the Turner Prize private view.

Yeah, the Turner Prize in those days was really, really, really worth watching and really wild. Something radical always happened, one way or another. That was what happened that was radical that evening, because it had all been quite tame, really. My friend had won it, Gillian Wearing won it, and it had all been very nice and very ordinary up until the *'Is Painting Dead?'* panel discussion!

And then, of course, in the Turner Prize show of 1999 you put your own bed. Was that a sudden decision on your part, because it came from this whole notion you had of inviting people in? The tent was to do with inviting people in, and here you're inviting people into your bedroom.

I wasn't really inviting people into my bedroom – that's very one-dimensional.

Oh, you weren't?

No.

OK, what were you doing?

First of all, I made the bed in 1998 and it was my bed. I'd been in it for four days in quite a bad way, and I got out of the bed, staggered to the kitchen, got some water, looked at the bed and thought: 'Oh, my god, that's disgusting! I could've died in there!'

How do you mean, in a bad way?

I'd been really depressed, and I drank so much. And I don't know whether anyone's ever done this: you go to bed, like, in the morning – you've been up all night – and you don't wake up until the next day! Has anyone ever done that? It's dangerous. That means you've been 30 or 32 hours without water. And if you've been drinking a lot, it's quite dangerous. And I never take drugs, ever, ever, I never do drugs at all – it's just drinking. And in those days we were kind of wild, you know. And I'd woken up out of this really weird drunken haze and god, I'd lost this whole 24 hours, I'd slept through it! And I got out of bed and staggered around, and then I had a moment of disgust at this dirty bed, sodden sheets, everything. And then I looked again and thought: 'I didn't die in there, I'm still alive, this bed kept me alive. This thing is really beautiful, you know.' And then, in my head, I visually took the bed out of the tiny little bedroom it was in, and put it in a large white space in a gallery in my head. And I thought: 'That will do – that's good.' And that was it. So for my part, there wasn't anything controversial or shocking intended. And I showed it in Japan, for the first time, and what really shocked the Japanese were my slippers, my dirty slippers. They stole two of the bloody condoms, they stole a pair of knickers, and that didn't shock them. But the dirty slippers were appalling for the Japanese people to look at. So d'you see what I mean? I showed it in Japan and I get one reaction. I showed it in America, and America has seen it all before in the 1970s, you know [laughs]. And then I originally wanted to show my beach hut in the Turner Prize, but it got stuck in San Francisco and I couldn't get it back in time. So I thought: 'Oh, I need a really large, square sculpture.' I don't like putting walls in shows – I think that's like a weakness. I needed a square sculpture to go in the middle of my show, so there's this sort of circular movement when people look. And I thought: 'Oh yeah, I'll put the bed there.' It was that simple.

The bed became linked to you at that time and everybody talked about it. And, of course, in those days a lot of British people used to rubbish the Turner Prize and get off on saying things like: 'A child of six could do it!' But actually, I remember going back to that Turner Prize exhibition and being very struck, and very impressed and very heartened, by the fact that there were loads of people there looking at your bed and all the other stuff, and they were treating

*it with incredible seriousness. They were not just going for a giggle at all.
They were treating it in the way that I'm sure you wanted them to treat it.
They were really thinking about it, and I thought: 'This is really getting through
to a lot of Brits who maybe need to have this kind of experience.'*

Yeah, but also there was the drawings, the blankets, there was a show-reel of films of, like, about fifteen films. And after the Chinese guys jumped on my bed, I went away. And the Tate changed my show without asking me. And they took the films down to just four films, because people were staying in the films for too long and the queue was going all the way outside the Tate to get into the Turner Prize. So it was really successful in lots of ways, my show. It wasn't just about the bed, there was other stuff going on.

Who were these Chinese guys?

I don't know – I still can't remember their names.

Were they artists?

I don't know – I think they were vandals.

They jumped on the bed and what did they do to it?

They shook up all the pillows, and got all the feathers to come out of the pillows, they drank the vodka and put my knickers on their heads. They were disgusting! And then they tried to make a career out of it. It was a career move, it was very stupid. It upset me a lot, actually.

I'm not surprised.

I think damaging art is like a crime. You know, it's terrible.

Yes, and we've had another example of it recently.

Yeah, with the Rothko.

*Awful, just terrible. Thinking of Margate, which we haven't done much, it's
really interesting that you went back to do a show there recently. That must
have been a very, very strange experience for you.*

It was really weird.

Because you're a London girl now, and have been for many years.

My mum still lives in Margate.

*But to go back there, to have a show by the sea in this beautiful new Turner
Contemporary gallery designed by David Chipperfield, that must have been intense.*

It was brilliant. 170,000 people went to see my show in Margate in the summer. Margate has a population of 60,000 – that includes old people, children, whatever – so I did all right to get that amount of people down to Margate, buying fish and chips, having cups of tea. You know, it was brilliant. I'm a local hero now [laughs]. No, it was brilliant showing in Margate, because it was definitely like the prodigal daughter returning home, and it was good. It was another thing I could tick off my list. I feel that I'd thanked Margate for everything that Margate's done for me. If you've got a backdrop to your life, a stage set or something, Margate is mine. Margate has done all these really positive and amazing things for me. Margate is really romantic, it looks beautiful, it's hard, it's gritty. I'm lucky to have that as my backdrop. A lot of people have, like, suburbia, you know, and whatever is in their head. I have this naturally made, fantastic backdrop. So my show this summer thanked Margate for what it's given me. And I felt it was really symbiotic, it was brilliant.

And Margate, of course, was incredibly important to another famous British
artist: Turner. Is he somebody who means much to you?

> Yeah, it was really good. Because in the Margate gallery, I could also curate
> works from the Tate, Turner's works. And so I took Turners and also Rodin's
> *The Kiss*. And I chose some of Rodin's erotic watercolours, and also some
> of Turner's. So it was really nice for people to see that it's not just me doing that
> kind of stuff. Their favourite old boys that they love so much were doing it a
> long time before I was. So it was good. Turner, I think, is fantastic – very sexy.

Yes, Ruskin tried to destroy Turner's pornographic work, didn't he?

> He did: he destroyed thousands and thousands.

I won't forgive him for that. Will you?

> No. Turner had a pub, and above the pub he had a brothel and above the
> brothel he had a studio, and he'd paint all the prostitutes. And when he
> died, Ruskin had the keys for the pub and the brothel and everything, and
> he went and destroyed every single work that Turner did. And the only ones
> that have survived, from the erotic works of Turner's, are the ones he'd given
> to other people.

Yes, that's awful. And Tracey, you really are very busy now. You're doing stuff
all over the place: you've gone global, I think one can say.

> Yeah!

Later on this month, you've got How it Feels *at MALBA, Buenos Aires, and on*
December 1st you've got You Don't Believe in Love but I Believe in You *opening*
at the new White Cube in São Paulo, and then on 14th December – you'll be a bit
breathless by then –

> I'll be knackered!

Just a bit!

> In between that I'm going to Miami as well, to discuss plans for my big new
> show there next year, and I'm going to New York and then I'm flying to Rome
> for my show.

That's right. The Roman show, which is called You Saved Me, *opens at the*
Galleria Lorcan O'Neill on 14th December. Why is it called You Saved Me,
and who is 'you'?

> Well, it's really funny. You know, like, 'you' – it's the way I speak, it's my
> colloquialism – I could say 'one' but it would make me sound a bit silly if
> I said: 'One saved me' [laughs]. You Saved Me – You Saved Me – You Saved
> Me! Someone saved me!

So you're not saying who?

> No. Art saved me! I told you earlier!

You did.

> Yeah. Totally, and often with my titles I'm ambiguous, and I change the 'I' and
> so *Love Is What You Want*. Oh god, was that a boring discussion? It went on
> for about two months: *Love Is What I Want, Love Is What You Want, Love*
> *Is What I Want, Love Is What You Want*, shall we take a vote in the studio?
> [Laughs.] So boring. And it actually more or less meant the same thing,
> but it didn't. 'You' and 'I' is not the same. But these stupid little philosophical
> arguments, I will spend hours and hours with myself, laying awake at night,

bouncing it backwards and forwards, till I decide what it's going to be.
Because I could've – OK, the really interesting one is the São Paulo title.

Yes: You Don't Believe in Love but I Believe in You.
Imagine how much fun that one was! [Laughs.] Everyone got so bored with it!

You must have incredible energy, Tracey.
I do. But also I'm an insomniac.

Are you?
Which is awful …

Well, you're not alone in that: Lucian Freud was an incredible insomniac.
It's really good because I've got friends all over the world, in different time
zones: 'Ah, China! Good!' And you start emailing or whatever. But when
I'm happy, I love being an insomniac. It means God has given me so many
more hours to be happy [laughs]. And when I'm unhappy, it's like the most
painful thing. If anyone here has been an insomniac, they'll know what I'm
talking about. Because your brain is just not at the right level to do things
properly. It'd be great if you could capitalise on the time, but you can't.
Your mind is just under par, it's just somewhere else, it's just not heightened
enough. So it's kind of difficult. Because there's not that much you can do
with that time. But I've started doing iPad drawings, thanks to David Hockney
[laughs]. And I've gone and got a new light bulb for my bedside lamp, which
is so bright that it means I can read much easier now. So I've started reading
again, furiously. A book a night, or whatever.

And you've got a massive new studio, in the East End.
Yeah, I've built my own studio in Spitalfields. It's got an 18-metres
swimming pool.

Well, that can't be bad, can it? [Laughs.]
The reason why I'm telling you this is because in all my wildest dreams, when
I was an art student, did I ever really think I was going to have an 18-metre
swimming pool in the bottom of my studio? No, I didn't. Did I ever think
I'd be sitting here? No, I didn't. You see, anything is possible, everything is
possible. Especially if you really believe in what you do, and love what you
do. A lot of people go into art, and especially now a lot of students say to me:
'Oh, how do you show at White Cube, or how do you do this, or how do you get
immediate success?' My tutor, when I was at the Royal College of Art, told me:
'It takes seven years, from being a student to actually having a realisation of
what you want to do.' And he was spot on with me. It was seven years. Seven
years in the wilderness!

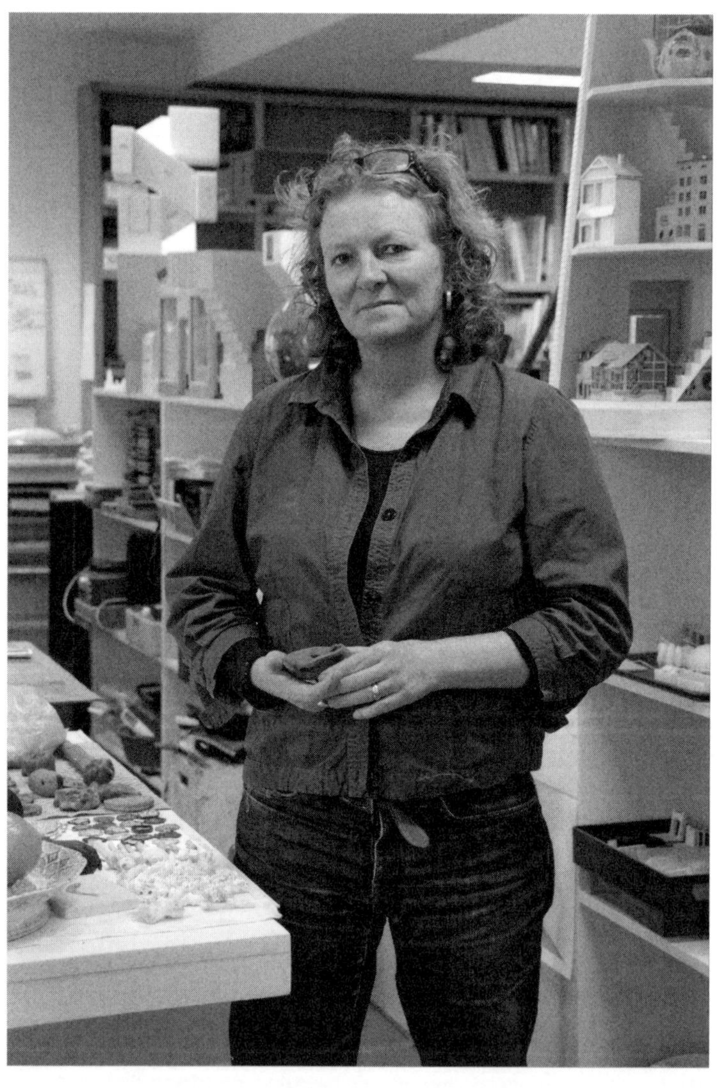

1997

Rachel Whiteread

'There were many stages when I thought I was mad. I felt very alien in the middle of it, and was going up on scaffolding with my head in bandages on the verge of a nervous breakdown. But I continued'

The paradox inherent in the whole idea of casting an empty space, of turning voids into solids, clearly fascinates you and lies at the centre of your work as a sculptor. The aptly entitled Ghost, *made in 1990, is an apparition in white plaster. Cast in sections from the interior space of a cramped north-London living room, this tour de force has a melancholy air. For all its magisterial presence,* Ghost *seems bound up with memories of a past beyond recall.*
So does House, *your life-sized cast of the interior of a condemned terraced house in east London. In my view,* House *was one of the most impressive pieces of sculpture made in Britain during the twentieth century. It brought you immense public attention in 1993, when you also became the first woman to win the Turner Prize. But* House *was tragically, and quite unnecessarily, demolished a few months later – an appalling act of Philistinism perpetrated by the local council. To your immense credit, though, the loss of* House *did not stop you developing as an artist.*

Your major exhibition last year at Tate Liverpool, the first substantial retrospective survey you have been given in Britain, showed just how much you have achieved, both before and after the House *debacle. In 1995 you moved away from the austerity of white plaster to explore the polychromatic splendour of* Untitled (One Hundred Spaces). *Ranged across the widest section of the Liverpool show, these compact resin units unfolded in a muted yet marvellously sensuous array of colours. Derived from the spaces underneath stools, chairs and tables, they transcended their commonplace origins and assumed the magnificence of temples. But they also resembled caskets fit for cremated ashes, and I remember walking up and down their ordered rows like someone visiting a military graveyard. The memorialising side of your imagination is as insistent as before. It shows that, ever since leaving the Slade School of Art in 1987, you have pursued a single-minded, clear course with great lucidity of purpose.*
I'd like to start by asking whether your work was very different before that.

Not really. In fact, I studied painting at Brighton Polytechnic and worked in the Painting Department for three years. But I actually painted for only one year, and I think it was towards the third year when I started to cast in one way: very, very simple casting, just by maybe pressing a spin into sand and pouring lead into it and making an object that was very like a spin, but wasn't a spin any more because it had no recess in it. Those ideas started maybe in 1983, and then I went to the Slade and worked with furniture and body cast. So really at that point, in my second year at the Slade, it was the beginning of what I do now. The work was obviously much more immature, and a little less coherent, but I think the genesis was there at that point.

What was it about casting which you found presumably more satisfying than the painting you had been doing?

When I was making paintings I got very frustrated with the edges of the canvas: you know, I started painting and I had to stop at the corner. It just irritated me, and I started to add things and they were going down to the floor. It is quite strange, because now really all I do is make edges. I am always filling things in and making edges, so I have gone full circle. Really what I am doing is painting! [Laughs.]

What were your paintings like?

Well, terrible sort of landscapes, I seem to remember.

Nothing like your subsequent concentration on ordinary, household objects?

No. I mean, they were abstracted. You know as a student how you walk through the landscape and make some drawings. You take that back to the studio and

then it goes off into something else. What you get involved with is the process
of the painting or putting paint on canvas. And that is really what I was doing
very early on, it was to do with process and colour.

I find it quite surprising that you were ever very interested in landscape.
It seems to me you are essentially an urban artist. Am I wrong about that?
You know, I was twenty-one at the time. In my last years at school I had got very
interested in art, went to Foundation to unlearn everything that I had learned
at school and then – you go to your first year at art school and it's like an open
book: you are like an open book. I was profoundly influenced by all sorts of
things, but I had no idea what I was really doing until maybe the third year
at college. I was an immature artist. I was learning, I was enjoying life and
I was playing. It wasn't until later that I was able to focus on certain areas
I was interested in.

The earliest work on view in your recent Tate Liverpool show was called Closet.
You made it in 1988 by taking an ordinary wardrobe and emptying the inside,
laying it on its back, drilling several holes in its doors and then filling it to
overflow with plaster. Finally, the shell of the wardrobe was jettisoned, leaving
a bleached cast of the interior in its place. But rather than leaving that naked,
as you might have done later on, you covered the plaster with black felt. Looking
back now, do you regard Closet *as a kind of turning point?*
Absolutely. I mean, when I made it, I regarded it as a turning point. It was
really, I think, the first sculpture I made. When I was at the Slade, I was trying
to make objects. I was desperately trying to make an object that would fit in the
middle of a room and you could walk around. But I never succeeded. It always
leant against the wall, or bore some relationship to an object that was next to
it. I was never able to make what I regarded as a kind of monolithic sculpture.
So when I made the *Closet* piece it was absolutely a turning point, yes. I drew
on childhood experience, I drew on all sorts of things as an excuse to make
that object, in a way. I was trying to illustrate a childhood experience of sitting
inside a wardrobe, of hiding inside wardrobes and finding these little dark
spaces to just go and dream in. I think I have described it before as a black,
furry space, like in a darkroom when you are developing film, how this is so
like a velvety darkness.

You make childhood experience sound quite idyllic, in a way. But it also seems
to me that, apart from suggesting perhaps an interest in Joseph Beuys's work,
the black felt gives the Closet *sculpture a sense of claustrophobia, almost?*
Yeah.

Funereal?
Absolutely. I think it's very sort of intentionally claustrophobic. It's like with
wallpaper, flocked wallpaper, for instance, you have this very strange surface
put on a wall. So you try to use things like that, which has relevance to your
own history, to parts of our lives – but also making quite an abstracted form.

How significant was it that Closet, *which you have already said was*
a very important moment for you, had some sort of a relationship with
childhood experience?
I think it was very important. When I was at the Slade, I made work that was
connected with both my own body and with furniture. I would go to my parents'
house and think: 'I'll borrow that table and bring it into college and do
something with it.' And it was very marked, it was very rooted in my own

language, what I had learnt, what I had understood. And I used that as a kind
of trampoline into the next stage. I had to go through that experience, I had
to make things that were very closely connected. It was really around that time
that I made *Closet* and I thought of making *Ghost*, but it took me a year and
a half to make it.

I would say that Ghost *was surely your masterpiece in 1990 – an extraordinary
year when you did several very important works, but I think* Ghost *is a
masterpiece. It makes me realise that your interest in something monumental
must have been very intense even then. Was it a very difficult task, setting about
casting an entire room in a house?*

Yes, it was difficult. In retrospect, it was one of the hardest things I have made
– for all sorts of reasons, partly because I had no money, I had to apply for
grants, I had to find a location to make the room in, and I had to find
somewhere for the piece to be exhibited after it was made. So I had these three
elements that for an unknown artist are very difficult to put together. But
gradually these things came together. I found this room in Archway, which was
ideal because it was actually very close to where I used to live. I was looking for
a room that was sort of connected with me – either a room that I lived in after
leaving college or that was connected with my childhood. And it had to have
three very important elements: a door, a fireplace and a skirting board.
I wanted these elements to be in the room, and obviously a window. So when
I found this house, there were maybe six rooms that I could have chosen from,
and I decided to choose this particular room because it wasn't so large. It was
quite humble in its origins, and I worked inside this place for maybe three or
four months, virtually entirely on my own. My partner helped me some of the
time, but a lot of the time I was there on my own and just confined to this room.
Working with the architecture and drawing the structure on the wall – which
was strangely enough connected for me, in my mind at the time, with the
paintings of Piero della Francesca. And it had very much a compositional
element which, I think, is apparent in all of my work. They are very clearly
defined blocks that fit together to make one element. So I spent a long time
composing the room and drawing it, seeing how it was going to finally look.
And then I literally cast every inch of it by hand. At one point I was in there
and had to cast the door. I said to the people next door – I used to borrow
their electricity – and in the morning I said to them: 'If you don't see me by six
o'clock, can you come and find me because I am casting the door and I may not
be able to get out!' It was quite strange. I felt like a kind of wicked nun who had
done something terrible, and I was going to be bricked into my cell.

It sounds quite frightening!

It kind of was. If you look at it now it is quite amusing, but at the time I was
a little bit scared.

However much you tried to figure out what Ghost *would finally look like, were
you nevertheless surprised when you stood back – and there it was?*

I was completely surprised. I mean, working within this comparatively small
space, every element that was cast was then put back against the wall in order
to cast the next element, so I was only seeing maybe 2 or 3 square feet of the
piece at a time and then it would go back into place. So I had this kind of jigsaw
puzzle of what it would look like in my mind, but it had all the pieces scattered
around and I couldn't put it together. Then we took it to my studio and built the
metal framework that holds the piece up. We'd been there – Max was helping
me – maybe two weeks of fiddling around with this thing. I came to the studio

and when I opened the door, there was the door of *Ghost* and I was completely
amazed at what I had done. Suddenly, I was the wall, and it was so strange
I couldn't quite believe it!

I know Ghost *well by now and I know what to expect, but whenever I see it,
I am always astonished. There is this feeling of something changed and
unexpected about it. And also, walking round it, I often experience a powerful
sense of frustration. Although the physical reality of the space has been,
I suppose you can say, faithfully memorialised, it actually can't be entered,
can it? It appears almost to have been silted up, and that seems to me to imply
– or maybe even to emphasise – that the lives once led inside that space have
somehow become irrecoverable. Does that make any sense to you?*

Yes, it does. When I made the piece, that was very much a part of it –
embalming lives, embalming the air, mummifying the space inside the room
is how I described it at the time. Now, after seven years, I have a sort of distance
from it. There is a sentence that someone said to me, a guy who had been in
prison, and he saw this piece and he said it reminded him of the inside of his
pocket. I thought that was a really beautiful way of describing it. This man,
who had obviously lived in this very small space for a long time. And that's
the way I like to look at the piece now – a kind of microcosm, it's like a mini-
universe inside your pocket.

*You talk about 'mummification' – there is another work which you also made in
1990, from the space around a bath. And looking at it, I get this feeling somehow
that it is like a sarcophagus. Although it's empty, the implication is that a body
may once have inhabited it. And it seems to me that you intensified this feeling
by placing a thick layer of glass on top, which almost looks like a coffin lid. Why
did you put the glass on top of something which in other respects you left more or
less raw and untouched?*

At that time, when I was making those bath pieces and some of the table pieces,
I was using parts of the original elements of the furniture. But with the bath
pieces, both had glass on the surface of them. One of them had two holes in
the glass, so it was almost like nostrils or, in a way, so it could breathe. Whereas
the other piece, *Valley*, had this glass straight over the top, and it was very
claustrophobic. When I first showed the piece, it wasn't completely dry and
the glass was put on top and it was amazing. I came in the next day and water
had collected on the glass, so it was really as if there was actually someone in
the bath and breathing in this kind of coffin.

*May I ask you whether, by the time you made that work, you had ever
undergone the experience of seeing a dead body?*

No, I had plenty of chances to see dead bodies and I have never seen one. I was
very clear about it when my father died: I didn't want to see him dead, because
I didn't want to live with that memory. I wanted to live with the memory of him
alive. And when I was a child, a friend of mine died and she was brought back
to the house. People came and went and visited her, and I didn't visit her. It was
for exactly those reasons, because I liked to keep a kind of clear memory of her
alive rather than dead.

How old were you when your father died?

Twenty-two, twenty-three …

Very young: that was obviously an important moment for you.

Yes, profoundly important …

Yes. But most people do have this desire, don't they, to see the dead person.
They find it almost reassuring.

I don't know how people react. People react in strange ways: some never
talk about it, they won't grieve, or they grieve in a very quiet way. Other people
scream and cry. People have very different ways of dealing with it. You know,
it's a personal thing. I chose to simply not see my father dead.

The central paradox in your work is the idea that you cast an empty space,
that you turn a void into a solid, almost that you make the hidden visible.
Why do you find that so fascinating?

I think it really started by trying to register in this world places that were
unregistered, that people had just forgotten about – giving an importance
to, for instance, this table that we are sitting at, the space underneath this table,
where you store things. All sorts of intimate things can happen under a table.
There are places I have always been fascinated with that are forgotten, and
I wanted somehow to bring them back into the world. That was certainly how
it started. Now, I think, it has become far more sculptural. It is not just to do
with casting space.

In terms of the art you may have seen at the moment when you began to define
your own direction, were you aware that way back, as early as 1965, Bruce
Nauman had made a plaster cast of the space underneath his chair?

I was, but not until probably when I was at the Slade. There was a Nauman
show at the Whitechapel, a great show, and I went to see it and quite frankly
I didn't really understand it. I saw the space underneath a chair, but Nauman's
work is incredibly complicated and incredibly varied.

It could hardly be more different from your work: it's always shooting off in
unexpected directions.

I really think he is one of the most extraordinary living artists. I know I have
seen this piece, but I sort of blanked it out. And when I made the *Closet* piece,
someone said to me: 'Do you remember this piece of Nauman's?' And I said:
'Yes, kind of.' And then I went to see it again, or looked at it again in a book.
But actually I am not going to worry about this, because what he was doing
with that particular piece is very different from what I am doing with my work.
So when I made *Closet* it was obviously a path for me that I was going to take
and continue down quite some time. I wasn't really fazed by it. But later on,
I think in about 1994, I decided to really take this on, that people would say
to me: 'What about Nauman?' I gave a lecture in America and someone would
say: 'Have you seen Nauman's work?' And I would say: 'Of course I have seen
Nauman's work.' So I felt that I would really take this up as a challenge and just
say: 'Look, I do know about Nauman.' I phoned the Canadian International,
which is one of the most public spaces in America that you could do something
like this. I decided to make a piece that was cast from a hundred chairs, in
different coloured resin, and it was like a repeat. I think there were nine chairs
cast and about seven different variants in the colour of resin, but really I was
using the chair as a block and as an architectural form. It was laid out on a grid
and you could walk through it, so it was almost like a miniature city. I decided
absolutely to take on a kind of Nauman challenge.

It is obviously important for you to invest even the most mundane and
overlooked aspects of life with some kind of unexpected dignity. But how
important is it that the viewer recognises or identifies what your starting
point was?

No, I think it's difficult. If I have a museum show, for instance at the Tate in
Liverpool, it's very clear in that exhibition – the work went from 1988 to 1996,
that's eight years with the work not changing that much – and I would hope
that someone would go and see an exhibition like this and really take care to
walk round and, as I do when I see an exhibition of someone that I am
interested in, follow the path and hopefully, from the little bit of information
taken from the first piece, then follow on to the next piece. Really, it's like
reading an encyclopedia. You gradually gather this information and try to
understand how the artist works. You know, I tend not to give too much away,
even though I am more and more asked to do interviews. But many people
are very lazy when they look at work, and I am also the same if I see something
that I am not that interested in. I may not really take it on board. But the work
I make is so simple and it's so clear in a way that I hope people would realise
that there must be something else about it. I want to make them look a little bit
harder, and this is why I don't use titles now. Everything is *Untitled*, and then
in brackets *(Yellow Bath)* or *(Black Books)*. It's just a description now, rather
than calling it *Yellow Leaf* or *Ether*, which were early titles that I used. They
were very poetic, but they also took you off onto another plane about how to
look at the piece. It's something that I personally hate when I go to a museum
and see something that I don't quite understand so I look at the title and think:
'Oh yes.' It's far too easy [laughs].

*That doesn't surprise me, because you are right: your work is on one level
very clear and that's one of its attractions, but on another level I think it
is very mysterious and you are fascinated by the whole notion of enigma.
Take, for example, the cast you made of the space underneath the bed. You
made the cast in rubber and then you burnished this amber oblong and
half-propped it against a wall. So when people first see it, maybe they feel
slightly thrown – partly because it departs so surprisingly from the
four-square presentation on a floor which sculpture in general, and your
work in particular, often adheres to. Your piece using the bed space transforms
a nondescript source into 'something rich and strange', like the submerged
coral-boned skeleton which Shakespeare writes about in* The Tempest.
Do you find his words potent, and close to your concerns?

Absolutely. You know, when I made that under-bed piece, it was cast flat.
I had this object in the studio and I was literally just playing with it, trying
to figure out what I was going to do, other than just have it lying on the floor.
It was like wrestling with a dead body in a way, there was a sort of strange,
inert weight to it. And when finally I put it up against the wall, it was finished.
Very often that happened in my work. With some of the pieces cast from
mortuary slabs, for instance, they were dust and I just had no idea what I was
going to do with them. They weren't finished, and I couldn't find the right place
for them. I don't think of the work as finished until I finally get it in my studio,
and I am looking at it, and it is sitting in the right kind of place that it needs
to be exhibited in.

*I just wonder if, to you, the objects that you make, although abstract in one
sense and removed from reality, are in a strange way more real to you than
what we think of as 'reality'. Simply because they have the permanence of art,
the distillation of art and all the satisfaction that can bring with them, rather
than the experience of reality, which is so often frustrating, so often hedged
around with a sense of transience. And when you start using resin, it helps
you to indulge some kind of appetite for colour which maybe your early
work had suppressed. I am thinking in particular of the multi-part piece,*

Untitled (One Hundred Spaces), *which unfolds in a fairly muted but
nonetheless extremely sensuous range of colours. Do you think colour is going
to become more important to you?*

Strangely enough, since making that piece I have gone back to using just
plaster. Colour has been very important to me, but from much earlier on by
using different-coloured plasters, dampy plasters, different kinds of rubbers,
and getting rubbers to be invented for me in order to somehow control the
colour. I have always been interested in colour, and even going back to some
of the early table pieces where parts of the tables were embedded in the
surface. One was quite yellow, so actually colour has always been there.
With the *Untitled (One Hundred Spaces)* I wanted to use the material which,
by very carefully using different types of resin, meant that I could mix to make
these very particular colours. I must just say that I have never actually coloured
something by adding pigment. It has always been very much part of the
material.

Is that important to you?

Yes. There is a piece that I am about to make using a plastic, and I am actually
dyeing a plastic. But because it is black, I think I can cope with that. It's not
like using plaster and adding loads and loads of pigment to change it to a
different colour. It's just simply going from white to make this very, very dense
black colour. With some of the other materials that I have been using, especially
the resin, I have managed to get a sort of transparency, translucency, to very
deep forms, so that the internal structure of the object is as important as
the external structure. When they are sitting in a space and the sun comes
in, they can virtually disappear. And in other light conditions, they are clearly
ever-present. I was really enjoying working with that.

Yes, I was very struck, when I saw a piece called Untitled (Floor) *in your
Tate Liverpool exhibition, that it started off looking very tough, with the seven
elements cast from the gaps between the floorboards' underlying supports. Lying
there on the floor, they looked very uncompromising. But then the sunlight came
through a big window from the Mersey and hit those resin forms. They seemed
to glow, almost like ingot, and revealed their transparency, which makes
absolute sense when you are an artist who is dealing with voids and emptiness.
So from that point of view, is resin perhaps more exciting to you than plaster?*

No, I like the dead or dense quality of plaster. I have actually stopped using
resin, because it is a really unpleasant material to work with. I persevered
with it for about a year and a half, and then just felt that, healthwise, it was
probably not very sensible to work with a material like this. I was also pushing
the boundaries of what you could do with a material, casting nearly half a ton
of it – it's very complicated to use, so I have gone away from that. I am looking
for another kind of plastic, clear plastic, that I can use. But it's a struggle finding
these materials.

I also remember thinking, when I looked at Untitled (One Hundred Spaces),
*that walking up and down those ordered rows was rather like visiting some
kind of graveyard, and I noticed that you had actually taken photographs
of war cemeteries. How do you use those photographs? How do images that
you record with a camera feed your work?*

I think they are simply to do with gelling the memory. I take a lot of
photographs, but I often think about a place I have been to and I can't
quite place what it was that I saw. If I had a 35mm slide, even if I didn't have
it to hand, I can remember looking through the sheets of slides I have taken.

I think it has to do with imprinting something on my memory: maybe if I didn't take the photographs, I would take a little more for granted.

Can we talk about House? *It seems to me that the memorialising side of your imagination – if I can call it that – is most insistent in* House. *It only stood for a few months on the otherwise demolished side of a road in East London, but I will never forget the experience of seeing it there. How did it come about?*

It actually came about very soon after I made *Ghost*. I almost immediately thought about mummifying a whole house. But it was a sort of dream at the back of my mind, really, and then James Lingwood from Artangel asked me – maybe a couple of years later – if I was interested in doing a project with them, and I said: 'Well, I have got this idea.' He said, over a cup of tea, 'OK, yeah, let's do that', and it started as simply as that. Little did we know what would ensue! I was living in Berlin, and I had a friend researching, looking for various kinds of properties. Then we would go and look at them. It was a very long and complicated process. But then eventually this house came up, which I knew very well because I cycled past this road every day on my way to the studio, and it was kind of perfect. I came to look at it, and there was a whole row of houses, maybe ten or twelve. I went back to Berlin, then came back about two weeks later and all of the houses had gone, apart from this one house. It was kind of unbelievable that they were building me a plinth for my piece to sit on! This whole area had been cleared.

Why was there only one house left?

Because there was a very stubborn and extraordinary man called Mr Gale. He refused to leave until he was really housed in another proper house, rather than pushed into some dreadful tower block. So he stayed and fought tooth and nail, and was rehoused in a house. When he and his son left, we moved in and worked for about three or four months just dealing with all the surfaces, from the attic to the basement, getting rid of a lot of the fitted cupboards and things that were in the house. We were really stripping it and covering the windows, dealing with undercrofts and putting a release agent on. We were building new foundations for the building that was being built within the building. Then we sprayed concrete and finally took the original house down, brick by brick, and revealed the inside-out concrete house.

That must have been a gruelling task! Was there any stage when you thought: 'I am mad to have embarked on this.' Or was it fairly pain-free?

No, there were many stages when I thought I was mad. It was very complicated dealing with all the building, and dealing with the demolition people – people that I normally have not very much to do with in my field of work, and they were completely trying to take advantage of me, at every single kind of opportunity. The whole situation was very complicated. I felt very alien in the middle of it, and was going up on scaffolding with my head in bandages on the verge of a nervous breakdown. But I continued. No, it was an incredibly complicated thing to make – emotionally, physically, and all of those things. But I am very pleased that I did it, and very proud.

Yes, and quite rightly, too. How far did you see House, *on one level anyway, as a kind of memorial to all the houses that had once lined this street – and, by extension, to all the houses in the East End which were destroyed by bombing or afterwards by wholesale and often very misguided post-war redevelopment?*

It has absolutely to do with all of those things. But interestingly enough, that's why it was destroyed as well. I was really making a comment about all those things you have just talked about. But because it was made out of concrete, there was this man called Councillor Flounders who made it his mission to get the piece destroyed. He said he had spent the past twenty years trying to rid Tower Hamlets of ugly concrete, and what was I doing giving them another great lump of concrete? He didn't understand the complex issues involved with the piece at all. He made it his mission to show 'the chattering classes' that he was better than they were.

I remember him calling them 'the chattering classes of Hampstead'!
I think that was his phrase, yes.

But the extraordinary thing about House *was that, although it became notorious and received an astonishing amount of press coverage not only in this country but elsewhere, it wasn't just a kind of Aunt Sally, was it? I think a lot of people were genuinely moved by it. Many people saw the point of it. One of the aspects of this sculpture was that it became a receptacle, almost, for emotions which the viewer could bring to it. Speaking for myself, what I remember most was a feeling of very understated vulnerability. Those projecting windows at the front were still clearly identifiable, you knew what was going on there architecturally, but they also looked sealed up – as if somehow the entire building had become engulfed, almost as if it had suffered from petrification after a lava flow descended. And there was a very strong preoccupation with death. Would you say that a sense of loss was right at the centre of your concerns here?*
Yes, I think it was. When I first started thinking of making the piece, obviously there were all sorts of engineering problems and some architectural problems involved with it. But eventually, I was trying to embalm this house. Working from the inside out, I was carefully going over every single surface – in a way, showing it respect before it died. Because the house was going to disappear. It's kind of confusing for me, because I can talk about the technical problems involved with making the piece, but there were also a great amount of emotional problems. I don't think that I ever really understood the piece when I was making it, and I never had the chance to see it when it was finally made because of the hoo-ha that was involved. I find it very strange talking about it now because it's a memory for me, as it is for you – even though I was the person who made it. I really had quite a strange relationship with it. I am almost more familiar with the inside of it, and the structure and skeleton of the house, as I am with the outside of it. Because I was involved with every cubic inch of it.

This desire to embalm and to lay to rest – which is another phrase you used earlier – how does that link up with this interest in the war cemeteries you photographed? It seems to me that they are all part and parcel of something.
Yes, I think they are. This stems from having worked in Highgate Cemetery as a teenager …

What was the work you did there?
The old part of the cemetery was derelict, and I helped to restore it – to enable people to walk round and look at it. It's incredibly peaceful. I love cemeteries. I love walking around cemeteries. I find them very calming, poetic places. I think they are so beautiful, and they are also incredibly sad. It's almost like walking into a cathedral when walking into a cemetery: you have this sense of awe, this sense of spirituality – however you want to explain it. Or it's like walking up to the top of a mountain. All those things for me are very clear, in my understanding of the world and how I somehow intensify that understanding for myself.

Were you surprised by the notoriety of House *and the hatred it aroused, at least in the circle of Councillor Flounders?*

> I knew that the piece would be controversial, but I had no idea it would be that controversial! You can't ever imagine that would happen to anything. I was surprised by the support, and I was amazed how everybody used it as a kind of soapbox. They all stood on their own little soapboxes and shouted about whether contemporary art was good or bad, or whether they thought housing policies were good or bad. And I hid as much as I could: I couldn't take it all in, it was out of control.

It seems to me that the act of ripping it down was tantamount to a criminal act of vandalism, and I deplore it. But the fact remains that it was initially intended as a temporary structure, wasn't it?

> Yes, it was always intended as a temporary structure, because there is no way you could ever have got planning permission to have it made from Tower Hamlets. And I was very specific about its location: it had to be around this site in the East End of London. Some other councils might have been a little more open to it, but I didn't want to make it in Kensington or Westminster. I think the struggle to make it was part of the piece.

The strange thing is that no public sculpture could have been more rooted in its context, in its locality, in an understanding of what that part of the East End of London actually is or was. So from that point of view, it wasn't as if you were coming along and imposing some weird, arbitrary piece of art which bore no relation to the neighbourhood.

> No, but I was making something that supposedly uneducated people hate, which is modern art. And that's what this man, Councillor Flounders, was banging on about: 'How dare you speak for everyone else!' But, you know, that is the nature of our political system. He was able to speak for everybody else! What made me so upset about its destruction was not that it happened, because I knew it would happen, but that it happened so quickly. I don't think it had a time in its life to have any sort of dignity. It was only up for six weeks, two months, something like that. I think if it had stayed up for maybe a year, people would have stopped staring at it and just come across it quietly and glanced at it – it would have become invisible, like a lot of urban architecture is. And I think that would have been nice, if it had a chance to have that moment of dignity.

I quite agree. You have also encountered enormous hostility in some quarters to your new monumental sculpture for the Judenplatz in Vienna: the Holocaust Memorial, *which was commissioned by the city. Why do you think the restrained image that you produced for this project – of a great book-lined library – provoked opposition?*

> I think whatever had been proposed for that square, and accepted by the committee of people who invited artists to make something, it would have been very, very complicated and wouldn't have been made by now. This is clear from the history of public monuments in Vienna. There is this man called Herr Lischker, he has made a really rather terrible piece of public sculpture against world fascism just opposite the Opera, about a mile away from my piece, or rather the site for my piece. And I think he waited for years for this piece to happen. But he is a citizen of Vienna, he lives there and he is involved with the politics day to day. I simply am not prepared to do that, to spend the next year and a half of my life fighting with the officials in the city of Vienna about this. They asked me to make the piece, and I think it is up to them whether or not it is going to happen.

Where did your idea of the library come from?

I went to see the site, and it's a very ornate square but quite domestic in scale. I always knew that I wanted to make a room that was somehow connected with the location, and then gradually the idea of books started to come in. I have been working with some smaller book pieces in my studio, and I was doing a lot of reading and thinking about this for Jewish heritage. I did some travelling, went to Normandy, Washington and saw memorials and monuments. I started to think about it in quite a clear way. I had also spent a lot of time, when I was living in Berlin, going to concentration camps. So I was going to build up the language that might try and deal with something as terrible as the holocaust ...

It's almost an impossible task, isn't it?

It is, and that was really the challenge: to see if I could come up with some sort of humane and poetic way of dealing with such a tragedy – such a dreadful, dreadful thing. And I feel that I did, but I don't know if the piece will ever be made. I don't know if it will ever sit in that square.

Can you say anything more about books and their importance?

Well, the Jews are known as the people of books. And also, during the Nazi time, there was an enormous amount of book burning, and that has happened throughout many, many centuries. So really it was using that as an idea and working from that. But I also wanted to make something that was quite severe, quite brutal in a way. And I didn't think that you deal with something like the holocaust with any kind of sentimentality or nostalgia. So I was really very clear that it had to be – I wouldn't say ugly, but brutal. And I hope that, if the piece is finally made, what will happen with erosion and weathering and all sorts of things – you know, pollution will gradually pick up, and birds will do their doings on them, and the weather will do something to them – and gradually, you will have this very, very complex surface, a repeated surface, and I think that will become over the years a testament to its own history, as a piece of sculpture.

Rachel Whiteread's *Holocaust Memorial* was finally unveiled in October 2000.

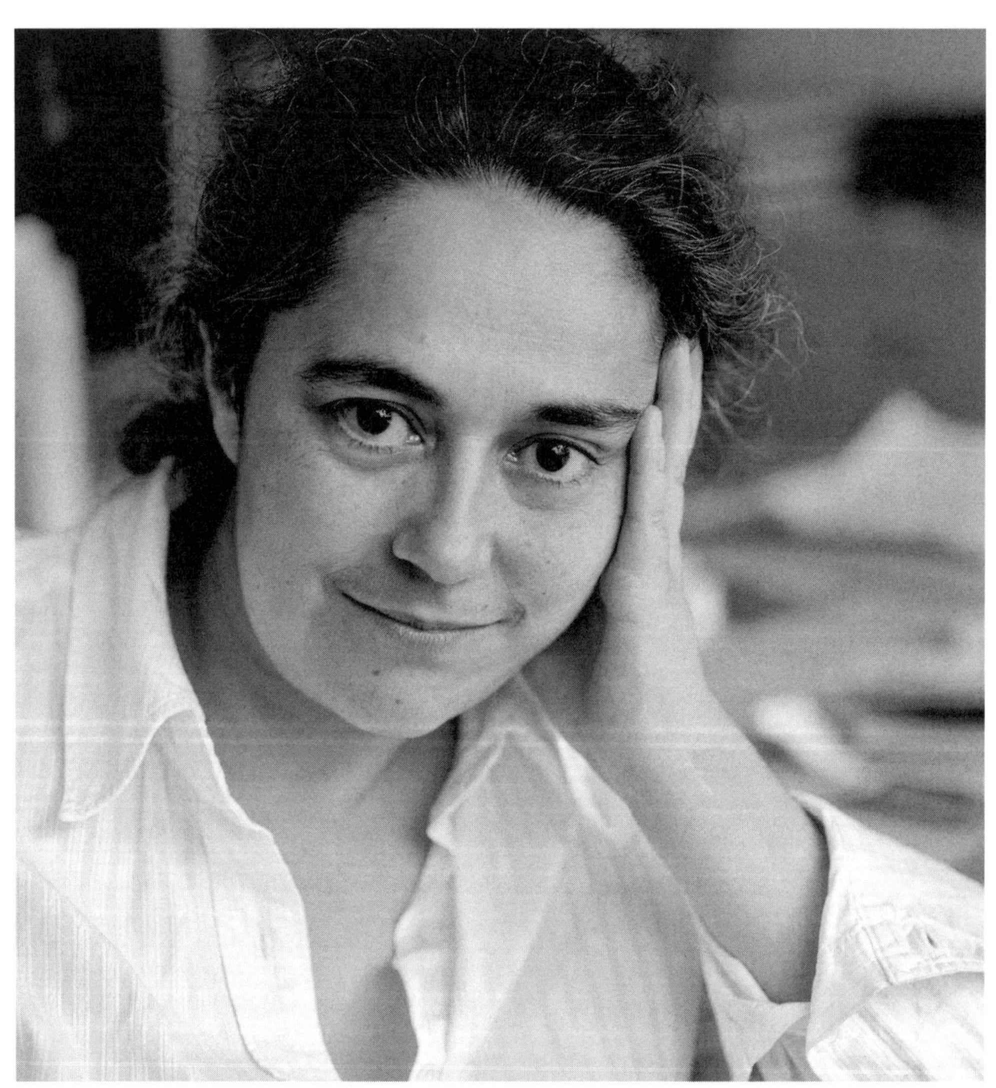

Tacita Dean

'What became more important was the fact that he got totally lost, and time-lost as well. He suffered from what was called "time madness", and so I was very interested in and attracted to being able to get completely lost'

*In many of your early works you see yourself as an amateur sleuth who
follows a trail of clues and amasses evidence. However possessed you may
become during the chase, though, the pursued story never quite fits together.
It remains incomplete, and this absurdity is enlivened by a spirit of wild
delight. But the quixotic oddity of your assignments does not prevent you
from relaying the findings in a sober, authoritative style.*

*After devoting your first film to the tale of a woman searching
for beards in different countries, you then turned your attention to* The
Martyrdom of St Agatha (in several parts). *The voice on the film's soundtrack
is quiet, almost professorial, describing with dignity how the devout Agatha
of Catania refused the lecherous advances of the Roman Consul Quintian.
The camera tracks across her native Sicily, searching for traces of the third-
century woman who became a legend after Quintian cut off her breasts.
Whatever eroticism and violence can be found in your St Agatha film is
tempered by understatement. The same approach characterises the even more
sober* Girl Stowaway, *although film here plays a smaller role in a work which
also relies on newspaper cuttings, photographs and the dubbing sheets from
a British feature film apparently prepared in 1928. You tease us with
coincidence and enigma throughout* Girl Stowaway, *but sound plays a far
more important role in your 1996 installation, arrestingly shot and succinctly
edited, on two Foley Artists. Beryl Mortimer and Stan Fiferman take their
quirky professional name from the original Mr Foley, who concocted sound
effects in the pioneering days of film post-production.*

And now you have made a work for BBC radio. Berlin Project
*was commissioned by Radio 3, and it concentrates on you, your family
and friends as well as the city where you now live. All the sound was recorded
personally by you in Berlin during the autumn of 2001. I found it a very
intense and haunting piece, especially listening to it here tonight with an
audience. In one sense it's difficult to define, but in another sense it's almost
tangible, in a strange way – or visceral, perhaps, is a better word. But anyway,
you've actually said that* Berlin Project *is 'the most personal piece I have ever
made, the most autobiographical'. I wonder if you could pin down some
at least of those references for us in the piece, and say why they reflect your
own life so closely?*

God, here we go: confessions! It is very strange hearing *Berlin Project* again,
because last time I heard it was some months ago. And how painfully
autobiographical it is, I have to say!

Really?

And also how much about radio it is, because I sat there feeling it was quite
fragmentary. But I knew in a way that was because, when you're in radio,
you drift in and out, which was part of the whole nature of it.

Yes indeed.

But back to the autobiography. What happened with this radio piece,
from the very beginning, is that I actually had no idea what I was going
to do. To the point where it became immensely painful. I was living in
Berlin and collecting sound, and I really had to reverse the way that I
worked before, which is that I find an idea and then, although I go through
a similar state of chaos, the chaos is distilled into some sort of order in
the editing process. This is completely reversed here: I was collecting
information blindly, and there are very, very strong threads going through
it which I will tell you in this intimate setting, but which nobody else
would normally know.

Just to give you some clues about it. Publicly, it says that it's about the dialogue
between the soul and the body – Andrew Marvell is a poet I've always been very
interested in. So for me there's a very, very strong dichotomy throughout this,
to do with the physical body which I transcribe into walking and the feet and
journeying. This is made manifest with – you often hear footsteps – but also
football: the last scene is Hertha Berlin beating Bayern Munich (a very rare
occasion) in the Olympic Stadium in Berlin, which, by the way, is beautiful
acoustically. And it was the first football match I've ever been to, except for one
in Ohio State, which doesn't quite count. But also the main character is a family
friend of ours, who we've known as 'Boots'. And he's called 'Boots' in the way
that you always name people after their disability. He has a huge boot because
he has a sort of withered leg. His name is Robert Steane, and he's my sister's
godfather. We've known him all our child life, and he's always been a very
important person, very dramatic-looking. Not only did he have a big false
boot, but he had a patch on his eye for most of our childhood. He's the most
charismatic person you could ever possibly meet. And it was just a chance
meeting at the very early stage of this *Berlin Project*: it was my father's eightieth
birthday, and I sat next to Boots. We both share the same birthday, and that's
why he said 'twin' at the end. His father was a silent movie actor called Jack
Trevor in Berlin, just in the 1920s and '30s. Then, with the rise of National
Socialism, he got enmeshed and stayed in Berlin. We don't really know the
true story, but he ended up broadcasting for the Nazis in some manner or other.
English-language propaganda broadcasts. He was eventually arrested, tried for
treason and spent four years in Pentonville Prison in Britain. And this is always
the story, half anecdote and half fact. When I did delve into the internet to find
out a bit more about it, I only found one mention of him which clearly stated
he was a traitor. So Boots has grown up with this terrible ambivalence about
his father, [whose story] from Boots's own stories, was very much that he
hadn't got a lot of choice, which I could quite understand. So Boots had this
relationship to Berlin, and as I delved further, one of the first things I did was
to go down and talk to Boots, who lives in Thanet. He told me this extraordinary
story, including the fact that he actually had his leg operated on in the Charité
Hospital, which is the hospital where I go because I have arthritis. So we had
this bond through time, and this was the hospital of the former party bosses
of East Berlin. It's situated in the centre of the new Berlin now, and there's a
moment when I actually recorded going up in the lift in Charité, and I became
a bit of an eavesdropper with my tape recorder. They didn't know that I was
recording, but fortunately the woman said 'Charité' so there's a connection
between the beginning and the end. And there's another connection, because
Boots is my sister's godfather and my sister's name is Antigone. Her historical
father was Oedipus, which means 'swollen foot' in Greek. And the other male
voice you hear is my father, in fact. That was a very old conversation about
years ago, when I asked him why he called Antigone 'Antigone'. I've always been
very interested in that story, which is the relationship between Antigone and
Oedipus. Years ago I was drawing swollen feet and all sorts of things, so that's
another narrative going throughout. And then there's Berlin, and bits of found
material like the Krakow radio, which is a beautiful thing I found on the radio
in Berlin: it sounds like a limping man going north, south, east, west, and
blowing a horn, which apparently symbolises the moment when the watchman
was killed by the invading Turks. So that's why it stops abruptly each time in all
four corners. But they play that every Saturday or Sunday at midday on Krakow

radio, and it's beautiful that they would allow that kind of expanse of time.
Apparently, it's extremely popular in Poland because it precedes the equivalent of
the shipping forecast, which is the level of the rivers in Poland. So that becomes
an incantation afterwards. But I also love those bits of radio that just take their
time. And also my name means 'silence', so that was another element in it.

A paradox there, I think.

Well, it's a silent work with sound. So that's also a personal narrative for me. I'm
very interested in silence and what's perceived as silence, and the gaps between
moments. It starts in my studio – I had a studio in the forest in Berlin, and
literally there was this silence before a storm. I sensed the storm was coming,
so I put on a recorder and then this wind comes, and that's a true piece of sound.
Then it goes to Porto Cathedral where there's the silence of praying, as it were.
Silence is also a big theme throughout it, so there's loads of different things.

*It's very rich. At one point, you talk about absolute thresholds of touching,
seeing, hearing and so forth. How do you think that impinges on what you're
doing in* Berlin Project? *I'm very interested in that word 'thresholds'.*

I wanted, radio-wise, to play with limits. And we won – we succeeded. But that
actual text I had written down a long time ago, from another spell in another
hospital, where I met this other woman who was studying for some degree.
She had a book on perception and I'd written down the quotation from there.

But there's quite a lot of 'thresholding' going on in this piece, I think.

Well, there's a lot of movement, from England to Berlin and back again. There's
a lot of transport trains, if that's what you mean, going from place to place.

*No, I didn't mean that, actually – although it's an interesting point. I meant
more that one of the things I like about the piece is that very often it's almost
silent, isn't it? You push it to a degree where you can hardly hear it, and you
hardly know what you're listening to. That makes it quite fascinating. Were
you consciously trying to do that?*

Oh yes, because I've always been interested in those bits of waste sound, as it
were. Like for example where you hear people coughing at four o'clock in the
morning in a courtyard, and at the beginning of the S-Bahn there's someone
blowing their nose. There is that kind of wind in all sorts of places. I don't
know if everyone noticed the fart in the ladies' loo, and then the hoover?

And the marvellous, very, very distant piano at one point.

Yes, that was my neighbour, who was a composer. None of it's fake. The
music that you keep hearing, which is repeated in four different ways – the
glockenspiel, and various versions – that's a famous Berlin song called 'Das
ist die Berliner Luft, Luft, Luft', which means 'That is Berlin Air, Air, Air',
and it's all about how foul-smelling Berlin air is [laughs]. So that's another
connection: the air is strong in relation to the soul.

*You've already mentioned the Andrew Marvell poem about the dialogue between
the soul and the body. Can I pursue you on this? What kind of tensions do you think
there are between those two alternatives as they're explored here? How do you see it?*

How I transcribe the soul is as air. And that goes back to my film *A Bag of Air*,
which was about rising up in the sky to catch the upper ether, which, when
transmuted, would become a remedy to all disharmonies in the soul. And
I've often made that parallel between air and the soul, which is an alchemical
parallel. It's emphasised by the Greek quote at the beginning, talking about air,

when made thicker, becoming wind. Anaximenes, a pre-Socratean philosopher.
And then the body for me was very much the sound of feet – corporeal sounds
as well, but particularly the feet. This all happened very, very late in the day.
My unconscious was extremely busy. My conscious didn't know what was going
on, because I was getting all these things that, at a certain point, suddenly made
perfect sense. But it took me right up to the point of the editing, with boxes
of sound, before I really understood what was going on. And I made a kind of
map in the end, drawing it all to try and connect it, to try and understand what
the hell I was going to do. It was quite a terrifying project in that sense, because
I felt totally stuck. Also, I didn't really want to make it pedantically narrative.
I wanted to make it elusive.

Absolutely. That's a very good word. It's exactly what you've done. But it makes
Berlin Project *gripping, too, because you're constantly in pursuit of it.*
I'd love to listen to it as somebody I didn't know, an ordinary person, not
having made it. Because I like difficult radio. Especially in Berlin, if you pick
up Russian radio and Polish radio, it's much more sophisticated somehow.
You can hear the most extraordinary things across the airwaves, which you
don't so much any more, here – things which do push against the thresholds
of perception, as it were.

How susceptible are you to music? Because it occurred to me at several points
in Berlin Project *that there was a musical, or certainly a percussive, thing going*
on. Terrific Ladies loo percussion, very intense and rhythmic. Do you listen to
a lot of music?
I do, but I can't pretend I'm any good at music.

No, no, I wasn't asking that.
No, I know, but I mean …

Music means a lot to you, does it?
It does, but it does to everybody.

No, not to everybody.
I think if anyone was asked that question, they'd say: 'Oh yes, music means a lot
to me' [laughs]. I was very attracted to the sound rhythms in the loo, because
it actually was my last chance to go there, and it was certainly quite difficult to
get there before it closed at four o'clock on a Saturday. So I knew I really wanted
that sound, with the coins and then the banging. It's just so beautiful, and it's
also very old-fashioned – and I'm quite old-fashioned, in that sense.

The BBC didn't like Berlin Project *at first. What was the problem?*
I'm trying to remember the word. It was a word that had two meanings. Oh,
yes: it was a matter of 'levels'. Which could have been taken in two ways – one
of them was audible levels, and another one was subject levels. The message
I got was that they were uncomfortable and it wasn't narrative enough. It was
suggested that I put more sound over what were, I think, called *longueurs*.
And these were exactly the bits that I wanted to try and push. But in the end
they played it, which was great.

Yes, that's great. A lot of artists have told me that, in their studios, they love to
have the radio on.
So there was an element of that in it. This is a captive audience here, you're all
sitting and listening to everything, but that's not how it was made and what it

was made for. For a lot of people it will be drifting in and out, and thinking: 'What's that? That's pretty bizarre to hear on a radio!' Or becoming engaged by it, or turning it off. I mean, the point is people walk out of exhibitions the whole time – you can't ever insist on people being there, however much I've tried. So people would turn it off. But the fact that you'd get half who might be more engaged by it than they would normally by evening radio, and then the other half will turn it off, I think that's quite successful.

And the Radio 3 audience is an adventurous audience almost by definition, otherwise they wouldn't be listening to it. You've actually been working with sound as a medium – one of your many media – for quite a while now. Listening to Berlin Project, *I remembered the ambitious sound-work that you made for a Thames-side location outside the Millennium Dome, where you took the ventilation shaft of the Blackwall Tunnel and transformed it into a kind of globe. Each side of this structure transmitted sounds that you had recorded in different time zones. How did you go about doing that, and why were you so interested in the Blackwall Tunnel's proximity to the Meridian Line?*

The Meridian Line went right through this air vent before they moved it. They moved it because they wanted it to be more obvious, but at the time when I was proposing this idea the Meridian Line went straight through this air vent, which had eight sides. And because the Meridian Line is longitude zero, I decided to make it into a sound world. And so one side was Greenwich, and the others were 45 degrees around the world. And then I went to each of these longitude lines, where it cut between land and sea – a port, effectively – and I recorded twenty-four hours of sound between midday Friday and Saturday that would play in its real time for the whole millennium year. For example, when midday in Greenwich is midnight in Fiji, and then is three in the afternoon in Yemen and six in Bangladesh and nine in the evening in Japan. And then it was Alaska, New Orleans and Brazil. I went to most of these places and recorded the sound, which was wild sound and a bit like how I recorded the sound here, and then it was all going simultaneously. Then the Millennium Dome sited those water fountains right next to it, and you couldn't hear a thing! It was such a disaster.

With their customary flair and care for the specially commissioned artworks in that location! I was one of the selectors of the Millennium show there, and it was a very mortifying experience for everyone concerned.

Yes, it was.

You are a great traveller, though. Another earlier sound piece that I remember charted a different kind of journey – this time in a car, with a patient driver called Greg – through a very remote area of Utah. You wanted to find Robert Smithson's great Spiral Jetty, *which is such an icon of American Land Art and once upon a time whirled out into the Great Salt Lake. It was a very entertaining but deeply frustrating expedition, wasn't it?*

Yes. I actually was in Sundance Filmmakers Lab with my film idea, which was Antigone the movie pic. And the driver was actually a film director who was also at the Lab. He had never heard of Smithson and didn't know what he was looking for. We hired a car, and we did follow these fax instructions that I'd rung up and got from Utah Arts Council trying to find Smithson's *Spiral Jetty*. It was an incredibly difficult journey: further and further into this absolute wasteland, and then at the end we didn't find it, or I thought we didn't find it, and now I've had it confirmed that I definitely did not find it! I don't know if anyone's read in *Artforum* this month that somebody else has done it again and gone there.

What, retraced your journey?

Yeah, well, he's done his own journey and told me categorically, through the written word, that I was nowhere near Smithson's jetty, and that what I was standing on the end of was this oil jetty built in 1985!

Oh, no!

I know, never mind. But apparently it has risen again: someone sent me an article from the *Utah Post* to say that, because of the drought, it has risen again.

But to me, the fact that you didn't find it is all of a piece with your other work. Because there is this preoccupation with projects, often very vaulting, that somehow get confounded – often in surroundings where, I notice, nature is at its most vast and elemental. This runs through a lot of your work, particularly in film.

What are you really thinking of there? Which one?

Well, let's talk about Donald Crowhurst, shall we?

People say to me that there is a strong element of disappearance in my work.

Definitely, yes.

I didn't notice that for a very long time.

It's certainly true of Crowhurst, this lone yachtsman who vanished during a 1969 race to sail around the world. You became very, very absorbed in him and his extraordinary desperation – that's the only word for it.

Well, what attracted me first about him was that he faked his logbooks, and so it was the whole element of fact and fiction. But then what became more important was the fact that he got totally lost, and time-lost as well. He suffered from what was called 'time madness', and so I was very interested in and attracted to being able to get completely lost in a fairly contemporary age, although it was a pre-satellite age – losing all sense of time and space, really.

One film that you explore him in is Disappearance at Sea. *Why did you decide there to use that lighthouse? I think it was at St Abb's Head – what a wonderful name – near Berwick-upon-Tweed. This is very much the focus of the whole film, isn't it?*

That was almost an accident. But what I wanted was what I never got, particularly, which was light searching the horizon. And I wanted an extended frame: it was the first time I ever used anamorphic.

Yes, it's very wide.

Yes, it's very long and thin. And therefore it takes longer for the things to pass through the frame, and that's what I was very interested in. We intended to go to two other lighthouses rather than Berwick, and St Abb's was in fact the first we went to. What was so attractive about this lighthouse was that it didn't have a tower, so it meant you could actually be up there with the bulbs. So it was really quite impressive at that moment, but through the sound which gets more and more desolate as the night grows and the light bulbs become lit. But the lighthouse is the last human place between land and sea, really. So sailors do rely on them completely and their different pulses of light. It was a commission for a lighthouse at the time as well, so that played an important part.

We were talking about thresholds earlier, and it certainly applies to that film – the visual threshold, the sense of the darkness and the void, and then the light every now and again alleviating it. But talking of travel, you adopted a more exploratory approach when you travelled to Cayman Brac in the Caribbean.

*You wanted to track down the trimaran that Crowhurst used for his ill-fated
voyage. Why did you want to look at the vessel itself and, as it turned out, film
it in great detail?*

Well, at a certain point it was the last thing I could do in relation to the story.
It was a commission I had from the National Maritime Museum, and I wanted
to make a book about Crowhurst. It was about the boat rather than him, and
I was very careful to try to use only photographs of the boat, because in a way
it was the last part of the puzzle. But the most amazing thing about going
to Cayman Brac was that it also led me to Bubble House, which was the other
place of neglect on this island. Both of them had incredible similarities: they
were both conceived in the 1960s when there was this incredible optimism.
I should explain that the Bubble House was built by a man who ended up being
convicted of fraud for embezzling money off the American government.

He was French, wasn't he?

And he's still doing – so far as I know – thirty-five years in prison. It was a
perfect house, the Bubble. It was completely deserted, but on this extremely
tax-haven, pampered island, Bubble House and the trimaran were the only
two pieces of neglect. It was extraordinary. Both had paid dearly for their fraud,
and both had the same quality: out-of-timeness. They were anachronisms.

And Bubble House was never finished.

No. Nor was the trimaran, actually.

*I remember during the filming there was a rainstorm, and the rain started
pouring in – which in a strange way links up with the sound we were getting
in the* Berlin Project. *You use that sort of event, don't you?*

Well, I was just very lucky, because I was filming out of the window.

It was very dramatic.

The storm came across the sea and got there just as my film ran out. I could
have done with ten seconds more, I really could. There was one drop of rain
on the lens and then I ran out of film. But it was truly luck: I am quite lucky.

*You do need luck in this kind of thing. Do you think your attraction to ruins,
and these awesome spectacles that you like in nature, links you in particular
with those late-eighteenth-century artists who became captivated by nature
at its most sublime, the word that came up during that period and meant
so much to artists? It means not just what we think of as sublime, which
is something exhilarating and awesome, but also something threatening.
I imagine this ambiguity might appeal to you quite a lot.*

Yes, I was thinking about follies just then.

Follies – yes, that's even better for you than ruins.

I'm attracted to anachronisms and things that don't function in their time
any more. I realise that usually they were built in the 1960s and they're now
dysfunctional. It's funny, I think it's something to do with my lifespan, maybe.
But I'm making a new film, with Boots actually, and I realise that he's a human
ruin. I haven't really used people before in my films. But why am I interested
in ruins? I don't know. There are a lot of things you don't question, you just
seem to be attracted to them.

Is it to do with the vanity of all our hopes, maybe?

Of course it is [laughs]. No, I don't know.

There is a strong sense of futility in your work. Or rather, you seem to be drawn to things, often on a colossal scale, that fill the screen in your films and somehow failed to live up to their intentions – like the Sound Mirrors built on the coast at Denge, near Dungeness. What were they intended to do?

They were intended to catch sound, actually.

Yes, but for military reasons.

Yes. They were built between the First and the Second World Wars, and they were facing out to sea, to track the sound of enemy aircraft. It was when aeroplanes began to become a menace, taking off from France. But the Sound Mirrors were useless: they had little listeners in them, like with stethoscopes, listening to vibrations. And then they would pick up traffic and passing propeller boats. They were completely non-directional, so it was totally useless. The mirrors would have been knocked down, had it not been for the Second World War which distracted the Ministry of Defence. Yes, I do like things that are failed visions. It's all the optimism in those things and then they 'dysfunction'. There is a sort of pathos.

And almost a bathos, too. I'm tempted to wonder whether you're essentially a tragic artist, in the sense that you do often deal with the destruction or frustration of hope. But I pause on the brink of that, because I think there's a lot of humour in your work as well. It's often extremely funny, in a very Tacita Dean kind of way, and there's a lot of beauty in your work. I'm thinking of that extraordinary film, again in Berlin, where you look at this oddly floating interior of the restaurant in the Berlin TV Tower. Or there's another film where you look at the Cornish eclipse of August 1999, with a cloud formation floating across the sun's dimmed surface.

Well, that wasn't what I wanted to be looking at [laughs]. I did hope for a sunny day!

Yes, it's the frustration of your hopes again, isn't it?

You know, often things go wrong in order to go right, and that was one of them, maybe. Because if I had made the sunny day eclipse film, it might not have worked so well. But that film was something else entirely. And on top of the television tower in Berlin, I was very much interested in the restaurant, not the outside. Because it's a rotating restaurant, and it was built in the 1960s when spheres were optimistic visions of the future. It's a beautiful time trap, because it's still a place where busloads from the former East go, and tourists. But people in West Berlin don't go there. It's quite strong and such an amazing place, because it really is defying the contemporary world. That's what I like about it.

Yes, and it has this very potent atmosphere which grips you. Then suddenly, I remember, the lights are switched on – these desperate neon lights – and the whole atmosphere is punctured.

But what was so beautiful about that was the waiting staff. I found out, while making it, that if you got a job there it meant that, somehow or other, you were connected with the Stasi, because it was the best job in Berlin. You had simply to observe and not be seen to be observing, so the most beautiful thing about this film is that they never look at the camera. When the lights go on at the end, they come in and clear the tables and never once look at the camera. Had they looked at the camera, the whole thing would have become very self-conscious. But it was the most extraordinary behaviour, the waitresses. So the fiction was complete, because they never, ever interrupted it, somehow. And again we were very lucky, because there were two groups scheduled in from the East, but they'd gone to the Forum Hotel where the top floor is a gambling – what do you call it?

A casino?

A casino, yes. It meant that these people were two and a half hours late, so all the front tables were empty, waiting for this huge party to come. It was beautiful for my film, but it was a gift from God because they were supposed to be there. It meant that we had the whole light moving on the empty tables and the distant group, all through the transition from daylight to sunset. And then the second group eventually arrived and the whole atmosphere changed. I mean, there were such shifts of atmosphere within that thing. It's quite amazing! It really is like the world: you have sun and shade. It was very difficult to cut together, because the tower would be moving into shade but the whole of the other side would be brilliantly illuminated. It was very difficult to pull off the editing from one to the other, because it'd look like I'd gone back in time or forward in time, but actually it was chronological. And it's that movement the whole time as well – it was extraordinary, that constant movement. That's why I really didn't want to do any movement of the cameras, because the restaurant was moving. And then the lights coming on at that point meant the windows became totally opaque. Where at the beginning you have this sense of the outside and translucent in a way, then the totally opaque meant that the whole atmosphere changed. The beautiful keyboard player was there as well, and uninvited, he played 'The Blue Danube' and the theme tune from *Dr Zhivago*. When I went there recently, he'd updated his keyboard and it was horrible. I was thinking: 'Oh god, that's progress, brand new.' He was very proud, and he'd been there twenty-five years – he was really in the fabric of that building.

You say that you're lucky and you have these moments, but it's a question in the end of how you use that luck, and how you build that into the artefact you're producing. Finally, I'd like to instance one marvellous bathetic moment in the Cornish eclipse film, when we see an idyllic panorama of cows dozing in a field near the cliff's edge. It's very peaceful, and then suddenly one of the cows stands up – or staggers up, really – raises her tail and shits all over this picturesque stretch of grass. It's a wonderful …

You've missed out the best bit: then she walks directly out of the picture frame, she walks without stopping, it's just beautiful!

Yes [laughs]. But you use that in the context of the entire film, it's not just a moment in itself. It's a question of where it's put, and what it's combined with. That's down to you, and the editing process, and being an artist.

The editing process is incredibly important, because you know I never pre-imagine things. It's the editing where everything happens.

Index